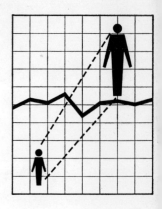

CHANGES IN

HOUGHTON MIFFLIN COMPANY · BOSTON

NEW YORK · ATLANTA · GENEVA, ILL. · DALLAS · PALO ALTO

INTELLIGENCE QUOTIENT

INFANCY TO MATURITY

New Insights from the Berkeley Growth Study
with
Implications for the Stanford-Binet Scales
and
Applications to Professional Practice

SAMUEL R. PINNEAU

DEPARTMENT OF PSYCHOLOGY · UNIVERSITY OF HOUSTON

PERMISSIONS

Profound gratitude is expressed to authors, publishers, and other copyright holders for permission to reprint from the copyright material listed here.

Bayley, Nancy, "Consistency and variability in the growth of intelligence from birth to eighteen years," *J. Genet. Psychol.*, 1949, 75, 165–196.

Terman, L. M., and Merrill, Maud A., *Measuring Intelligence. A guide to the administration of the new revised Stanford-Binet Tests of intelligence.* Boston: Houghton Mifflin, 1937.

Terman, L. M., and Merrill, Maud A., *Stanford-Binet Intelligence Scale. Manual for the Third Revision Form L–M.* Boston: Houghton Mifflin, 1960.

Wechsler, D., "Equivalent test and mental ages for the WISC," *J. Consult. Psychol.*, 1951, 15, 381–384.

The Riverside Press

CAMBRIDGE, MASSACHUSETTS

PRINTED IN THE U.S.A.

Acknowledgments

To Professor Harold E. Jones. His stimulating criticisms and careful guidance during the progress of the study added materially to the scope of the investigation.

To Dr. Nancy Bayley. Her contribution to the investigation included not only the Berkeley Growth Study data but suggestions, criticisms and encouragement during the analyses of data and preparation of the manuscript.

To Ruth A. Pinneau and James L. Wright. Their assistance made possible the establishment of the Deviation IQ tables and the tables of change in IQ with age.

To the others who helped in different phases of the study and in the preparation of the final manuscript: Dr. Herbert S. Conrad, Dr. Alexander Milton, Dr. Orville G. Brim, Jr., Dr. Gordon E. Patterson, and Mrs. Katherine Eardley.

To the Russell Sage Foundation whose original interest in the proposal made the investigation possible.

Samuel R. Pinneau

Houston, Texas

TO

RICHARD, LINDA, MARCIA,

BRUCE AND JAMES

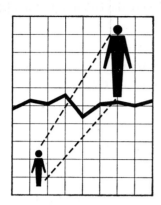

Contents

List of Tables

List of Figures

1

INTRODUCTION [1]

Reports of research investigations which examine the IQ (*Intelligence Quotient*) are legion. Recording the results of one more investigation into the subject would serve little purpose if the opus only contributed supporting bulk to the existing literature. *However,* the study reported here reveals *new* information which is critical in reading and using this number, *the IQ,* so extensively used by many disciplines.

There are four topics of major concern in this work. The consistency of the intelligence quotient from early infancy to late adolescence is analyzed. Accurate mental age scores and revised IQ tables are developed for the Stanford-Binet Intelligence scales. IQ changes with age are tabulated and the use of these tables is explained. Finally, the rate of mental maturation by subjects of different levels of ability is considered.

A BACKDROP FOR THE PRESENT WORK

Conclusions as to the stability of mental test scores (relative to age) were based on meager evidence until longitudinal studies were available which covered the life span from early childhood to adulthood. The results of these long-term studies indicate that the stability of intelligence test performance depends on three variables: the age at which the earlier of the two tests is given; the interval between tests; and the intelligence level of the subject (8, 17, 28, 39, 41). Results from these studies also indicate that intelligence is not a homogeneous entity but consists of a number of functions (6, 8, 16, 26), and that the composition of mentality varies not only from individual to individual but also with the age of the individual (6, 8, 26, 41, 45).

Theoretical attempts have been made to explain the phenomena of stability and change in the IQ, and studies have been directed at determining how

[1] During early phases of work on the manuscript the writer was a Public Health Service Research Fellow of the National Institute of Mental Health.

different environmental conditions affect mental test performance. Of the theoretical explanations, one of the most ingenious is found in Anderson's discussion of year-to-year relationships in terms of overlap of common elements (5). The more detailed analyses of variation in mental test performance have emphasized not merely psychometric factors but also test-taking attitudes, the environment, parent-child relationships, personal experiences, and inherited potentials [see (31) for a comprehensive review of studies].

These and other problems of intellectual growth constitute one area investigated in the longitudinal studies conducted under the directorship of the late Professor Harold E. Jones at the Institute of Child Welfare (now Institute of Human Development), University of California. The present report utilizes a segment of the data obtained in one of these investigations, the Berkeley Growth Study (BGS).

AREAS INVESTIGATED

Stability of Scores

The extent to which subjects maintain their same relative standing in their age group is usually measured by the correlation coefficient. This measure of relationship is preferred by some research workers. However, it has little practical significance for a large number of individuals who use mental test scores. An alternative way of indicating the stability of the IQ, and one which is more functional for many non-research workers, is the number of points of change which are likely to occur with age. In view of this, tables were developed for estimating the amount of change in IQ which a subject is likely to show subsequent to a test at a given age. Because amount of change depends on how old the subject is when the assessment is made, different values are required at different age levels. In the present work, a table is provided for each of nineteen different ages between birth and age seventeen.

Deviation IQs

Conventional IQs for the 1937 Stanford-Binet scale have a somewhat different meaning at different ages. A given IQ obtained with this test may indicate at one age that a subject is superior to ten per cent, at another to twenty per cent, and at still another to fifteen per cent, of his age group. In such instances the subject's IQ must change if the same relative position in the age group is maintained. To avoid this difficulty a derived IQ was developed for this and the 1960 revision of the scale, namely the *deviation IQ (DIQ)*. In addition, the range of ages covered was extended from 16 to 18 years of age by the deviation IQ tables.

The deviation IQ is computed so that a subject obtains the same score on successive testings unless his position in the age group changes. The tables for estimating the stability of scores with age, referred to in the preceding section, include the changes with age for both the conventional and deviation IQs. In a later chapter the conventional is compared with the deviation IQ, both in terms of methodological soundness and usefulness.

Corrected Mental Ages

An analysis of the 1937 standardization data of the Stanford-Binet scale reveals that mental age scores obtained with this test are somewhat high at most ages (54, p. 36). Because these scores are used practically in interpreting performance on intelligence tests, especially to individuals who have limited training in psychometric methods, more accurate mental ages were derived and tabulated for this as well as the 1960 revision of the scale. The table not only provides corrected mental ages for subjects from chronological ages 2 years–0 months to 13 years–0 months, it also furnishes the average mental age scores for chronological ages 13 years–1 month to 18 years–0 months. The clinical use of these scores is illustrated in Part Two.

Rate of Mental Maturing as Related to Intellectual Level

An issue of basic importance in theories of mental development is whether a subject's rate of mental growth is related to his level of intelligence; that is, whether the bright children at a given age grow at the same or a faster rate than the dull. If, on the average, subjects of all ability levels were found to grow at the same rate in terms of mental age units, the more intelligent and the less intelligent would maintain their relative superior or inferior status as indicated by mental age differences. While mental age differences would remain the same, differences in IQ would become smaller at the higher chronological ages. If the amount of gain were positively correlated with intellectual level, relative measures such as the IQ would be more stable with age, and individual differences in mental age would increase. In the detailed investigation of this problem we will find that the latter is the case; by age six, bright children are making larger gains each year than are children of less mental ability.

ORGANIZATION OF THE REPORT

This manuscript is both a research report and a handbook for members of professional groups who evaluate the performance of individuals on the Stanford-Binet or comparable tests of intelligence. Part One presents the methodologies used in the investigations, the results which were obtained, the procedures utilized in determining change with age in conventional and deviation IQ, and those used in deriving corrected mental ages and deviation IQs for the revised Stanford-Binet scales. Those aspects of the book which deal with the practical applications of the findings and developments of the study are included in Part Two. Part Three, the appendices, consists of the tables for determining amount of change in IQ and DIQ with age, the table of corrected mental ages for the 1937 and 1960 Stanford-Binet scales, and the tables for determining deviation IQs for these scales.

PART ONE

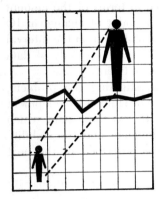

Research Findings

A major purpose of this study was to determine systematically the stability of intelligence from early infancy to late adolescence in terms of the amount of change in IQ scores between testings. Since the amount of change in IQ depends both on the age at which the initial testing is made and on the interval of time between testings, the attainment of this goal required a body of data collected on the same subjects for a span of from fifteen to twenty years.

At the time the writer became interested in investigating the problem, data of this kind were already available at the Institute of Human Development on the Berkeley Growth Study sample of subjects. It was these data which were used in investigating the rate of mental development and the stability of mental test scores with age. The BGS sample is described in the next chapter.

It became evident early in this study that a change in the conventional IQ does not always indicate a change in relative position and, on the other hand, that a change in relative standing is not always accompanied by a change in the conventional IQ. As a consequence the IQs of the BGS sample were transformed into standard score, or deviation, IQs, utilizing the means and standard deviations obtained on the standardization samples of the tests involved.[2]

In the case of the 1937 revision of the Stanford-Binet, tables for determining deviation IQs were developed for all ages from 2 to 18 years although this scale was not used with the BGS sample until the age of eight years and subsequently. Analyses of data from the standardization of the 1937 revision are presented only where they bear directly on the problems of the meaning and stability of scores obtained with this scale since the statistics are given in readily available sources (39, 54).

[2] Deviation IQs were derived so that, so far as possible, representative samples at each age level would obtain a mean score of 100 and a standard deviation of 16.

2

THE BERKELEY GROWTH

STUDY SAMPLE

The sixty-one cases originally comprising the Berkeley Growth Study sample were "normal" Berkeley, California, children born in hospitals between September 25, 1928 and May 15, 1929. "The families selected included only white, English-speaking parents who could be regarded as permanent residents of Berkeley and who were willing to cooperate in bringing their children to the Institute for the required series of examinations. In consequence of the selective factors involved, the group tends to be somewhat above average in measures of socio-economic status (parental occupation, income, and education)" (33, p. 167).

At the end of 18 years the sample had diminished to forty subjects (20 boys and 20 girls) who were available for most of the regular examinations. This reduction in sample size was due primarily to families' moving out of town. However, relationships with some of the other subjects were maintained through correspondence, with occasional opportunities to renew contact for interviews and tests.

RESEARCH PROGRAM

During the major period of data collection in childhood and adolescence, the primary responsibility for the study as well as for administration of the tests rested with Dr. Nancy Bayley.[3] The research program included mental

[3] Investigators who collaborated with Dr. Bayley include Dr. Lotta V. Wolff, Dr. Mary E. Shirley, Dr. Herbert S. Conrad, and Dr. Herbert Stolz. Extensive data were also collected on these subjects' motor and physical development. The detailed procedures of the program are presented in a description of the study by Jones and Bayley (33).

7

tests at thirty-nine different periods within the first 18 years — monthly for the first 15 months, at three-month intervals through 3 years, semi-annually through 5 years, and annually through 18 years. The schedule of tests used is given in Table 1 together with the obtained measures of central tendency and of variability. While the number of subjects was not large, the results are of exceptional interest because of the continuity of the sample and the long age-span covered.

TABLE 1

Means and SDs of Mental Age and IQ, by Age and Test:
Berkeley Growth Study Sample (from 8, p. 170)

	Age	Test	N	Mental age in months* Mean	SD	IQ Mean	SD
Mo.	1	Calif. First-Year	52	1.04	.195	103.8	19.5
	2	Calif. First-Year	58	1.998	.34	101.8	16.9
	3	Calif. First-Year	61	2.92	.41	97.5	13.6
	4	Calif. First-Year	58	4.01	.51	101.0	12.9
	5	Calif. First-Year	58	5.00	.60	100.3	12.3
	6	Calif. First-Year	57	5.96	.79	99.1	13.2
	7	Calif. First-Year	52	7.03	.705	100.7	10.2
	8	Calif. First-Year	53	8.08	.77	100.9	9.7
	9	Calif. First-Year	56	9.01	.77	100.1	8.5
	10	Calif. First-Year	56	10.13	.75	101.3	7.6
	11	Calif. First-Year	52	11.03	.78	100.9	7.5
	12	Calif. First-Year	53	12.06	.82	100.7	6.7
	13	Calif. First-Year	53	13.04	1.07	100.3	8.4
	14	Calif. First-Year	46	14.08	1.12	100.7	8.1
	15	Calif. First-Year	52	15.00	1.38	100.0	9.3
	18	Calif. Preschool I	49	18.38	2.20	102.4	12.0
	21	Calif. Preschool I	52	22.59	2.47	107.6	11.7
	24	Calif. Preschool I	47	26.29	3.09	109.5	13.3
	27	Calif. Preschool I	48	30.48	3.69	112.6	13.6
	30	Calif. Preschool I	46	33.96	4.11	113.1	13.6
	33	Calif. Preschool II	44	37.04	4.87	111.6	15.0
	36	Calif. Preschool I	47	42.83	5.20	118.8	14.4
	42	Calif. Preschool I	39	49.39	5.50	117.6	13.2
	48	Calif. Preschool I	44	52.28	6.64	109.4	14.1
	54	Calif. Preschool I	43	62.28	8.03	115.0	15.2
	60	Calif. Preschool I	46	70.60	9.90	117.8	16.9
Yr.	6	Stanford-Binet '16	48	88.71	11.01	123.4	15.6
	7	Stanford-Binet '16	46	103.65	12.64	123.0	15.1
	8	Stanford-Binet L	47	120.00	18.91	122.6	20.1
	9	Stanford-Binet L	45	139.40	23.56	129.0	22.2
	10	Stanford-Binet M	47	157.96	28.75	131.9	23.6
	11	Stanford-Binet L	45	174.51	30.22	132.5	22.1
	12	Stanford-Binet M	43	186.93	31.71	130.3	22.1
	13	Terman-McNemar C	36	—	—	115.6	21.4
	14	Stanford-Binet L	37	213.08	31.85	129.9	19.2
	15	Terman-McNemar D	37	—	—	121.7	19.1
	16	Wechsler-Bellevue	39	—	—	117.4	16.2
	17	Stanford-Binet M	40	231.55	36.08	129.1	19.9
	18	Wechsler-Bellevue	37	—	—	122.1	16.1

*Data ungrouped.

3

THE STABILITY OF IQS

Evidence regarding the stability of mental test performance has usually been presented in terms of the correlation between scores at different ages or in terms of the average number of points of IQ change. These two kinds of findings are not related by any simple statistical formula and may seem at times to be in disagreement. For example, for the subjects of the Berkeley Growth Study the correlations between test scores at age 2 and scores at 3, 4, and 17 years were respectively .72, .60, and .58, while the mean IQ changes for the same periods were 8.5, 8.8, and 18.9. Thus, relative to the correlation coefficients, it appears that the score changes are "too small" from two years to four years and "too large" from two years to seventeen years. An inspection of Table 1 indicates systematic changes with age in the magnitude of the means and standard deviations. Such changes would result in apparent disagreement between these two different measures of stability. The issue as to whether the discrepancies are due to characteristics of the sample or whether they are a function of features of the tests will be considered in Chapter 4.

CORRELATION BETWEEN SCORES AT DIFFERENT AGE LEVELS

Correlational results from several longitudinal studies of mental development have been published in recent years. Among the major reports are those by Bayley on the Berkeley Growth Study (6, 8, 9); by Honzik (28), and by Honzik, Macfarlane and Allen (29) on the Guidance Study; by Ebert and Simmons (17) on the Brush Foundation Study; by Sontag, Baker and Nelson (50) on the Fels Study; by Anderson (5) on the Harvard Growth Study data; and by Bradway, Thompson and Cravens (12) on sub-groups of the 1937 standardization sample of the Stanford-Binet scale.

In determining for the BGS sample the relationships between tests given at different ages, Bayley increased the reliability of her measures by using

10

averages for three successive ages.[4] The results she obtained are presented in Table 2. This table may be compared with Table 3, which gives the coefficients obtained between single-test IQs for ages 6 through 18 years. [The difficulties involved in using tables such as these in the practical situation are discussed later (see pages 81–82).]

The relationships presented in these tables are consonant with those reported in other longitudinal studies, in indicating that the greater the interval between tests, the greater is the tendency for the individual child to shift in relative position, and that there is greater constancy of relative standing with increasing age. These findings suggest the importance, in the practical evaluation of mental test performance, of reporting the stability of scores for the particular test used not merely in general terms, but for the ages at which the subjects are tested.

[4] Sigma scores were used for this purpose in order to eliminate attenuating effects of age changes in means and variabilities.

TABLE 2

Correlation Coefficients between Average Age-Level Standard Scores of Intelligence: Berkeley Growth Study Sample (from 8, p. 181)*

Av. of Months, or Years	Av. of Months							Av. of Years				
	4, 5, 6	7, 8, 9	10, 11, 12	13, 14, 15	18, 21, 24	27, 30, 36	42, 48, 54	5, 6, 7	8, 9, 10	11, 12, 13	14, 15, 16	17, 18
Months												
1, 2, 3	.57	.42	.28	.10	−.04	−.09	−.21	−.13	−.03	.02	−.01	.05
4, 5, 6	—	.72	.52	.50	.23	.10	−.16	−.07	−.06	−.08	−.04	−.01
7, 8, 9	—	—	.81	.67	.39	.22	.02	.02	.07	.16	.006	.20
10, 11, 12	—	—	—	.81	.60	.45	.27	.20	.19	.30	.23	.41
13, 14, 15	—	—	—	—	.70	.54	.35	.30	.19	.19	.09	.23
18, 21, 24	—	—	—	—	—	.80	.49	.50	.37	.43	.45	.55
27, 30, 36	—	—	—	—	—	—	.72	.70	.58	.53	.46	.54
42, 48, 54	—	—	—	—	—	—	—	.82	.71	.64	.70	.62
Years												
5, 6, 7	—	—	—	—	—	—	—	—	.92	.85	.87	.86
8, 9, 10	—	—	—	—	—	—	—	—	—	.94	.92	.89
11, 12, 13	—	—	—	—	—	—	—	—	—	—	.96	.96
14, 15, 16	—	—	—	—	—	—	—	—	—	—	—	.96

*These scores are the means of standard scores for three consecutive test-ages, e.g., months 1, 2, & 3; 4, 5, & 6, etc., and years 5, 6, & 7, etc. The last level is composed of only two test ages, 17 & 18 years. Each child's score is the average of all tests taken by him for the ages included in that level.

TABLE 3

Correlations between Single Test IQs at Different Ages: Berkeley Growth Study Sample (from 8, p. 183)

Years \ Age	Form of Stanford-Binet						Terman-McNemar	Stanford-Binet	Terman-McNemar	Wechsler-Bellevue	Stanford-Binet	Wechsler-Bellevue
	1916	L	L	M	L	M	Form C	Form L	Form D		Form M	
Age	7	8	9	10	11	12	13	14	15	16	17	18
6	.86	.85	.84	.90	.78	.81	.82	.74	.72	.79	.78	.77
7	—	.88	.83	.87	.82	.83	.88	.79	.75	.83	.83	.80
8	—	—	.91	.89	.89	.91	.88	.91	.85	.88	.84	.85
9	—	—	—	.88	.90	.82	.87	.86	.82	.87	.85	.87
10	—	—	—	—	.92	.90	.88	.92	.83	.88	.86	.86
11	—	—	—	—	—	.93	.91	.93	.89	.89	.92	.93
12	—	—	—	—	—	—	.87	.94	.85	.88	.90	.89
13	—	—	—	—	—	—	—	.89	.95	.90	.94	.93
14	—	—	—	—	—	—	—	—	.87	.92	.89	.89
15	—	—	—	—	—	—	—	—	—	.88	.89	.88
16	—	—	—	—	—	—	—	—	—	—	.89	.94
17	—	—	—	—	—	—	—	—	—	—	—	.90

In the report (8) which originally presented Tables 1, 2, and 3, Bayley was primarily concerned with problems of consistency of the IQ, as affected by unsystematic variability of mental age scores. In that work she quantified individual differences in constancy through the use of Intelligence Lability Scores. The subject's Lability Score for a given age interval is the standard deviation of his standard scores; thus, the measure provides a means of quantifying the fluctuations of scores with age shown by subjects in longitudinal studies. This method of assessing the variability of performance appears to have special promise in investigations directed at evaluating the effects of changing environmental variables on mental test scores.

CHANGES IN CONVENTIONAL IQS WITH AGE

The second method of assessing the stability of mental measurements is determining the amount of change in score between tests. Reports on age change in the IQ are available (e.g., 2, 14, 18, 24, 25, 49). The subjects of such studies frequently have been heterogeneous either with respect to age at the first test, or with respect to interval between test and retest, or both. Since the amount of IQ change depends both on the subject's age and on the period of time which has elapsed since the earlier test, the reported values deviate an unknown amount from the true changes of specific age groups and of specific testing intervals. Reports of some studies have presented findings on subjects homogeneous as to age and interval between tests (11, 12, 18). However, these rarely permit direct comparison, since only infrequently are the samples at both testings comparable as to age.

At the present writing no tables in the literature systematically present for any major longitudinal study the changes in IQ for subjects tested at specific ages and for specific intervals. Such information was obtained by analyzing the data of the Berkeley Growth Study in terms of amount of change in IQ from one test to another at different ages. Though mental tests were administered to these subjects on thirty-nine different occasions between birth and maturity, only results obtained on the following tests and at the ages specified were used: the *California First-Year Mental Scale* (7) at 1, 3, 6, 9, and 12 months; the *California Preschool Scale* (30) at 18 months and thereafter at six-month intervals through three years, and then at yearly intervals through age 5; the *Stanford-Binet Intelligence Scale*, 1916 Revision (52), given at 6 and 7 years; and the *Stanford-Binet Intelligence Scale*, 1937 Revision (54), Form L or M, given at yearly intervals from age 8 through age 12, and again at 14 and 17 years.

Following the directions provided in the manuals for the appropriate tests, conventional IQs were computed at each of the twenty ages for these subjects. For each subject the difference was determined between his IQ at each testing and his IQ at each of the subsequent testings. Since in this study the concern was with the amount of change in IQ regardless of whether it was an increase or decrease, the absolute values of the changes were used.

The next step in the procedure was to determine the median, the first and third quartiles, the range, mean and standard deviation of these changes for each age comparison. These values are presented in Section A of the tables in Appendix E.[5] For statistical reasons considered in detail in the next chapter, changes in the conventional IQs should not be used in the practical evaluation of intelligence test scores.

[5] It might be argued that the results presented in Appendix E could have been predicted using the standard errors of estimate for the various age comparisons. To use these measures, it would have been necessary to assume that the array distributions of the scores were both equal in dispersion and normal. The findings of Terman and Merrill indicate that such an assumption is not warranted. In their computation of reliabilities for Form L and Form M of the 1937 Stanford-Binet, they found that the array distributions were not equal. As a consequence, they estimated the reliabilities of the test scores at different IQ levels (54). This finding would lead one to expect that the distribution of algebraic changes would be anormal. Inspection of the IQ changes for the BGS sample supports this position — at many of the ages the distributions of change tend to be either rectangular or bimodal.

4

THE DEVIATION IQ

ERRORS INHERENT IN CHANGE IN THE CONVENTIONAL IQ

Somewhat different conclusions regarding the stability of intelligence test scores may be drawn from investigations presenting correlations between IQs and those giving number of points of IQ change. An illustration in addition to the one discussed in Chapter 3 involves comparing, for the BGS subjects, correlations between IQs with the number of points of IQ changes at age 6 on the one hand and at age 10, 11, and 17 on the other. The correlations were respectively .90, .78, and .78; while the mean IQ changes for the same age comparisons were 12.4, 14.8, and 11.4. As in the earlier example, the apparent disagreement is accounted for in terms of variations in the magnitude of the means and standard deviations (see Table 1). This raises the question as to whether the group's changes in mean score and in IQ variability are greater than would normally be expected.

To determine whether variability of the IQ changes significantly with age for this group, the standard deviations of IQs at various ages were compared with the median standard deviation of 15.6. The differences were significant at a number of ages, as can be observed in the first two columns of Table 4. These results indicate that the greater instability suggested by the IQ changes (as compared with the correlations) is not due to just chance fluctuations in the homogeneity of the group. However, these findings still do not answer the question as to whether the group actually changes in homogeneity of ability or whether the age changes in variability are a function of the tests used.

An inspection of the mean IQs of the BGS sample (Table 1) suggests that some of the disagreement between the two measures of stability is due to shifts with age in the average score of the group. These shifts may be due to actual changes in the performance of the subjects, relative to that of the standardization samples. On the other hand, since the sample is for the most part a

TABLE 4

Changes in IQ Variability with Age on Tests Used in the Berkeley Growth Study

The median variability for a given sample is compared with the variabilities of the sample at other ages

	Age	Berkeley Growth Study		California First-Year‡	California Preschool	1937 Stanford-Binet (Forms L and M combined)	
		SD	F	F	SD	SD	z'
Mo.	1	19.5	1.56	2.18**			
	3	13.6	1.32	1.06			
	6	13.2	1.40	Mdn.			
	9	8.5	3.37**	2.41**			
	12	6.7	5.42**	3.88**			
	18	12.0	1.69*		10.44		
	24	13.3	1.38		8.89	16.2	.18
	30	13.6	1.32		11.48	20.7	2.97††
	36	14.4	1.17		23.38	18.8	1.79
	42	13.2	1.40		15.71	16.8	.34
	48	14.1	1.22		11.36	16.3	.09
	54	15.2	1.05		10.32	15.8	.54
	60	16.9	1.17		9.98	14.2	2.30†
	66					14.2	2.31†
Yr.	6	15.6	Mdn.			12.8	5.48††
	7	15.1	1.07			15.9	.63
	8	20.1	1.66*			15.7	.90
	9	22.2	2.02**			16.6	.24
	10	23.6	2.29**			16.2	.25
	11	22.1	2.01*			17.7	1.49
	12	22.1	2.01*			19.8	3.46††
	13	21.4	1.88*			17.8	1.58
	14	19.2	1.52			16.4	Mdn.
	15	19.1	1.50			19.2	2.14†
	16	16.2	1.08			17.0	.50
	17	19.9	1.63			14.4	2.05†
	18					16.9	.42

'Use of the variabilities for the two scales combined has not increased the size of the z's over that obtained with either scale treated separately.

*F-values significant at the .10 level. (The variance ratio, $\left(F = \dfrac{SD_1^2}{SD_2^2} \right)$, was used to test the significance of the difference between the variabilities because the size of the sample did not warrant the use of the large sample formula. This formula does not take into account the lack of independence of the variances. The writer chose to ignore this fact rather than to reduce the number of subjects in each age comparison to only those who were tested at both ages.)

**F-values significant at the .02 level.

†z-values significant at the .05 level. ("z" is the ratio of the difference between the standard deviations to the standard error of this difference.)

††z-values significant at the .01 level.

‡The California First-Year Scale was standardized on the Berkeley Growth Study sample; consequently, the SDs in the first column for ages 1 to 12 months are the SDs for the standardization sample of this test.

superior one composed at each level of practically the same cases, the fluctuations in means may reflect chiefly the age variations in the standard deviations of the tests.

The age changes in the standard deviations of the sample could also be due to psychometric characteristics of the test. Fluctuations such as are present would result if there were inter-test differences in the measures of dispersion or if the IQ variabilities for each of the tests actually change with age. The evidence indicated that both of these conditions exist.

Standard deviations obtained on the standardization samples of the three tests are presented in Table 4. The comparison of the standard deviations for a given test with the median value shows that there are significant age changes in the intra-test variabilities. [Statistical comparisons were not possible in the case of the *California Preschool Scale*, since Jaffa did not indicate what proportion of the 2,000 tests fall at each age level (30).] In addition, Bayley (8) has shown that other investigators have found trends in variability on the *California First-Year Mental Scale* similar to those of the Berkeley Growth Study, furthermore, Terman and Merrill (54) and McNemar (39) have granted that age changes in variability are characteristic of IQs on the 1937 revision of the Stanford-Binet.

Since standard deviations of conventional IQs for a given test characteristically vary from age to age, a number of conclusions may be drawn.

(a) The same relative standing may at different ages be designated by quite different numerical scores. The practical significance of this conclusion can be seen if the results obtained with the 1937 standardization sample for the Stanford-Binet are considered. It is shown in Table 5 that the standard deviation for Form L at 6 years is 12.5 points and at 12 years, 20.0 points. Hence, for this scale and form (assuming that these standard deviations represent the true values), the IQ point is equivalent to one-twelfth of a standard deviation at age 6 and one-twentieth of a standard deviation at age 12. Or, stated in terms which may have more practical meaning, if a subject were to remain at the 98th percentile relative to his age group, assuming a mean IQ of 100 at different ages for the Stanford-Binet and a normal probability distribution, his IQ would be 125 at age 6 and 140 at age 12. In contrast, a subject who was at the second percentile at both ages would have an IQ of 75 at 6 years and an IQ of 60 at 12 years.

(b) Amount of change in the conventional IQ from one testing to another is an inaccurate measure of change in relative position because it confounds this change with that due to fluctuations in the size of the variabilities. In the example just considered both subjects showed a 15 point change in IQ, but they maintained the same relative position in their age groups. The change in score was purely a function of fluctuations in the size of the variabilities.

(c) A specified change in conventional IQ may indicate a different amount of change in relative standing for subjects differing in level of ability. Suppose the two 6-year-olds in the example both show a 15 point drop in IQ by age 12. The child whose IQ dropped from 75 to 60 has not changed in relative position, but the one whose IQ dropped from 125 to 110 has changed from the 87th to the 69th percentile of his age group.

TABLE 5

Stanford-Binet IQ Variability in Relation to Age: 1937 Standardization Sample (54, p. 40)*

C.A.	N	$\sigma_{L_{IQ}}$	$\sigma_{M_{IQ}}$	σ_{IQ} for Composite L-M (Smoothed)
2	102	16.7	15.5	18.2**
$2\frac{1}{2}$	102	20.6	20.7	18.4
3	99	19.0	18.7	18.2
$3\frac{1}{2}$	103	17.3	16.3	17.4
4	105	16.9	15.6	16.3
$4\frac{1}{2}$	101	16.2	15.3	15.5
5	109	14.2	14.1	14.7
$5\frac{1}{2}$	110	14.3	14.0	14.2
6	203	12.5	13.2	14.4
7	202	16.2	15.6	15.0
8	203	15.8	15.5	15.7
9	204	16.4	16.7	16.3
10	201	16.5	15.9	16.9
11	204	18.0	17.3	17.7
12	202	20.0	19.5	18.1
13	204	17.9	17.8	18.0
14	202	16.1	16.7	17.7
15	107	19.0	19.3	17.4
16	102	16.5	17.4	16.8
17	109	14.5	14.3	16.2
18	101	17.2	16.6	16.0

*Modified so as to include the values of the SDs used in deriving deviation IQs.
**For reasons explained in the text, the mean SD of 16.1 was used in computing deviation IQs at two years rather than the smoothed value.

(d) If children are tested at ages where the conventional IQ variabilities are large, a given IQ change designates a different amount of change in relative position from that designated by the same IQ change at ages where the variabilities are small. Making the same assumptions as in the preceding illustration and using standard deviations obtained on the 1937 revision of the Stanford-Binet (Table 5), consider two subjects with conventional IQs of 90 who show a 20 point increase on a second test. The first subject was tested at ages 2 and 12, and the second at ages 5 and 17. The first child changes in his standing in his age group from the 31st to the 69th percentile. The second subject, who at 5 years was at the 24th percentile, is at the 76th percentile on the second test. Thus while the subjects had the same IQ on both tests and showed the same number of points of change, a striking difference is present in the changes in relative position, the second subject being further below average on the first test and further above average on the second.

THE DEVIATION IQ TRANSFORMATION USED WITH THE BGS DATA

If it were possible for a given numerical score on a mental scale to indicate the same relative standing at all ages, a given *change* in score would have a constant significance as to change in relative position regardless of age at initial test or of interval between tests. The suggestion that standard scores should be used to accomplish this result has had little appeal because of the importance attached to the IQ during the past several decades. This obstacle is, of course, overcome by the deviation IQ transformation since the properties of the DIQ conform to the traditional notions concerning the Stanford-Binet IQ; that is, at each age, for samples representative of the general population, the IQs are given a *mean of 100* and a *standard deviation of 16*.[6]

In determining deviation IQs for the BGS subjects on the *California First-Year Mental Scale*, the obtained means and standard deviations were used since this group constituted the sample on which the scale was standardized. Consequently, the DIQ means and standard deviations closely approximate the chosen values of 100 and 16 respectively (see Table 6). (The mean values deviate from one- to five-tenths of a point from 100 because the scores were

TABLE 6

Means and SDs of Deviation IQs in Relation to Age:
Berkeley Growth Study Sample*

Age (Months)	Test	N	Mean	SD
1	Calif. First Year	52	100.1	16.0
3	Calif. First Year	61	100.1	16.0
6	Calif. First Year	57	100.3	16.0
9	Calif. First Year	56	100.1	16.0
12	Calif. First Year	53	99.5	16.0
18	Calif. Preschool I	51	104.5	18.9
24	Calif. Preschool I	48	123.0	18.4
30	Calif. Preschool I	47	118.2	13.9
36	Calif. Preschool I	48	120.0	13.2
48	Calif. Preschool I	45	120.8	15.7
60	Calif. Preschool I	47	115.0	20.1
72	Stanford-Binet '16	48	128.0	21.5
84	Stanford-Binet '16	46	127.8	19.6
96	Stanford-Binet L	47	122.9	19.9
108	Stanford-Binet L	45	126.3	22.0
120	Stanford-Binet M	47	126.9	22.9
132	Stanford-Binet L	45	127.4	20.8
144	Stanford-Binet M	43	124.9	19.7
168	Stanford-Binet L	37	125.7	17.8
204	Stanford-Binet M	40	124.2	19.3

*Deviation IQs were not derived at 156, 170, or 182 months, ages at which the Terman-McNemar or the Wechsler-Bellevue were administered.

computed to only one decimal point.) Since this is an intellectually superior group in the later years, it might be argued that their DIQs in the first year should average above 100. This may be the case, but the necessary adjustments cannot be determined inasmuch as data on representative samples are not

[6] Details of the development of deviation IQs for the Stanford-Binet scales are presented in Chapter 6, pp. 48–53.

available for this scale. There seemed to be little reason to expect the average score during the first year to be comparable to that obtained at later ages since relationships between first year scores and scores at 2 years and thereafter are slight. Consequently, there appeared to be little choice but to assume, tentatively, a mean IQ of 100 during the first year for the BGS (standardization) sample.

The *California Preschool Mental Scale* was also standardized on a superior sample. However, a large number of these subjects were tested, in addition, on scales standardized on more representative groups. Therefore, Jaffa (30) was able to adjust the norms for the scale so that samplings of the general population would obtain mean IQs of approximately 100 at preschool ages. Since she does not present the standard deviations of IQs at various ages, it was necessary to utilize the point score means (corrected by the factor she had used) and the variabilities of these point scores to obtain standard scores in terms of the normal population. These scores were then transformed into deviation IQs.

An inspection of the means and variabilities of the BGS subjects' DIQs for this test (Table 6) indicates that a number of the fluctuations exceed chance. The smaller variabilities between 2 years–6 months and 4 years suggest that this sample became more homogeneous in its performance during these years. Alternatively, the decreased size of the variabilities could reflect sampling errors in the standardization sample of the Preschool Scale since their standard deviations were used in deriving the DIQs at these ages. If this were the explanation, the heterogeneity of the standardization samples for this scale would be greatest during these years. The standard deviations for these groups (Table 4) suggest that this is the case.

If, due to sampling errors, the standardization samples of the Preschool Scale are too heterogeneous between 2 years–6 months and 4 years, one would expect that at these ages the means for the BGS sample would be somewhat low. This condition exists, as can be observed from Table 6.

The DIQ standard deviations of the BGS sample on the *California Preschool Scale* are consistently smaller than those obtained on the Stanford-Binet (Table 6). Since no consistent age changes in intra-test variability are apparent, it seems likely that the standardization samples of the Preschool Scale were more hetereogeneous than those used in standardizing the Stanford-Binet. Hence, the variabilities of the Preschool Scale would have to be corrected in computing standard scores with respect to the general population. Such corrections would increase the variabilities of the DIQs for the BGS sample on the Preschool Scale and, as a consequence, they would be more in line with those obtained on the Stanford-Binet. In addition, these corrections would increase the mean DIQs for this superior sample by several points, especially between the ages of 2 years–6 months and 4, thus making the DIQ means on the two tests more comparable.

Differences in the intra-test variabilities of the Preschool Scale would not account for the depression in mean DIQ at 18 and 60 months. With respect to the scores at 18 months it should be noted that Jaffa's correction assumes that the standardization sample was less than a third of a standard deviation above the mean of the general population, whereas at the later ages at which the test was used the magnitude of the correction ranged between .72 and 1.33 standard deviations. The mean DIQ of the BGS sample at 18 months is 104 as compared with a mean of 123 at 2 years. Since it is not readily credible that relative to the mean of the general population the BGS sample as a whole moved out more than one standard deviation during this six month period, it may be that Jaffa's correction at 18 months is insufficient. The depression in the mean at 60 months is not due to an inadequate correction; rather, it appears probable that it is the result of this relatively superior group reaching the ceiling of the *California Preschool Scale*.

The mean DIQ for the BGS sample is remarkably stable between 2 and 18 years in view of the differences between the standardization samples of the tests involved. In this connection it is interesting to note that the average DIQ for these subjects at 2 years of age is 123, only one point below their terminal Stanford-Binet DIQ at 17 years (204 months) of age (see Table 6). Thus the group as a whole at 2 years approximated its relative standing at the end of high school. This finding is in contrast to the inference likely to be drawn from Table 1, namely, that approximating this standing is a gradual process which requires at least the first six years. It might also be pointed out that this information will give little comfort to those who would like to interpret the increase in conventional IQs during this period in terms of the gradual accumulation of practice effects in the repeated testing of the same subjects.

EFFECTS OF THE TRANSFORMATION ON SCORE CHANGES

Subsequent to the transformation into deviation IQs, the amount of change in score between tests was determined in the same manner as for the conventional IQs. The results are entered in Section B of the tables in Appendix E. If the deviation IQ transformation overcomes some of the inadequacies in the conventional IQ, it might be expected that point changes in the deviation IQ would be more in agreement with the intercorrelations than are the conventional IQ changes. This is the case. For example, in the illustration considered on page 10, the correlations between test scores at year 2 and ages 3, 4, and 17 years were .72, .60, and .58, while the average IQ changes were 8.5, 8.8, and 18.9 respectively. In comparison, the average DIQ changes were respectively 10.6, 13.5, and 14.5. This example illustrates the point that amount of change in conventional IQ depends on the ages at which the tests are administered as well as on change in relative position. In contrast, when the deviation IQ is used, the changes are directly related to the correlations between the scores regardless of age of testing — a given DIQ change between any two tests indicated the same amount of change in relative standing regardless of the initial age of testing or of the interval between tests.

A comparison of the changes in the conventional IQ with the changes in deviation IQ (Section A versus Section B of the tables in Appendix E) indicates that, prior to age 8, the former are the smaller. After age 8, the converse is true.

The difference in change obtained when conventional and deviation IQs are used is illustrated in Figure 1. The first three graphs compare the mean

FIGURE 1

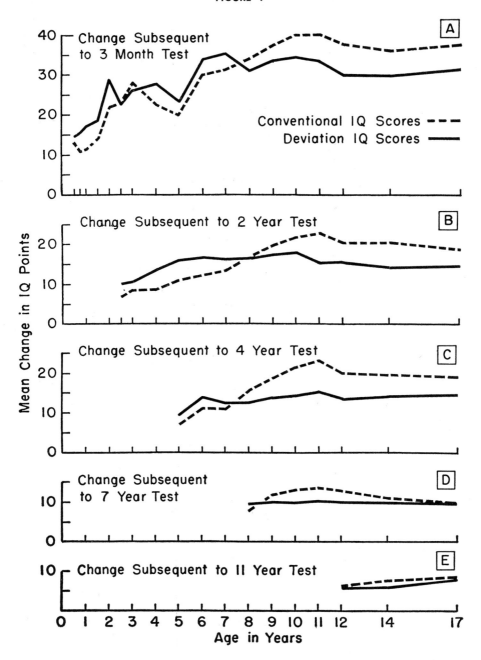

Changes in conventional and deviation IQs subsequent
to tests at various ages: Berkeley Growth Study sample

changes subsequent to tests in the preschool years and the other two changes in score subsequent to tests in the school years. The graphs illustrate the greater changes in deviation IQs prior to 8 years as compared to the conventional IQ changes. The smaller changes in relative position suggested by the latter values result from the relatively small variability of scores in the earlier years (see Table 4). Thus, the changes in the conventional IQs for this group give the impression of greater stability of performance before the 8 year test than is actually the case.

Figure 1 shows that the opposite tendency is just as strong after 8 years; that is, the changes in conventional IQ between tests suggest greater changes in relative position than are actually present. This is the result of the relatively larger variabilities after that age.

CORRECTED TABLES OF CHANGE FOR THE EARLIER AGES

While the fluctuations in the means of the Berkeley Growth Study are reduced by the deviation IQ transformation, some variations are still evident (see Table 6). Earlier considerations suggest that the change in the means of this sample are to a considerable extent a function of characteristics of the tests and of the standardization samples rather than of changes in the group's standing relative to the general population. Therefore, it seemed appropriate to correct the IQ changes at ages where the variations in the means appeared to distort the score changes. Since tables were desired which would be applicable to samples representative of the general population, that is, for samples whose average IQ at each age is 100, the corrections would seem to be necessary. The difference between BGS means, at the two ages involved in a given comparison, was subtracted from each subject's score change between the two testings. The means, standard deviations, and other statistics were then recomputed.

The fluctuations in means materially affected the DIQ changes from tests administered in the first year and a half. Therefore, at these ages the corrected values were used in the tables in Appendix E. The average DIQ changes from tests at 2, 3, and 4 years, corrected for change in mean DIQ, differed in less than 10 per cent of the instances by more than three points in either direction from the original DIQ changes; consequently, the values obtained for these ages were not corrected. The mean DIQ of the sample dropped considerably at age 5, probably because the subjects were reaching the ceiling of the preschool test used. Since the changes were materially affected, the corrected values were used at this age (Table .11 of Appendix E). The corrected mean changes from tests administered subsequent to 5 years in no instance differed by more than one or two points from the earlier obtained values; hence, the original tables appear adequate.

For the purposes of basic research, tables of the uncorrected values for tests administered during the first year and a half and again at age 5 are presented here as Tables 7.1 to 7.7.

TABLE 7.1

**Change in Deviation IQs with Age when Subjects were Tested at 1 Month:
Berkeley Growth Study Sample**

Years and Months	N	Median	Quartiles I	Quartiles III	Range	Mean	SD
0–3	52	9	3	18	1–30	11.5	9.0
0–6	48	14	4	21	1–45	14.8	11.8
0–9	47	13	6	23	0–47	15.2	10.6
1–0	45	16	9	21	0–54	16.1	11.2
1–6	45	13	6	27	1–65	17.5	15.4
2–0	41	21	9	37	1–75	23.9	18.6
2–6	41	20	8	32	2–56	20.6	14.0
3–0	40	20	7	34	1–58	22.1	15.8
4–0	37	26	8	38	0–63	25.6	18.0
5–0	39	17	7	33	1–62	20.6	16.1
6–0	40	32	18	53	0–83	34.5	21.4
7–0	39	35	14	52	2–78	34.8	21.1
8–0	39	29	20	40	2–80	31.3	19.3
9–0	37	32	17	45	0–74	32.2	20.8
10–0	40	32	18	44	1–99	33.8	23.4
11–0	37	30	20	43	0–82	32.5	19.5
12–0	35	25	12	43	1–76	29.1	20.7
14–0	33	27	18	38	0–74	30.1	18.6
17–0	34	30	19	42	6–61	29.8	16.7

THE VALIDITY OF THE TABLES OF CHANGE

The tables of change in score with age which are provided (Appendix E) represent the actual amounts of change which were found for the Berkeley Growth Study sample, with the exceptions noted above. These are changes for a select group, and hence the question arises as to whether similar changes would be expected for a sample representative of the general population. To obtain evidence on this point these results were compared with those which Bradway (11) obtained on two samples of subjects used in the 1937 standardization of the Stanford-Binet.

Bradway reports a mean difference of 12 points between IQs obtained on the sample composed of children of ages 2, 3, and 3 years–6 months and IQs for the same children tested again with the 1937 Stanford-Binet after ten years (on the average). In contrast, subjects of the Berkeley Growth Study show a mean change of 20 points in conventional IQ from tests at 2 years with the *California Preschool Scale* to the tests at 12 years, at which age the 1937 Stanford-Binet was administered. The difference in results is to be explained in part by the tendency of the BGS subjects to show an increase in mean IQ with age. However, as can be seen by comparing the results in Table 1 with those in Table 6, the major portion of the changes in mean IQ between the 2

TABLE 7.2

Change in Deviation IQs with Age when Subjects were Tested at 3 Months: Berkeley Growth Study Sample

Years and Months	N	Median	Quartiles I	Quartiles III	Range	Mean	SD
0–6	57	12	8	21	0–45	14.6	10.2
0–9	56	13	7	22	0–56	15.5	11.7
1–0	53	12	6	25	1–50	17.0	13.5
1–6	51	15	3	28	0–67	18.4	16.8
2–0	48	29	12	39	0–83	29.0	21.3
2–6	47	19	9	32	1–68	22.8	17.8
3–0	48	26	11	37	0–66	26.1	16.6
4–0	45	28	15	42	0–61	27.8	17.2
5–0	47	20	11	39	1–61	23.3	15.3
6–0	48	37	16	47	0–84	34.1	21.7
7–0	46	38	22	49	0–77	35.4	19.2
8–0	47	29	18	43	3–78	31.4	17.8
9–0	45	33	20	47	1–79	33.7	19.0
10–0	47	29	20	47	1–91	34.2	20.6
11–0	45	31	18	45	1–83	33.2	19.7
12–0	43	26	18	45	1–81	30.1	18.9
14–0	37	25	17	41	0–76	29.7	18.3
17–0	40	30	18	44	0–66	31.2	18.1

TABLE 7.3

Change in Deviation IQs with Age when Subjects were Tested at 6 Months: Berkeley Growth Study Sample

Years and Months	N	Median	Quartiles I	Quartiles III	Range	Mean	SD
0–9	52	10	4	13	0–43	10.2	8.4
1–0	49	8	4	15	0–34	10.4	8.7
1–6	47	14	8	26	0–48	16.8	11.5
2–0	45	16	7	36	0–76	23.6	21.0
2–6	44	18	7	29	0–55	19.6	15.2
3–0	44	17	7	35	1–57	21.0	16.9
4–0	41	20	14	36	2–76	25.0	16.1
5–0	43	17	6	31	0–59	20.7	16.3
6–0	44	30	10	49	0–96	32.0	23.1
7–0	42	31	15	50	0–87	32.4	21.6
8–0	43	23	11	41	1–87	27.8	20.6
9–0	42	25	15	42	0–80	30.3	21.7
10–0	43	32	10	44	1–113	32.4	24.6
11–0	42	32	14	45	1–76	31.6	21.2
12–0	40	26	12	46	0–70	28.5	20.6
14–0	34	28	13	40	1–68	28.5	18.8
17–0	36	27	17	46	1–73	29.8	18.5

and 12 year tests (17 of the 21 points) is a function of the age changes in variability. This effect on the score changes can be ruled out (to a great extent) by subtracting the difference between the means at ages 2 and 12 from each subject's score change and redetermining the mean change, or it can be

TABLE 7.4

Change in Deviation IQs with Age when Subjects were Tested at 9 Months: Berkeley Growth Study Sample

Years and Months	N	Median	Quartiles I	Quartiles III	Range	Mean	SD
1–0	52	8	4	14	0–28	9.7	7.1
1–6	49	13	6	24	0–59	16.1	12.7
2–0	46	20	10	40	3–81	25.6	18.0
2–6	45	18	15	31	0–49	20.6	12.4
3–0	46	19	8	31	0–48	19.7	13.8
4–0	44	23	12	31	1–66	22.6	14.3
5–0	45	15	9	25	0–59	18.3	13.1
6–0	46	28	9	41	0–87	29.2	20.7
7–0	44	29	15	43	0–78	29.2	19.1
8–0	45	25	11	36	0–76	25.4	17.8
9–0	43	29	11	42	3–73	28.4	18.0
10–0	45	30	12	38	3–102	30.0	21.8
11–0	43	32	14	40	0–86	29.0	18.2
12–0	42	28	11	35	0–77	26.1	16.8
14–0	35	27	10	36	1–78	26.2	16.4
17–0	38	28	16	35	2–65	26.4	15.0

TABLE 7.5

Change in Deviation IQs with Age when Subjects were Tested at 1 Year: Berkeley Growth Study Sample

Years and Months	N	Median	Quartiles I	Quartiles III	Range	Mean	SD
1–6	49	10	6	20	0–47	14.5	12.1
2–0	46	22	11	32	0–68	24.5	17.0
2–6	45	19	8	31	0–50	19.2	13.1
3–0	46	16	11	30	1–53	20.4	12.8
4–0	44	21	11	27	1–72	22.4	14.3
5–0	45	13	6	23	0–55	17.7	14.3
6–0	46	24	14	44	2–92	30.0	21.1
7–0	44	29	13	44	2–83	30.1	19.7
8–0	45	22	12	34	0–81	26.1	19.2
9–0	43	27	11	44	0–74	28.6	19.8
10–0	45	27	15	43	1–107	31.3	21.9
11–0	43	30	19	41	3–77	30.9	18.0
12–0	42	24	12	40	2–74	27.3	18.5
14–0	35	27	16	41	2–69	29.2	16.4
17–0	38	28	13	42	0–63	28.2	16.2

TABLE 7.6

Change in Deviation IQs with Age when Subjects were Tested at 18 Months: Berkeley Growth Study Sample

Years and Months	N	Median	Quartiles I	Quartiles III	Range	Mean	SD
2–0	45	16	10	29	0–77	21.0	15.6
2–6	46	14	10	23	2–45	17.7	11.3
3–0	45	16	9	26	0–46	18.5	12.0
4–0	43	18	9	27	0–57	19.3	13.5
5–0	45	14	7	19	1–61	15.2	12.2
6–0	45	22	13	42	1–75	27.7	19.6
7–0	43	24	11	39	1–68	27.0	17.9
8–0	44	24	12	34	1–79	25.6	18.1
9–0	42	20	11	37	1–76	27.1	20.6
10–0	44	21	12	42	0–87	28.4	21.6
11–0	42	24	17	41	2–83	28.9	19.6
12–0	41	21	11	36	0–74	26.6	19.3
14–0	37	27	18	32	0–75	27.0	16.9
17–0	38	22	12	32	0–62	25.5	17.5

TABLE 7.7

Change in Deviation IQs with Age when Subjects were Tested at 5 Years: Berkeley Growth Study Sample

Years and Months	N	Median	Quartiles I	Quartiles III	Range	Mean	SD
6–0	46	15	8	22	0–40	16.0	10.0
7–0	44	14	6	22	0–39	15.0	10.6
8–0	45	11	8	19	1–42	13.7	8.8
9–0	43	13	7	22	1–43	15.0	10.2
10–0	45	13	6	22	1–46	16.1	12.4
11–0	43	14	7	27	0–45	16.5	11.1
12–0	42	12	4	20	1–47	14.0	10.4
14–0	36	12	5	20	1–36	14.4	10.3
17–0	39	12	3	20	0–36	13.3	10.2

eliminated by transforming the conventional IQ scores into deviation IQs. The mean score change was reduced to 16 points by both procedures.

Different tests were used at the two ages in the case of the BGS subjects whereas different age levels of the *same* test were used in the Bradway study. This may explain why the means and variabilities of the conventional IQs change somewhat less for Bradway's group than do the DIQs for the BGS sample. The difference in means and variabilities could readily account for the slightly greater change in the scores of the Berkeley Growth Study subjects;

or, the four-point difference may be due either to the somewhat greater mean age of Bradway's subjects or to the fact that in her study the test-retest interval varied somewhat, a certain proportion of the subjects being tested at a shorter interval than 10 years.[7]

Similar results were obtained in the comparison of the BGS subjects tested at 4 and 14 years and Bradway's second sample, children initially tested between 4 years and 5 years–6 months of age and retested with the Stanford-Binet after a mean interval of 10 years. The mean change for the Berkeley Growth Study sample (corrected for age changes in the means due to variations in the magnitudes of the standard deviations) was 14 points. The mean change in the Bradway study was 10 points. As before, Bradway's group averaged somewhat older and the interval between tests varied for her subjects. Alternatively the differences may be due to the use of different tests with the BGS subjects at the two ages and/or to the greater instability of measures of relative ability on superior children.

The comparison of BGS results with those which Bradway obtained (11) on samples used in the 1937 standardization of the Stanford-Binet suggests that the BGS changes in DIQ may not differ to any great extent from those which would be obtained from a random sample of the population. Hence, they can be taken as a fairly adequate guide as to how much change to expect in relative position over a period of years, and will thus, it is hoped, keep the practitioner from putting too much (or too little) faith in test results obtained early in the child's development (43).

SUMMARY

Evidence presented in this chapter shows that on several available tests a given conventional IQ value indicates a different relative position at different ages. As a consequence, a child's IQ on such tests must change as he grows older if he maintains his same standing relative to those his age. These changes are a function of the construction of the tests and of the method of computing the IQ, not of developmental processes within the child as has previously been thought (8, 42, 50). Consequently, if one is told only that a subject's conventional IQ has increased 10 points, it is impossible to determine whether the subject has maintained his same relative position, whether there is an increase in his ability relative to others his age, or whether his relative position is actually somewhat lower.

In contrast to the conventional IQ is the deviation IQ which indicates the same relative standing at all ages. Consequently, a subject's DIQ will not change unless he changes in the age group. In addition, a given change in DIQ indicates at different ages and at different levels of ability the same amount of change in relative position in standard score terms.

---

[7] The greater instability of scores of bright as compared with more nearly average subjects is an additional factor which may account for the greater IQ change of the BGS sample as compared with Bradway's group. While greater instability of the scores of bright subjects may chiefly be dependent upon psychological features of the test (cf., pp. 40–41), it may also be partially a function of the more rapid rate of mental growth of bright as compared with average or dull subjects (cf., p. 63).

5

THE EFFECT OF AGE CHANGES IN

VARIABILITY ON STABILITY

OF STANFORD–BINET IQS

In this and the next chapter the derivation of the deviation IQ will be considered in more detail as it affects interpretations of results obtained with the 1937 Stanford-Binet and as its rationale and theoretical basis provide a foundation for developments in the 1960 revision. The concern will be with age changes in the means and standard deviation of conventional IQs for the standardization samples of the 1937 revision; the relation of the fluctuations in variability to the reliability of IQ scores obtained with the test; and the presentation of graphs comparing conventional and deviation IQs for individual subjects during elementary school years and adolescence.

FLUCTUATIONS IN IQ VARIABILITIES OF THE 1937 REVISION OF THE STANFORD-BINET

Terman and Merrill in *Measuring Intelligence* (54) note that the variability of IQ scores for the 1937 revision at such ages as 6 and 12 differ so much from those obtained at other ages that it may be doubted if this deviation is due purely to chance. They add, "In the lack of positive proof to the contrary we are probably justified in assuming that the true variability is approximately constant from age to age. Repeated tests of the same subjects from early childhood to maturity will be necessary to determine whether this assumption is in accord with the facts" (Ibid., p. 41).

The standard deviations for the 1937 Stanford-Binet (Forms L and M combined) which were obtained on the standardization samples are plotted in Figure 2. The curve of these values, arithmetically smoothed three times to

FIGURE 2

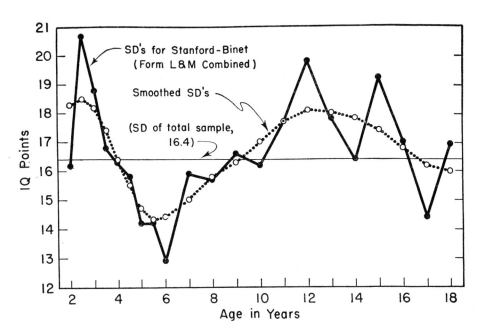

IQ variability for the Stanford-Binet for ages
2 to 18: 1937 standardization sample

remove irregularities, is also included in this figure. The departure of the values obtained at the different ages from the median standard deviation of 16.4 for the composite L-M variabilities is too large to be explained in terms of chance (see Table 4). The question arises as to how to account for these fluctuations. They may be due to selective factors in the samplings (greater heterogeneity at some ages), to actual variations of mental growth processes with age as suggested by Bayley (8), to variations in test composition at the different age levels, or to a combination of these factors.

McNemar, in his analysis of the standardization data (39) discounts the first explanation, which is that selective factors in sampling are causative of the major variations in the standard deviations. The second, the possibility that the major fluctuations reflect true variations or cycles in mental growth, will be considered in detail in a later section (see p. 61). However, it can be stated that the second explanation appears unlikely in the light of an analysis of BGS data (42).

McNemar, in agreement with the position held by Goodenough (22, 23) and others (1, 13), suggested that they are due primarily to the manner in which the tests at the various age levels are constituted. As is shown later, the analysis of BGS data supports this point of view.

McNemar's Corrections

In his analysis McNemar reports that the greater variability at the early pre-school ages and again at 11 and 12 years is probably to be accounted for by the larger concentration of items of medium difficulty at these ages, and that the restriction in variability at ages 5, 5 years–6 months, and 6 years is probably to be accounted for by the small number of items of medium difficulty at these ages. He presents corrections for a number of the ages at which such variations in difficulty level were most pronounced, for example, ages 4 years–10 months to 6 years–6 months and ages 11 years–6 months to 12 years–5 months.

If the corrections suggested by McNemar are adequate, it might be expected that their application will result in *corrected* mean IQs that are more stable from age to age than *conventional* mean IQs. One of the administrations of the 1937 Stanford-Binet scale to the BGS sample occurred at an age for which he presents corrections, year twelve. Appropriate application of McNemar's correction to this sample's scores should, presumably, bring the mean IQ at this age more in line with the mean IQs for other ages. It can be observed in Figure 3

FIGURE 3

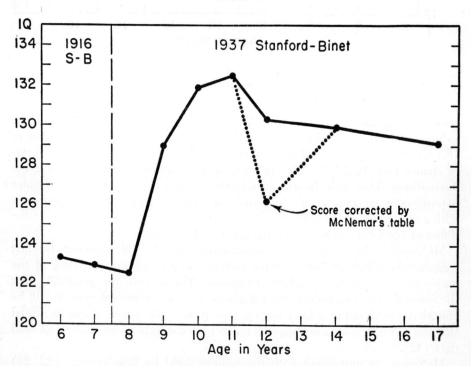

Effect of McNemar's correction on mean IQs
of the Berkeley Growth Study sample

that the correction increases rather than reduces the fluctuations in the means for the BGS sample. Yet, as results presented later show, this should not be interpreted to indicate that correction of the scores at twelve years is unsound.[8]

It might be expected that the concentration of easy or difficult items at a given age level would tend to apply not only to subjects at that age, but also to subjects of adjoining ages since they are also tested with these items. If so, the concentrations would affect the variabilities of scores at the adjoining ages. The congruent declines and increases in variabilities around these areas (as shown in Figure 2) suggest that this is the case; that is, the standard deviations at adjacent ages are being systematically affected. This finding suggests that the fluctuations in the smoothed standard deviations reflect actual age changes in variability, and hence that corrections should be employed at all ages.

Variability Corrections at All Ages

If, as McNemar contends, the extreme fluctuations in variability reflect unevenness in concentrations of difficult and average-difficulty items, and if, as the present investigator has suggested, the variations in the adjacent years are also meaningful, then the variabilities in another sample should show similar trends (1, 23, 41).

The standard deviations for the Berkeley Growth Study for those ages at which the Stanford-Binet was used are shown in Figure 4. Also included for comparison are those of the standardization samples for the same forms of the Stanford-Binet.[9] The comparison suggests that the variability changes are not just random fluctuations. However, it should be noted that the peak of variability for the BGS sample comes somewhat earlier than for the standardization group. This is to be expected since the mentally superior BGS subjects are successful, some two years earlier than average, on the concentration of average-difficulty items around the age of 12.

If the fluctuations in the 1937 Stanford-Binet mean IQs for this relatively superior group were reduced when the IQs were transformed into deviation IQs, there would be additional evidence that the fluctuations in the variabilities are meaningful. Figure 5 compares for the BGS sample the mean deviation IQs with the mean conventional IQs for the ages at which these tests were administered. The range of fluctuations of the means is reduced from 10 to 4 points. (It should be noted that the mean of the 12 year scores, corrected according to McNemar's method, falls in line with the means of the deviation, rather than with the means of the conventional, IQs.)

It is apparent from Figure 5 that a considerable portion of the fluctuations of the conventional IQ means for this superior group is accounted for by fluctuations in the size of the standard deviations. That is, the increased stability of the mean scores obtained when the DIQ is utilized with this group supports the conclusion that the fluctuations in the smoothed standard deviations for

---

[8] Elwood presents (18) data which appear on the surface to contradict McNemar's contention that corrections should be applied. However, it appears that if the scores were corrected in the manner subsequently described, the amount of change would compare favorably with that expected on the basis of regression toward the mean.

[9] In the case of the 1916 Stanford-Binet scale, standard deviations were computed from the six and seven year frequency distributions (53).

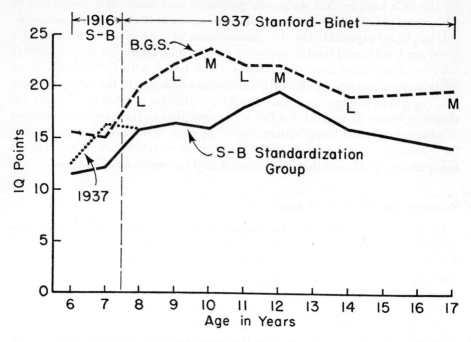

FIGURE 4

Stanford-Binet IQ variabilities obtained on the 1937 standardization sample and on the Berkeley Growth Study sample [adapted from Bayley (8)]

the standardization sample represent actual age changes in variability of performance for this test. [Analysis of the data indicates that the socio-economic adjustment has contributed little to the reduction in range of variation of the means (cf., p. 48).]

If, in the BGS sample, part of the IQ change with age is due to fluctuations in the variabilities, then the magnitude of the *changes* should be reduced when the scores are transformed into DIQs. Figure 6 compares the conventional and deviation IQ changes in score subsequent to year 8, the first age at which the 1937 revision was administered. As is to be expected, the reductions are greatest at those ages at which the means were most out of line. Of special significance is the finding that the marked increases in variability at ages 10, 11, and 12 cause the changes in conventional IQ from the 8 year test to the tests at these ages to exceed those obtained for an interval more than twice as long, that is, from 8 to 17 years. Also included in Figure 6 are the standard errors of estimate for the same ages. In deriving these the writer utilized the standard deviation obtained on the total 1937 Stanford-Binet standardization sample, 16.4 (54), and he used the BGS correlations as estimates of the relationships which would have been obtained between scores if the 8 year standardization sample had been retested at these later ages. Assuming this constancy of variability for the test, the fluctuations of change in DIQs of the more heterogeneous BGS sample follow much more closely the pattern of changes expected

EFFECT OF AGE CHANGES   34

FIGURE 5

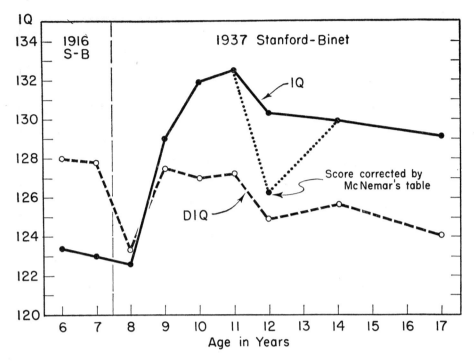

**Mean conventional and mean deviation IQs on the 1916 and
1937 Stanford-Binet scales: Berkeley Growth Study sample**

on the basis of the standard errors of estimate than do the changes in conventional IQ.

The evidence in this section indicates that the corrections provided by McNemar do not adequately reduce the spurious changes found between the repeated testings of the BGS sample with the 1937 Stanford-Binet because the corrections were limited only to the ages at which the variability fluctuations were most extreme. When corrections were employed at all ages at which the 1937 Stanford-Binet revision was administered, instability in the mean IQ of the BGS decreased, the IQ changes were reduced, and with age the pattern of changes was more in line with those expected on the basis of predicted standard errors of estimate for the standardization sample.

THE RELIABILITY OF IQS AT DIFFERENT LEVELS OF ABILITY

Terman and Merrill recognized in *Measuring Intelligence* that the amount of change in IQ from test to retest tends to be greater among high ability subjects than among those of lower ability (54, p. 46). This greater instability of scores for bright subjects can be explained in several ways: (a) it may be a a function of the method of calculating the IQ, that is, of the $\frac{\text{MA}}{\text{CA}}$ ratio, as

FIGURE 6

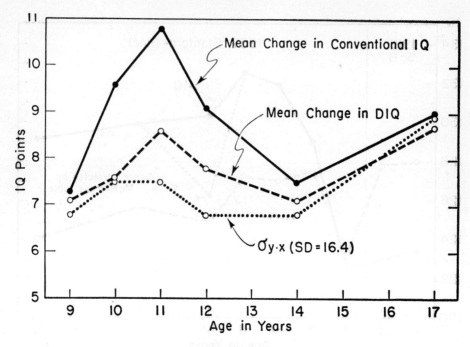

Average change in conventional and deviation IQs subsequent
to year eight tests: Berkeley Growth Study sample

suggested by Terman and Merrill (Ibid.) and McNemar (39); (b) it may be
related to the number of items on which the IQ is based (fewer items for
higher IQs, in terms of the way the test is constructed); or (c) it may be that
among bright subjects the expression of ability is actually more variable from
one time to another.

In his analysis of the standardization data of the 1937 revision of the Stanford-
Binet, McNemar gave considerable attention to this finding (Ibid.). He considered the age samples individually, and in various age groupings — 2 years–
6 months to 5 years–6 months, 6 to 13 years, etc. One procedure involved the
correlation of IQ level and IQ differences in retests. The correlations were
significant for the various age groupings and for the total age range, but (with
one exception) not for the individual groups. The question may be raised as to
whether these results would have been predicted on the basis of the construction of the Stanford-Binet. The issues which are considered in answering this
question are as applicable to the 1960 revision of the Stanford-Binet as to the
1937 revision since they are comparable in structure.

Consider the items on which the subjects between the ages of 2 years–6
months and 5 years–6 months are tested. All subjects who pass items through
Year V will obtain 1 month credit toward a mental age score per each test
passed whereas those who pass items above this level will receive 2 months of
credit per each item. This is because in the 1937 Stanford-Binet there are twice

as many items per year below Year VI as for Year VI and subsequently.[10] Consequently, if due to chance factors a subject fails a given item at the VI Year level, he will be penalized more heavily than for the failure of an item at the V Year level.

In view of the differential weighting of the items one would, assuming that the items are comparably reliable, predict greater reliability of scores for children who obtain their scores on Year V items or below, than for those who obtain their score on Year VI items or above where subjects are given double credit for passing an item. Consider next the group of items for Year VI through Year XIII. Assume again that each item at Year V and below is comparable in reliability to each item at Year VI and above. The mental ages of below average 6– and 7–year-olds will depend on their performance on items at Year V or at lower levels where subjects receive 1 month credit per item, while more nearly average subjects will obtain less reliable scores because their mental ages are based at least in part on items which are given weights of 2 months each.

At the other end of this age grouping one finds that the very bright 11-year-olds, the very superior 12–year-olds, and the superior 13–year-olds will be obtaining their scores in part by passing items for which they receive 4, 5, or in the more unusual cases, 6 months credit. As a result one would expect the bright children's scores to be less reliable than those of the below average or average subjects whose performance scores (at lower mental age levels) are based on a larger number of items per mental age unit. Results presented in the next section indicate that there is no reason to believe that an increase in item reliability adequately compensates for the increased weighting given each item at the higher ages.

The preceding considerations, which apply similarly to age levels beyond 13, indicate that the lower reliability of scores of more intelligent subjects is to be explained to a considerable extent by the increased mental age weight which is given to individual items at later age levels as compared to earlier age levels. The combining of all age samples as in the 2 year–6 month to 18 year grouping will, of course, merely make this factor more evident.

The Reliability of Mental Age Scores

Age changes in the reliability of mental age scores on the 1937 revision are directly related to age changes in the reliability of IQs (see subsequent section on reliability, p. 39). McNemar (39) has shown that the standard error of measurement for Stanford-Binet mental age scores increases with mental age level — from 1.9 months at the 2 year–6 month level to 7.0 months at a mental age of 15 years; that is, the higher mental ages are assessed less reliably than the lower mental ages. This empirical finding shows, as was suggested in the preceding paragraphs, that the increased unreliability of mental age scores which results from the increased weight given items at higher age levels is not offset by any increase in the reliability of the items.

[10] The tests at each level pertain to the preceding age period. For example, the six tests at Year V relate to the period from IV–6 to V, while the period from Year V to Year VI is covered by the tests under the heading of Year VI (54, p. 65).

An increase in the range of mental age distribution with chronological age (cf., Figure 14) does not in and of itself result in a concomitant increase in the errors of measurement for conventional IQs on the 1937 revision of the Stanford-Binet scale, as has been suggested (39, 54). Instead, the increase in the standard errors of measurement is a function of the increased weight given the items at higher mental age levels. The Stanford-Binet scales give each item mental age weights as follows: 1 month, Year II through Year V; 2 months, Year VI through Average Adult; and 4, 5, and 6 months, respectively, as Superior Adult I, II, and III.

In view of the weighting of items on the Stanford-Binet scales, steps in the magnitude of standard errors of measurement of mental age might be expected. However, such an expectation ignores the fact that a subject's mental age score is based on performance at a number of age levels. Hence, the closer subjects are to an age level at which item weighting changes, the more their scores will be based on fewer item successes. Consequently, it is not surprising that the increases in the standard errors of measurement of mental ages for the Stanford-Binet scales are fairly regular.

A further question which might be raised with respect to the reliability of mental age scores is whether or not a given mental age assessment is more reliably made for subjects of superior intellect than for subjects of below normal intellect. For example, is a mental age of 10–00 years more reliably determined for eight-year-olds with an IQ of 125, or for twelve-year-olds with an IQ of 83? In general, the latter tends to be true. That is, the standard error of measurement for a given mental age tends to decrease the older the subject is at time of testing. If the performance of an older subject of the same mental age tends to be based on a smaller range of items the score will be more reliable, on the average, than that of a younger subject whose score is based on items at the later levels where they receive greater weight. This suggestion receives little support from McNemar's analysis of the spread of performance at different age levels. (Still, the formula on page 39 indicates that in IQ terms the older subject's score will be more reliable since the divisor is larger.)

Investigating the spread of individual performances, McNemar (39) uses as a measure of variability the distance, in terms of age levels, from an individual's basal mental age to the highest level at which tests are passed. At several mental age levels, he correlates these variability scores with the subjects' IQs. While the correlations are generally negative, none are significant and none exceed a value of −.10. Thus the spread of performance at a given mental age level does not vary significantly with brightness nor with chronological age. It seems likely, at least when the standard error of measurement is based on test-retest administrations, that the greater unreliability of scores for bright subjects is due in a large measure to their more rapid rate of mental growth.

Reliability Estimates via the Average-difference Method and via the Variance Method

Because subjects of above average ability tend to be more variable in IQ from test to retest on the 1937 Stanford-Binet than subjects of lesser ability, a correlational plot of the scores on two different testings will tend to be fan-shaped at the upper IQ levels; that is, the scatter plots will lack homoscedasticity. Because of this, the conventional form-versus-form coefficient of reliability was deemed inapplicable (39, 54) in determining reliabilities for the 1937 revision of the Stanford-Binet. Therefore, McNemar (39) determined the reliability of scores at different IQ levels by means of the average-difference method and via the variance method. The developments in the present work have a number of implications for these relationships.

In combining the various age groups to estimate reliabilities, for example, from 2 years–6 months to 5 years–6 months, the assumption is necessarily made that the reliability of the IQ does not change with age. However, the available evidence indicates that it does (Ibid., pp. 62–63, 67). Consequently, the computed reliabilities tend to be too high for the 2– and 3–year-olds and too low for subjects between 4 years and 5 years–6 months. They are especially inadequate at the distribution extremes for the latter group because the standard deviations indicate that subjects between the ages of 4 years and 5 years–6 months are not adequately represented at these IQ levels (see Figure 2). Indeed, the differences among the standard deviations for the samples at the various ages between 2 years–6 months and 5 years–6 months are so great that it is doubtful that these groups should be combined. Similar difficulties are inherent in the combining of the 6 to 13 year age groups.

The findings of the present study, that variability of the IQ fluctuates with age, makes another point evident with respect to these age groupings. The subjects within a given IQ interval, especially at the distribution extremes, are not homogeneous with respect to relative mental ability. For example, the interval of conventional IQs from 140 to 149 include the subjects 2 years–6 months of age whose DIQs fall between 132 to 141, whereas at 5 years–6 months of age it includes those whose DIQs fall between 144–156. At 6 years of age this interval of IQs includes subjects whose DIQs fall between 145 and 154, and at 12 years of age those whose DIQs fall between 134 and 142. Thus for subjects between the ages of 2 years–6 months and 5 years–6 months and for those between 6 and 13 years the reliability estimates and the standard errors of measurement for a given range of relative ability are in error to an unknown extent, especially near the distribution extremes.

Reliability — a Function of the IQ Technique

It has been suggested that the errors of measurement for IQs should vary with the magnitude of the IQ because the variability of the mental age distributions increases with chronological age (39, 54). In this connection McNemar has pointed out (39) that if a measure is transformed by multiplication or division, its error must likewise be transformed,[11]

$$\sigma_{e_{(MA)}} = \frac{CA}{100}\, \sigma_{e_{(IQ)}}.$$

[11] The formula which follows is the same as that suggested by McNemar (39) with the exception that division of the second half of the equation by 100 is specified rather than left implicit. In the formula, $\sigma_{e_{(MA)}}$ is the standard error of measurement of the mental age and $\sigma_{e_{(IQ)}}$ is the standard error of measurement of the intelligence quotient.

39 RELIABILITY OF IQS

Let us assume at every chronological age that the standard error of measurement is the same for each mental age of a hypothetical Stanford-Binet scale, that there is one item for each month of mental age, and that the variability of the conventional IQ is 16 points. Under such circumstances the standard error of measurement of a given IQ score will decrease with age (as can be seen from the preceding formula), although at any one age the standard error of measurement will be the same for all IQs. Thinking in more traditional terms, this is because a given month of mental age represents a larger number of IQ points at earlier than at later ages. In this instance it is noted that the errors of measurement for IQs vary inversely with the age of the subject tested. It should also be noted that the increase in variability of the mental age distribution from earlier to later ages would not, however, result in a tendency for the size of errors of measurement of IQs to vary with the magnitude of the IQ for a given chronological age.

Suppose in this example that every other item at the Year VI and subsequent levels is dropped, and that the weight of the retained items is doubled. The standard error of measurement must also be doubled. The consequences are evident. Scores based on items at Year VI and subsequent levels will have a larger standard error of measurement than scores based on items before Year VI. Essentially this condition prevails with respect to weighting in the cases of the 1937 and 1960 revisions of the Stanford-Binet — double weight is assigned to items at and after Year VI until at the upper age levels the weight per item can be four, five, or six times as great as at the preschool levels.

Errors of measurement for conventional IQs on the Stanford-Binet scales vary with the magnitude of the IQ. This is not because the variability of the mental age distribution increases with chronological age, but because the increased weighting given to individual items at later age levels is not accompanied by a corresponding increase in their reliability.

It should perhaps be noted again that the standard error of measurement for a given mental age score is not a constant for all chronological ages. Because there is in general an increase with age in reliability of performance on an item, the standard errors of measurement for a given mental age score tend to decrease in magnitude for older subjects. This increase in reliability with age, based on test-retest data, appears to be chiefly a function of the decline with age in the rate of mental growth between birth and maturity.

AGE CHANGES IN THE IQS OF BRIGHT AND DULL SUBJECTS

At most ages the scores of bright subjects on the 1937 Stanford-Binet tend to change somewhat more from test to retest than the scores of dull subjects because of the construction of the scale. However, the available evidence (39, 54) suggests that rarely will the standard errors of measurement for bright subjects be more than one or two points greater than those for dull subjects at the same age, even when the mean conventional IQs for the groups differ by 50 or more points.

The conclusions presented in the preceding paragraph have to do with the test-retest reliability of conventional IQs; that is, of IQs obtained on two tests given at approximately the same age. Attention will now be directed to the finding that, as compared with dull subjects, the conventional IQs of bright subjects tend to change more with age than one would expect on the basis of reliability estimates. This result, as analyses presented later indicate, is expected in the case of the conventional IQ but not in the case of the deviation IQ.

Evidence previously presented (p. 17, ff.) indicate that the mean conventional IQ for subjects on the 1937 Stanford-Binet tends at some ages to be too high. This is especially evident at ages where the variabilities are large. The rank-difference correlation between smoothed means (54, p. 36) and smoothed standard deviations (Table 5) is .57 for ages 2 years–6 months to 17 years (see Figure 2). As a consequence, there will be less numerical discrepancy between the IQ of low ability subjects who maintain their same relative standing with age than there will be for comparably high ability subjects. As shown in Figure 19, a subject who, at ages 2 years–6 months, 6 years, and 12 years, is consistently three standard deviations above the mean will reveal a loss of 15 points and then a gain of 13 points. In contrast, a comparably stable subject three standard deviations below the mean will reveal considerably less change in conventional IQ — an increase of 9 points and then a decrease of 9 points.

It is apparent, because the elevation of the means tends to offset the variability changes, that dull subjects will obtain more stable conventional IQs on the Stanford-Binet scales than will bright subjects. When the deviation IQ is used, bright subjects will *not* be less stable than dull subjects except to the extent that their scores tend to be less reliable. If a subject maintains with age the same relative standing on the Stanford-Binet, the DIQ will be the same at every age regardless of his level of ability.

The differences in reliability of DIQs earned by bright and dull subjects at a given age are, generally, small. Therefore, for practical purposes there is no necessity to qualify the results presented in the tables of change in deviation IQ (Appendix E) when they are used with subjects at different levels of ability.

THE RELATIVE STABILITY OF CONVENTIONAL AND DEVIATION IQS FOR INDIVIDUALS

The deviation IQ transformation of the Stanford-Binet IQs reduces the fluctuations in the mean scores of the BGS subjects and the average changes in scores on tests administered at various ages. However, it reduces to a less extent the changes in an individual's scores since the changes are also a function of actual variations in the subject's rate of development and of errors of measurement. In figures 7 through 12 conventional and deviation IQs are compared by means of individual age-curves for those ages at which the Stanford-Binet was administered.

The differences between a subject's conventional and deviation IQs are a function both of the corrections for age changes in the variabilities and of the adjustments in the means required to yield a mean of 100 at all ages for representative samples. (Only corrections for changes in variability were used in the case of the 1916 Stanford-Binet.) With respect to the adjustments in the means it should be noted that while they lowered the mean score of the BGS sample by one to three points at every age, they did not reduce the fluctuations of the means. Thus on the average the adjustments in the means do not account for any reduction in the variation in an individual's deviation IQs (as compared with his conventional IQs) although they do account for part of the difference between the two kinds of IQ scores at each age.

The individual BGS cases presented in Figures 7 through 12 are chosen to illustrate the effects of the DIQ transformation on the stability of the IQ at various levels of ability above the mean of the general population. As noted earlier (p. 14), Bayley suggests that intra-individual differences in constancy be measured quantitatively in terms of standard deviation of the subject's standard score for a given age interval (Intelligence Lability Scores). Essentially this method was used to compare the stability of IQs for the individual cases presented in the figures; namely, standard deviations of the individual's conventional and deviation IQs. For each individual case the standard deviation of the conventional IQs was larger than that of the deviation IQs when both the 1916 and 1937 Stanford-Binet scales were considered. The differences between the Lability Scores were less marked when only the 1937 Stanford-Binet scores were utilized, although all but one of the cases (Case 32F, Figure 7) showed a greater Lability Score for the conventional than the deviation IQ. (Only the Lability Scores for the conventional and deviation IQs obtained on the 1937 revision of the Stanford-Binet are presented here.)

Age curves are presented in Figures 7 and 8 for two subjects whose scores vary around a DIQ of 150; that is, these subjects are approximately three standard deviations above the mean. One would expect to find only fourteen individuals of such exceptional ability in a representative sample of 10,000 subjects from the general population (assuming a normal distribution of DIQs at each age). The Lability Score for Case 32F (Figure 7) was 6.0 for the DIQ and 5.8 for the conventional IQ. Thus, as noted above, the variability of the conventional IQs of this subject suggests greater stability of relative standing with age than is actually present. For Case 7M (Figure 8) the Lability Scores for conventional and deviation IQs were 7.8 and 7.0, respectively. In this instance, as in the case of the other individual records considered, the variability of the conventional IQs is greater than that of the DIQs and thus suggests greater variations in relative standing than actually occur.

Age-curves for subjects whose scores vary around a DIQ of approximately 140 are presented in Figures 9 and 10. The first of these subjects, Case 23F, is the most consistent of the six individual cases in maintaining the same relative position throughout the age span of 8 to 17 years, whereas the second subject at this level (Case 9M) is one of the more variable subjects in mental growth during this period. (The Lability Scores for the conventional and deviation IQs were 3.1 and 2.1 for Case 23 F, and 8.4 and 7.2 for Case 9M.)

Age curves are presented in Figures 11 and 12 for subjects at levels of ability much more frequently encountered in the usual testing situation. The first of these presents scores for Case 17M, the subject in this series whose

FIGURE 7

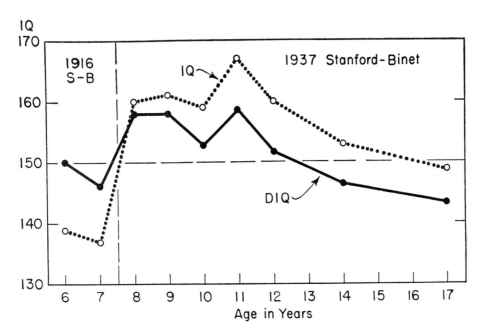

Conventional and deviation IQ curves for Case 32 F

FIGURE 8

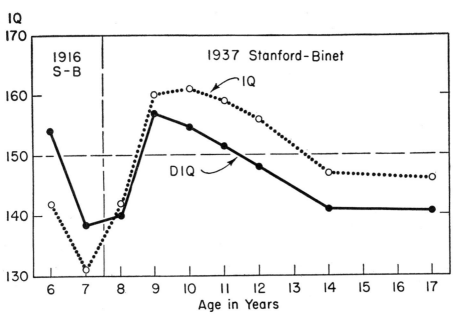

Conventional and deviation IQ curves for Case 7 M

INDIVIDUAL IQ STABILITY

FIGURE 9

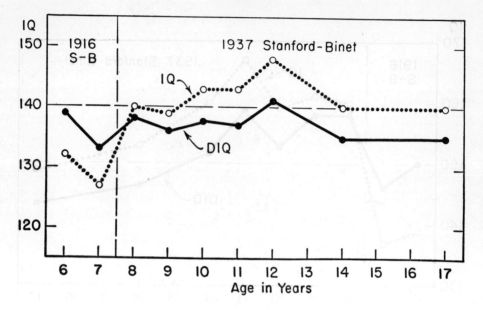

Conventional and deviation IQ curves for Case 23 F

FIGURE 10

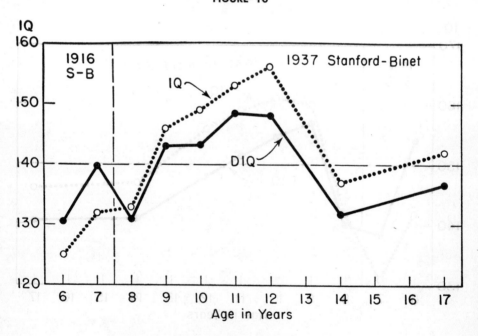

Conventional and deviation IQ curves for Case 9 M

FIGURE 11

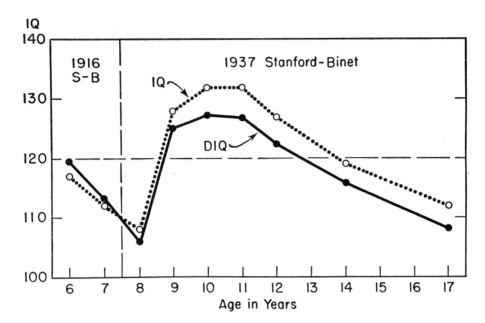

Conventional and deviation IQ curves for Case 17 M

FIGURE 12

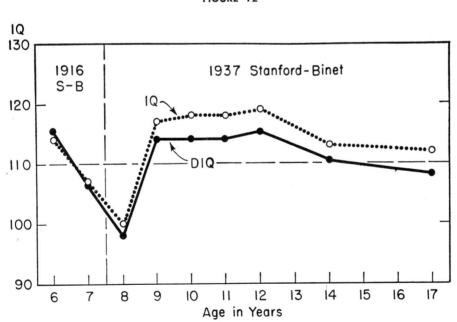

Conventional and deviation IQ curves for Case 42 M

performance showed the greatest variability at those ages at which the 1937 revision of the Stanford-Binet was administered. The second of these two figures presents the age curves for a subject (Case 42M) whose performance is more nearly average and whose fluctuations in relative standing with age are intermediate. The Lability Score for the conventional IQs were 9.7 for Case 17M and 6.8 for Case 42M. The Lability Scores for their DIQs were 8.9 and 6.1 respectively.

The impression gained from an inspection of the individual age curves is corroborated by the Lability Scores. The DIQ transformation increases the stability of individuals' scores with age. While it is to be expected that this standard score transformation will be most effective in increasing the stability of scores for bright subjects, it is evident from the individual comparisons that it also increases the stability of scores for subjects well within the range usually encountered in individual testing.

SUMMARY

There are fluctuations with age in the size of the standard deviations of conventional IQs for the Stanford-Binet scales, apparently because of varying concentrations of average difficulty items at different levels of the test. Consequently, IQ scores obtained with these scales must be corrected if they are to have consistent meaning from one age to another. When corrections are applied only at those ages at which the variabilities are the most out of line, the fluctuations in the mean IQs for the BGS sample increase rather than decrease. However, when the age change in variability (as represented by the smoothed values of the SDs) is taken into account at each age by transforming the conventional IQs into DIQs, the range of changes in mean score is reduced by half. These results, taken together with the findings on the 1937 standardization data, indicate the need for standard scores or deviation IQs for the Stanford-Binet scales.

On the average there is greater change in conventional IQ for bright children from test to retest on a Stanford-Binet scale than for those of less ability of the same age. This greater instability of scores on the test for bright subjects is not a consequence of the increased variability of the mental age distribution with increased chronological age, as has been contended, but is a function of the construction of the scale. It results from the increased weighting given items at later as compared with earlier mental ages and to an even greater extent from age changes in the means and standard deviations of the conventional IQ. (The age variations in the means tend to accentuate the effects of variability fluctuations on IQ change in the case of bright subjects and to offset them in the case of subjects of low ability.) The deviation IQ rules out this second and major source of instability in scores of high ability subjects.

For individual subjects the DIQ transformation rules out, of course, only part of the change in conventional IQ with age, namely that part due to age changes in the means and variabilities. Hence, the fluctuations in score which are not attributable to these factors will be present after the transformation. In the latter part of the chapter figures are presented comparing conventional and deviation IQs for selected subjects. These figures illustrate that, in general, DIQs are more stable with age than are conventional IQs. The greater stability of DIQs is indicated quantitatively by means of a comparison of Lability Scores; that is, by means of the contrast of the standard deviations of a subject's conventional and deviation IQs.

6

THE DEVELOPMENT OF REVISED

IQ TABLES FOR THE

STANFORD–BINET SCALES

In contrast to the conventional IQ, a given deviation IQ indicates the same relative standing at different ages. Ignoring unreliability of measurements, any subject's DIQ score will remain the same from one age to another unless there is a change in his relative position. Also, a given change in DIQ indicates the same amount of change in relative position, regardless of the subject's standing in his group or of the ages at which the tests are given. In view of these advantages, it seemed desirable to provide tables for determining deviation IQs for the 1937 as well as for the 1960 revision of the Stanford-Binet Scale.

CHOICE OF MEANS

It is usually assumed that the mean IQs on Forms L and M of the 1937 revision is 100 for representative samples of subjects at different ages. The results which Terman and Merrill present (54, p. 36) indicate that this is only approximately true and that at most ages such samples actually obtain average scores from one to four IQ points above 100. While these differences are small, it would appear that they should not be ignored in deriving an IQ score which would vary with age *only* in relation to changes in relative standing. Consequently, in establishing deviation IQs for these scales, corrections were made for the departure of the means from 100, utilizing Terman and Merrill's table of ". . . values that would have been obtained for a representative sampling of the native-born white population. . ." (Ibid., pp. 35–36).

The mean IQs for the 1937 revision average slightly above 100 because the mental age scores are somewhat larger (on the average) than the chronological age divisors. When subjects at ages 4, 8, and 12 receive mental age scores of 4, 8, and 12, respectively, their performance is actually slightly below the mean for their age group in the general population. Terman and Merrill's table, referred to above, was used in establishing the mental age corrections required to yield mean IQs of 100 for representative age samples. These corrections are presented in Table 8. In order to avoid the necessity of correcting the mental age scores obtained on the Stanford-Binet before determining the deviation IQ scores, these corrections were built into the DIQ tables as is indicated in the text which accompanies them (see Appendices B and C).

The individual's mental age score on a Stanford-Binet scale is a summary statement of his total performance. In addition to serving as the dividend in determining the conventional IQ, the mental age score indicates the age group for which the performance is typical. Those mental age scores between ages 2 and 13 on the 1937 and 1960 revisions of the scale indicate an age level slightly higher than the age group for which the performance is average. Those above 13 serve only the first function; that is, they are of value only in determining the conventional IQ. In order to provide more adequate estimates of the age group for which a given performance is average through a mental age of 13, and in order to relate mental age scores above this level to the average performance of subjects between 13 and 18 years of age, a table of *Corrected Mental Ages* was prepared and is presented in Appendix A.

CHOICE OF STANDARD DEVIATIONS

Evidence previously presented indicates that deviation IQs for the Stanford-Binet are needed in order to take account of the age changes in variability. Although it has been previously suggested that the variations of the standard deviations around the smoothed values (see Figure 2) could be due to chance, there still may be some question as to whether the actual or smoothed values should be used in deriving DIQs.

Berkeley Growth Study data provide evidence on this point subsequent to age 8 years. A comparison of the BGS mean DIQs computed from the raw and from the smoothed standard deviations indicates less fluctuation in the means when the smoothed standard deviations are used. Thus the comparison supports the hypothesis that in general the variations of the raw standard deviations around the smoothed values are due to chance (see Figure 13).

Before the age of 8 the differences between the raw and smoothed variabilities were relatively small except at 2 years, 2 years–6 months, and 6 years. In the absence of longitudinal data negating their importance, it seems desirable to consider these differences in more detail.

Since there are no items below the II Year level, the scale is almost certain to be short on items of medium difficulty at this age. An inspection of the percentages passing items by age (39) confirms this expectation; there are fewer items between the 35 and 65 per cent levels of difficulty than for any other age at which the standard deviations equal or exceed the II Year raw value. Since extent of variability is partly a function of item difficulty, it is to be expected that variability at this age would be relatively small. In view

TABLE 8

Mental age corrections for the Stanford-Binet scales:
Based on 1937 standardization data*

Corrections in months required to yield Mean IQs of 100 at different ages for
representative samples of the "native-born white population" (54, p. 36)

MONTHS

YEARS	0	1	2	3	4	5	6	7	8	9	10	11
2	—.53	—.60	—.68	—.73	—.81	—.90	—.99	—1.05	—1.15	—1.22	—1.29	—1.40
3	—1.48	—1.41	—1.33	—1.25	—1.12	—1.02	—.92	—.90	—.88	—.86	—.83	—.80
4	—.77	—.74	—.65	—.61	—.57	—.48	—.43	—.38	—.39	—.34	—.29	—.30
5	—.24	—.18	—.19	—.13	—.06	—.06	—.00	—.00	.07	.07	.07	.14
6	.14	.07	.00	.00	—.08	—.15	—.23	—.32	—.40	—.40	—.49	—.58
7	—.67	—.76	—.86	—.96	—1.06	—1.16	—1.26	—1.36	—1.47	—1.58	—1.69	—1.80
8	—1.92	—1.94	—2.06	—2.18	—2.20	—2.32	—2.35	—2.47	—2.60	—2.62	—2.76	—2.78
9	—2.92	—2.94	—3.08	—3.11	—3.14	—3.16	—3.19	—3.34	—3.36	—3.39	—3.54	—3.57
10	—3.60	—3.51	—3.54	—3.44	—3.35	—3.38	—3.28	—3.18	—3.20	—3.10	—2.99	—3.01
11	—2.90	—2.93	—2.81	—2.70	—2.72	—2.74	—2.62	—2.50	—2.52	—2.54	—2.41	—2.29
12	—2.30	—2.32	—2.19	—2.06	—2.07	—2.09	—1.95	—1.81	—1.82	—1.84	—1.69	—1.55
13	—1.56	—1.57	—1.57	—1.74	—1.75	—1.75	—1.92	—1.93	—1.93	—1.94	—1.96	—2.12
14	—2.13	—2.14	—2.14	—2.16	—2.17	—2.17	—2.18	—2.20	—2.20	—2.21	—2.22	—2.22
15	—2.24	—2.60	—2.77	—3.13	—3.50	—3.68	—4.05	—4.42	—4.60	—4.98	—5.37	—5.55
16	—5.94	—6.02	—6.09	—6.17	—6.24	—6.32	—6.40	—6.47	—6.55	—6.62	—6.70	—6.86
17	—7.03	—7.19	—7.36	—7.52	—7.74	—7.97	—8.19	—8.42	—8.64	—8.86	—9.09	—9.32
18	—9.54											

*To be read as follows: For child tested at 2 yr.-0 mo., deduct .53 mo. from the obtained mental age; for child tested at 2 yr.-1 mo., deduct .60 mo., etc.

of these considerations it seemed desirable to utilize the raw value rather than the larger value obtained by smoothing.

At 2 years–6 months there is a significant sex difference in mean performance. This is also the age at which the sex differences in variability are greatest. The standard deviation for the total group is 20.7 as compared with the value of 20.8 for the girls and 17.2 for the boys. If the total group value of 20.7 were used, studies of change in DIQ from tests at Year II to tests at later ages would indicate, other things being equal, greater stability of the DIQ for the girls than for the boys, since the SDs at the two ages would be more comparable for the girls. Use of the smoothed value, which falls intermediate between the variabilities for the sexes, will yield scores in which the apparent effect of sex bias tends to be reduced, and hence this was chosen as the appropriate value.

If one utilizes the uncorrected SDs rather than the smoothed values one finds that a seven-year-old with a mental age of 3–00 has a higher standard score IQ than a six-year-old of the same mental age; that a fifteen-year-old with a mental age of 7–00 has a higher standard score IQ than a fourteen-year-old of the same mental age; and so on. It is evident that use of the actual values overcorrects at some ages for age changes in variability. Therefore, Year VI, as at other ages except Year II, the smoothed value of the standard deviation was used in computing deviation IQs. This is in keeping with the writer's position that the true age changes in variability should follow a fairly

FIGURE 13

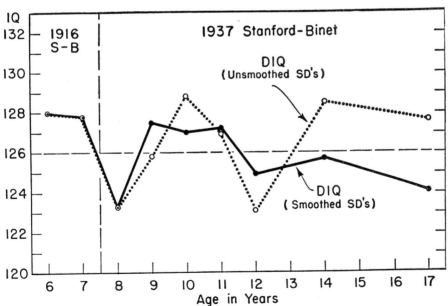

Mean deviation IQs obtained from raw and smoothed standard deviations: Berkeley Growth Study sample

smooth curve. The basis for this assertion being that the scores of subjects at adjoining levels are based to a great extent on the same items; and that, in general, the per cent passing an item with age does not reveal large or abrupt shifts. Results from the stratified samples used in the assessment of the 1960 scale support the decision of utilizing smoothed SDs rather than the uncorrected values (55, p. 38).

DEVIATION IQS FOR LATER AGES

In 1933, Jones and Conrad reported (35) their finding that mental growth continues through adolescence and into early adulthood. This finding is confirmed not only by various other studies available in the literature but by the 1937 standardization data of the Stanford-Binet itself. The yearly gains in performance which began to decrease by age 13 were quite small by 16 years; however, they were still evident at age 18. To provide conventional IQs beyond 16 years would have required small but troublesome corrections in the CA divisor, and hence these gains were disregarded. Because of the desirability of having the Stanford-Binet applicable throughout the high school years, DIQs were derived for the scales for ages 16 to 18 using the data on the 17– and 18–year-old subjects of the 1937 standardization samples. These DIQs are included (Appendix B) as part of the revised IQ tables for the Stanford-Binet scales.

REVISED IQ TABLES

Tables for computing deviation IQs were prepared, utilizing the smoothed standard deviations (except at Year II as indicated above) and utilizing the smoothed values of the means, adjusted for socio-economic bias in the standardization samplings (54). Monthly values were interpolated in all instances. The means are presented in Appendix C together with other information required to transform conventional IQs already obtained into deviation IQs. The tables for obtaining DIQs from a knowledge of the subject's chronological age and mental age score are presented in Appendix B. [These tables are included in the manual for the 1960 revision of the Stanford-Binet scale (55).]

Deviation IQs at the mean and at ± 2 and ± 4 standard deviations are related to mental age scores at various ages in Figure 14. It is evident from this figure that the mental age gains of a 7-year-old subject 4 standard deviations below the mean will be approximately 2 months per year during the next six years if he maintains the same relative position during this period. It is also clear from this figure that the subject will have to obtain a higher mental age score at 10 years than at 11, to obtain DIQs much below 36. Such reversals reflect fluctuations in the concentration of average difficulty items with age and the reduced rate of mental growth as maturity is approached. For IQs of 32 or below these reversals amount to one or two points at some ages. In order to avoid such reversals, a table of corrected constants was established to use in computing DIQs of 32 or less for subjects between the ages of 7 and 14 years. This table, to be used in conjunction with Appendix C, is provided in Appendix D.

FIGURE 14

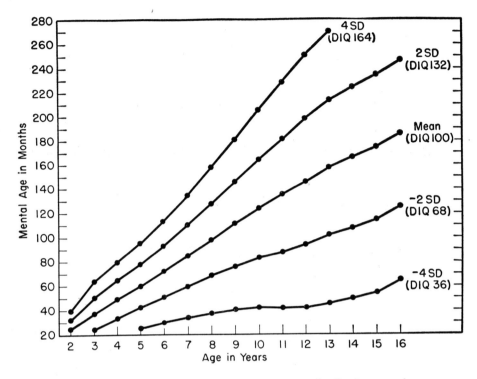

Mental age SDs from 2 to 16 years: 1937 standardization sample

SUMMARY

In Chapter 5 the findings presented show that the deviation IQ is a more stable measure of relative standing on the revised Stanford-Binet scales than the conventional IQ. This is evident even when conventional IQs are corrected at ages for which the variabilities are most deviant. In the latter part of the chapter the stability of conventional and deviation IQs are compared in individual age curves.

The results from this phase of the study indicate that the performance of a subject on the Stanford-Binet should be reported in terms of the deviation IQ, and that the expected change in his relative standing with age should be estimated in terms of deviation IQ change. To make it feasible to determine deviation IQs for both the 1937 and 1960 revisions of the Stanford-Binet, tables comparable to those presented by Terman and Merrill in their 1937 manual (54) are provided in Appendix B. Tables are provided in Appendix C which facilitate the direct transformation of conventional IQs into deviation IQs. The tables in these two appendices, with slight modifications, are those which are included in the manual for the 1960 revision of the scale (55). A third appendix, D, provides constants to facilitate the computation of DIQs below 32.

7

RATE OF MENTAL MATURING

AS RELATED TO LEVEL OF

INTELLIGENCE

Previously cited findings of longitudinal studies indicate that individuals over the age of 4 or 5 tend to maintain, relative to their age group, their same intellectual standing. Some psychologists believe that as a consequence of this tendency, bright children grow at a more rapid rate mentally than dull; that is, that rate of mental growth is positively related to relative standing. However, Anderson (5) has suggested that growth subsequent to a given intellectual assessment need not be related to the subject's relative standing in order for him to maintain essentially the same position relative to his age group. A third condition under which an individual could maintain essentially the same relative position might also be mentioned, namely that mental-growth-gains subsequent to a given assessment, if not too large relative to the individual differences in ability, could be negatively related to relative standing.

MENTAL GROWTH AS RANDOMLY ACCRUING GAINS

In demonstrating how the consistency of intellectual standing could be accounted for in terms of an overlapping of common elements, Anderson assigned scores to a number of hypothetical subjects from a table of random numbers. He added random numbers to the subjects' scores until each had been assigned 300 increments. At any time in this procedure a subject's total score represented the sum of all the increments assigned to him. Anderson then correlated the total scores of the subjects at specified intervals with their initial

54

and final scores. He found that these results, when plotted against per cent of common elements, agreed well with a curve in which correlation coefficients were plotted against per cent of overlap defined as r^2.

Anderson subsequently showed that data available from the California Guidance Study — and the Harvard Growth Study — were fairly consistent with this interpretation when the correlations between first and final tests were plotted against per cent of overlap (a) defined in terms of the proportion of final mental age achievement that score at any one age represents, or (b) defined in terms of the proportion that mental age at any specified testing is of performance at each testing at later ages.

In the light of his analysis Anderson states, "Moreover, it is clear that the constancy of the intelligence quotient is in a large measure a matter of the part-whole or overlap relation, since the growing individual does not lose what he already has attained" (Ibid., p. 336). If an individual's mental development is conceived of as the accretion of random elements, it is obvious that there is no consistency to mental development despite the consistency of intelligence test performance.

MENTAL INCREMENT GAINS AS RELATED TO INTELLECTUAL LEVEL

If mental growth subsequent to a given intellectual assessment were positively related to the subject's relative standing, the more intelligent subjects would become increasingly different in ability from the less intelligent; if negatively related, individual differences would decrease. Assuming that the age changes in variability of the IQ, as shown in Figure 2, reflect underlying growth processes, a negative relationship might be used to account for the decrease in variability from ages 2 to 6 and from 12 to 18 years, while a positive relationship might be used to account for the increase from 6 to 12 years. However, this interpretation is not consistent with the explanation of the fluctuations in standard deviations in terms of change in the concentrations of average-difficulty items at different ages or, as shown later, with the results obtained in a more detailed analysis of the Berkeley Growth Study data.

MENTAL AGE GAINS

In order to determine whether rate of mental growth is related to intellectual level, the BGS sample as of age 6 was divided into upper and lower halves in terms of performance on the 1916 Stanford-Binet. The mean yearly changes in mental age during the first 17 years were determined for both groups. These results, presented in Figure 15-A, indicate that through age 10 the upper half was showing larger gains, the gains from 7 to 8 and from 9 to 10 being significantly greater at the .02 level of confidence. Subsequently the yearly gains were essentially the same for both groups.

It is conceivable that the reduction in differential gain after age 10 could be accounted for in terms of change in relative position, that is, perhaps by 10 years of age the groups set up on the basis of 6 year intelligence no longer differ in ability. To determine whether this is the case, the sample was divided into upper and lower halves on the basis of mental test performance at age 10 and the mean yearly mental age increments were computed as in the preceding analysis. The results, presented in Figure 15–B, indicate that subsequent to year 10 the mental age gains are of about the same magnitude for the lower half of subjects as for the upper half. (The composition of the groups at 6 and 10 years was essentially the same, only two subjects having changed from one group to the other.)

FIGURE 15

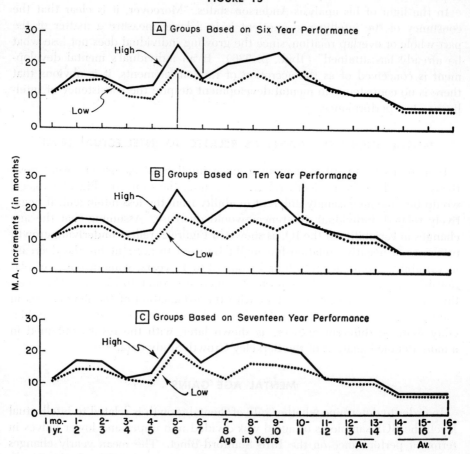

Mental age gains of upper and lower halves as established at chronological ages 6, 10, and 17 years: Berkeley Growth Study sample

While the children who are more intelligent at the age of 6 make larger gains in the next 4 years than the less intelligent, the hypothesis must be considered that the more intelligent children at 6 are not the more intelligent individuals at maturity. It may be that a different group of subjects make up the more intelligent half of the sample at ages 6 and 17. Needless to say, the consistency coefficients presented in Tables 2 and 3 would seem to militate against this hypothesis. To obtain further evidence on this point the 40 subjects who were tested at age 17 were divided into upper and lower halves on the basis of their test performance, and the number of subjects changing from their age 6 groupings was determined. One-fourth of the subjects in the upper half at 17 years were in the lower half at age 6 and vice versa. Such a finding suggests considerable change in the rate of mental growth for these subjects. However, a comparison of the average yearly mental age gains for the subjects changing from the lower to the upper half with those of the subjects changing in the reverse manner indicates that the subjects changing to the upper half tend to make consistently larger mental age gains at all ages subsequent to their 6 year test.

The average mental age gains per year for the upper and lower halves of the BGS sample, established on the basis of 17 year performance on the 1937 Stanford-Binet, are presented in Figure 15-C. This figure indicates that the mental age differential favoring the upper half as of 17 years has resulted from the gradual accumulation of greater average mental age gains at all ages since the first tests on *The California First-Year Mental Scale* at 1 month of age.

The means, standard deviations and *t* values for the three different age groupings are presented in Table 9. It should be noted that the comparisons of the groups (based on performance at 10 and 17 years) are not independent of the 6 year groupings. However, the comparisons made on the 10 and 17 year groupings cannot yield any evidence with respect to the original hypothesis; namely, that the upper half as of age 6 will show larger gains than the lower half in subsequent testings. Chiefly, the comparisons made on the 10 and 17 year groupings demonstrate that the ages at which the numerical gains are significantly different for the more and less intelligent of this sample are essentially the same when the basis of groupings involved tests administered four and eleven years later.

The results presented in Figure 15 do not take into consideration the varying size of *standard deviations of mental age gains* at different ages, and thus the figure may give a distorted picture of the importance of the gains in the later years. To avoid this possible distortion, the mental age *gains* were transformed into standard score values at each age and the mean of these was determined for the high and low groups as established on the basis of 6 and 17 year performance. These mean standard score gains are presented in Figures 16-A ′ and 16-C ′, respectively, and may be compared with the mental age gains of the two groups as presented in Figure 15. The figures for the standard score gains indicate the consistency with which the brighter group makes relatively larger gains at practically all ages, the preschool gains being as marked as at any subsequent period, except perhaps between the ages of 7 and 10 years.

Equivalence of Mental Age Gains

In the preceding analysis mental growth was considered in terms of *numerical* gain in mental age. Such an analysis at least implicitly assumes that mental

TABLE 9

Mean Yearly Mental Age Increments for Upper and Lower Halves of BGS Sample

Established on the basis of intelligence test performance at 6, 10, and 17 years

Age interval	Group	a. Groupings based on 6 year performance				b. Groupings based on 10 year performance				c. Groupings based on 17 year performance			
		N	Mean	SD	t	N	Mean	SD	t	N	Mean	SD	t
1 mo.–1 year	Upper	21	11.0	.82		18	11.0	.82		16	11.2	.78	
	Lower	17	10.8	.59	.86	17	10.7	.51	1.26	16	10.6	.65	1.98
1–2 years	Upper	20	16.8	3.01		18	16.7	3.00		16	16.9	2.70	
	Lower	21	14.6	1.97	2.84**	19	14.2	5.53	3.01**	18	14.2	1.75	3.48**
2–3 years	Upper	21	16.1	3.95		19	16.3	3.92		17	16.6	3.66	
	Lower	21	15.1	3.02	.92	20	14.3	7.99	1.90	19	14.1	2.62	2.45*
3–4 years	Upper	23	12.6	4.08		21	11.7	3.97		19	11.5	3.84	
	Lower	21	10.0	3.10	2.34*	20	10.5	3.52	1.04	19	11.1	3.92	.32
4–5 years	Upper	23	13.4	5.14		21	13.2	5.44		19	13.0	5.92	
	Lower	20	9.3	4.08	2.82**	19	9.2	3.29	2.80**	18	9.9	3.68	1.87
5–6 years	Upper	24	26.1	5.64		22	25.8	5.34		20	23.7	7.08	
	Lower	22	18.4	5.38	4.70**	19	18.2	5.05	4.65**	18	19.8	6.86	1.82
6–7 years	Upper	22	15.6	6.05		21	15.4	6.04		20	16.6	6.10	
	Lower	23	14.8	4.54	.48	21	14.6	5.56	.42	19	14.7	5.48	1.03

TABLE 9 (Continued)

Age interval	Group	a. Groupings based on 6 year performance				b. Groupings based on 10 year performance				c. Groupings based on 17 year performance			
		N	Mean	SD	t	N	Mean	SD	t	N	Mean	SD	t
7–8 years	Upper	21	20.6	10.10	2.59*	20	21.2	10.03	3.72**	20	21.6	10.36	3.33**
	Lower	23	13.0	9.52		22	11.0	7.66		19	11.5	8.61	
8–9 years	Upper	22	21.7	9.56	1.54	21	21.0	11.68	1.37	19	23.3	8.82	2.45*
	Lower	22	17.3	9.40		21	16.4	9.88		19	16.3	8.93	
9–10 years	Upper	22	23.8	14.49	2.62*	21	22.9	10.76	2.93**	17	21.5	13.32	1.46
	Lower	21	14.0	9.48		21	13.5	9.98		19	15.8	9.98	
10–11 years	Upper	21	16.0	10.70	.68	22	15.8	10.39	.64	18	19.9	10.48	1.64
	Lower	22	18.0	9.09		22	17.8	9.42		20	14.7	8.83	
11–12 years	Upper	20	13.1	11.59	.24	21	13.4	11.50	.14	18	12.5	11.12	.11
	Lower	21	12.3	9.14		20	13.0	8.40		19	12.8	8.44	
12–14 years	Upper	18	21.6	11.83	.07	18	23.0	12.99	.82	16	22.8	14.08	.72
	Lower	16	21.9	12.79		16	19.6	11.21		18	19.9	9.82	
14–17 years	Upper	19	20.3	12.44	.70	19	19.0	12.35	.06	17	20.2	14.37	.67
	Lower	16	17.3	12.28		16	19.3	12.15		19	17.5	9.92	

*Values significant at .05 level.

**Values significant at .01 level.

MA GAINS

FIGURE 16

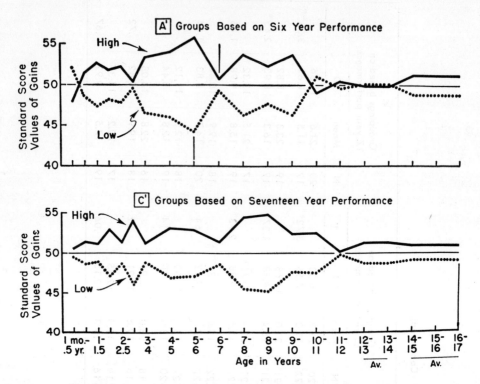

Standard score values of gains in mental age for upper and lower
halves of various age groups: Berkeley Growth Study sample

age units (months) are equivalent throughout the scale. If one makes this
assumption and if one also assumes that mental growth consists of the accretion of random elements, one would expect that on the average it would take
one year for any group of children to show a gain of 12 months of mental age.

Suppose a 7–year-old boy obtained a DIQ of 36; his mental age in years and
months would be 2–10. If he maintained this same relative position throughout
life, how long would it be after the test at seven years before he showed a
gain of 12 months of mental age? By reference to Appendix B one finds that
a mental age of 3–10 is not attained by a subject with a DIQ of 36 until he is
13 years–1 month of age. Thus, theoretically it takes a period of six years,
rather than one, for a 7–year-old boy with a DIQ of 36 to gain twelve months
of mental age. Consider as a contrasting example a 7–year-old with a DIQ of
164; the mental age is 11–3. If he maintains the same relative standing as he
grows older, his mental age score will increase by twelve months in half a
year. Thus, if stability tends to characterize the DIQ, one predicts a very rapid
growth for the bright child and very slow growth for the dull child. This
prediction is not in keeping with the assumption that it should take a year
for subjects, regardless of ability level, to show a gain of twelve months of
mental age.

Further evidence as to which of these alternatives is more likely to be correct is provided by predicting these two boys' DIQs at 13 years rather than assuming constancy of the DIQ from 7 to 13. Assuming means of 100 for the population from which they are drawn and using the correlation of .88 obtained between the 7 and 13 year conventional IQs of the sample (Table 3), predicted DIQs for these two subjects are 44 and 156. The predicted mental age scores, derived from these DIQs, are 4–11 and 20–4. Hence, rather than predicting that both subjects will gain seventy-two months in the next six years, one expects to find that the dull subject will have gained only twenty-five months of mental age while the bright subject will have gained 109 months. Thus more rapid gains are expected for bright than for dull subjects. This is necessarily the case if, as Anderson contends (5, p. 366), ". . . the growing individual does not lose what he has already attained," and if the average gains per year are twelve months and the variabilities for the conventional IQs do not decrease with age.

It might be maintained that there is actually no basis for assuming equivalence of months of mental age at various levels of the mental age scale and that the preceding results, rather than suggesting more rapid mental growth in the case of bright subjects, point up the lack of equivalence of mental age units at the various mental age levels. Furthermore, it might be argued that an appropriate question is whether the gain for bright subjects is greater than for those with less ability in the year following performance at a given mental age level. Consider as an example two subjects who both receive a mental age of 8 years. One, at age 6, has a DIQ of 137; the other, at age 10, has a DIQ of 78. If one assumed that they maintained the same relative standing in their age groups during the next two years, the first subject will show a gain of 37 months while the less able one will have shown a gain of only 15 months. Similar conclusions would be reached (assuming a mean of 100) if the correlations obtained on the BGS data (Table 3) were used to predict the subjects' performances at these later ages — gains of 31 months and 13 months respectively. Actual data on the development of a group of subjects are needed to be sure that bright subjects do grow at a faster rate.

An adequate answer to the question posed above would be obtained if annual gains were determined for a group of subjects subsequent to a given mental age, and if these gains were then correlated with the DIQ level of the subjects. Because of the difficulty of obtaining a sample composed of subjects who all have the same mental age, it would usually be necessary to approximate such a group by interpolating mental age values, mental age gains, and deviation IQs. Essentially, a variation of this procedure is used in the present study.

If the mental age unit has the same significance at different ages, it would seem appropriate to conclude from the data presented in Figures 15-A and 16-A ' that the rate of mental growth of the upper and lower BGS ability groups, was essentially the same subsequent to 10 years of age. However, the yearly gains of these two groups were made in different parts of the scale and the points considered earlier in this section raise question as to the validity of the assumption that months of mental age in the different areas of the scale have equivalent meaning. Thus, although numerically the gains are the same subsequent to age 10, mental growth of the upper half may have been at a faster or slower rate than of the lower half. If, in comparison with the group which was upper at age 6, the lower half is growing after age 10 at as rapid a rate on the same items, one would expect them to make equivalent gains when they were equated for mental maturity.

To obtain evidence about the yearly gains when the two halves were equated for ability, the average mental age was determined at each age for the upper and lower groupings and the yearly gains previously computed were then related to these values rather than to chronological age. The results are presented in Figures 17 A″ and C″, where the level of the mental maturity scale is represented on the abscissae. These comparisons are in contrast to those made of the same two groupings where the gains are plotted according to

FIGURE 17

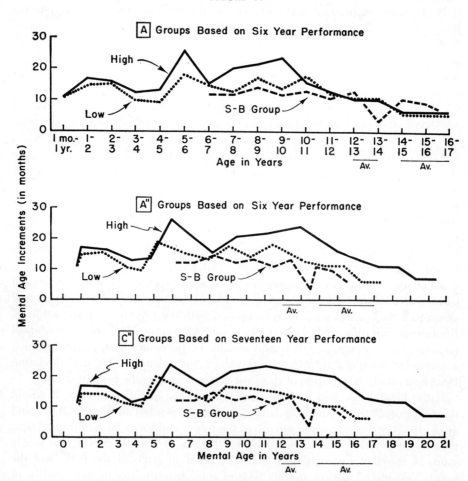

Mental age gains of upper and lower halves when equated
for mental age: Berkeley Growth Study sample

chronological age, as in the top portion of the figure. Also included for comparison in these figures are the differences in mental age between the Stanford-Binet standardization groups for those levels at which mental age data were available (39, p. 32). At every age after 10 years, when the BGS upper half (at age 6 or 17) is matched with the lower half for ability, the upper half makes larger mental gains in the following years. Taken in conjunction with the finding that larger mental gains also characterize the upper half before the age of 10, this indicates that, at least at all ages prior to maturity, the upper half are growing mentally at a faster rate than the lower half. Consequently, the actual differences in ability between bright and dull steadily increase after the early years, even though relative standing remains essentially constant. A similar conclusion was reached by Jones (32) from an analysis of data on subjects of the Oakland (Adolescent) Growth Study.

The results presented in this section provide further evidence that the consistency of mental test results cannot be explained in terms of the accumulation of randomly accruing elements of test performance, as has been suggested (5, 27). The analysis indicates that, when difficulty of the items is taken into consideration, more intelligent subjects have made larger yearly mental gains at all ages after the first year than the less intelligent. Such increasing individual differences in ability are, of course, masked in relative measures of ability such as the IQ or standard score.

SUMMARY

Intelligence tests serve two major functions. They indicate the subject's present standing in mental ability relative to others his age and relative to other age groups, and they indicate something of his level of ability at later ages. The developments of the present study facilitate the practical achievement of these functions for subjects through age 18. A DIQ from a Stanford-Binet administration provides an unambiguous estimate of a subject's standing relative to others his age; that is, a given score has the same relative significance at all ages. And the tables of DIQ changes provide a practical means of estimating the probable stability of a subject's standing with age.

One cannot, however, determine from a subject's DIQ score on two different occasions whether there has been any absolute change in his performance; that is, whether there has been any change in the number of items passed. For example, suppose a subject who, at 10 years of age, obtained a DIQ of 100, shows an eight point drop by age 11, and an additional twelve point drop by 13 years. What has been the absolute change in his performance? Since his mental age score is 10 years–3 months at all three ages, in absolute terms there has been neither an increase nor a decrease. Thus, mental age scores are important, not only if one wishes to determine the age group of which a subject's performance is typical, but also if one wishes to compare individuals or groups in terms of absolute amount of gain or loss in performance. In the present chapter, groups of different levels of relative ability were compared in terms of their yearly gains in mental age.

A question frequently raised is why subjects tend to maintain their same relative standing with age. One answer which has been suggested is that the consistency is to be explained in terms of the overlapping of performance at different ages. Another is that subjects at different levels of ability grow at different rates. These alternative answers were investigated in detail in the present chapter with data from the Berkeley Growth Study and with the standardization data of the 1937 Stanford-Binet.

The evidence indicates that subjects bright at age 6 grow at a faster rate mentally than subjects of less ability at all except the earliest ages. Hence, with age the bright subjects become increasingly different in ability from those of low ability. As a consequence, subjects can become increasingly different in ability even though their DIQs are somewhat closer together.

PART TWO

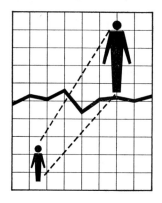

Practical Applications of Scores On Intelligence Tests

In this section the practical functions of intelligence tests are considered in relation to research findings presented in Part One. These findings lead to a stable assessment of relative ability, as well as to a systematic means of reporting the stability of scores with age. It is expected that they will be of value to psychologists, sociologists, social workers, and to members of other professional groups who work in clinics, adoption agencies, counseling centers, social welfare agencies, educational institutions, and other centers in which intelligence tests are used.

It has been pointed out that intelligence tests have two major functions. They indicate the standing of the individual relative to others of his age and the age group of which his performance is typical. Secondly, they yield information about the performance that can be expected of the subject at a later date. How much information the tests yield about a subject's future performance depends on the age at which the tests are administered and on the time interval in question.

Concern in this section focuses on the meaning of the individual's mental test score in terms of these functions. Thus a child's test score will be interpreted in a practical way with respect to (a) his standing among others his age, (b) the age group which he most resembles in performance, and (c) the amount of change which can be expected in his position (relative to others his own age) as he grows older.

8

THE DEVIATION IQ AND THE

MENTAL AGE AS MEASURES

OF ABILITY

A subject's performance on an intelligence test may be reported in a number of different ways. The score may be expressed in terms of absolute mental growth units (31), in standard deviation units (9), in relative measures such as percentiles, standard scores, and IQs, or in terms of mental age score in years and/or months. Since the examiner's concern in most practical situations is knowing a subject's standing relative to others of the same age and to the performance of different age groups, the score is usually given in terms of both IQ and mental age. The assumptions customarily made in using these measures are that a given conventional IQ has the same significance at all age levels and, in the case of the mental age, that the score is the average performance for the age group specified.

THE DEVIATION IQ AS A MEASURE OF RELATIVE ABILITY

Intelligence quotients obtained on a large sample of subjects will be distributed according to a normal probability curve, as shown in Figure 18[12]. When scores of different age groups are normally distributed, the proportion in each group who obtain scores above or below a given division of the normal

[12] If a truly random sample of subjects from the population is tested at a given age, the distribution of IQs or DIQs will vary slightly from normality because of the subjects with scores below −3 standard deviations. Because of brain damage, defective germ plasm, and other abnormalities, the number of mentally retarded subjects exceeds the number that might be expected on the basis of a normal probability distribution.

FIGURE 18

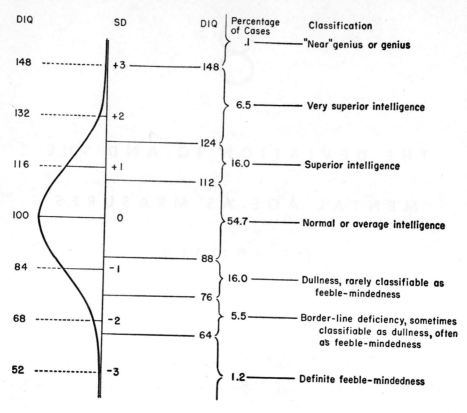

Theoretical distribution and classification of deviation
IQs for the Stanford-Binet scales

curve will always be the same. The divisions of the curve with which we are concerned are standard deviations (SDs) or proportions of a standard deviation, several of which are indicated in the figure. For normally distributed IQs, 16 per cent of each group will always fall more than one standard deviation above the mean, 7 per cent more than one-and-a-half standard deviations, and so on. However, for the conventional IQ, a given number of standard deviations above the mean is represented by different IQ values at the various age levels. It was for purposes of avoiding this problem for the Stanford-Binet scales that revised IQ tables were developed. As was indicated earlier, the IQ values in these tables are deviation, or standard score, IQs derived so that representative samples of the general population would, at each age, obtain a mean of 100 and a standard deviation of 16.

The difficulties inherent in the use of the conventional IQ can be illustrated by considering two representative samples of different ages who obtain average scores of 100 and standard deviations of 10 and 20 points, respectively. Sixteen per cent of the subjects in the group with the larger variability will obtain scores above an IQ of 120. However, to include the top 16 per cent of subjects in the other group, one will need to include all subjects obtaining an IQ above 110. Thus, while the proportion of subjects above one standard deviation is the same in both groups, there is a different proportion above a given IQ score.

This example illustrates in a practical way that when variability fluctuates with age, the conventional IQ does not have the same meaning at different ages. This point is further illustrated by Figure 19, where conventional IQs for the 1937 revision of the Stanford-Binet are positioned on the normal curve

FIGURE 19

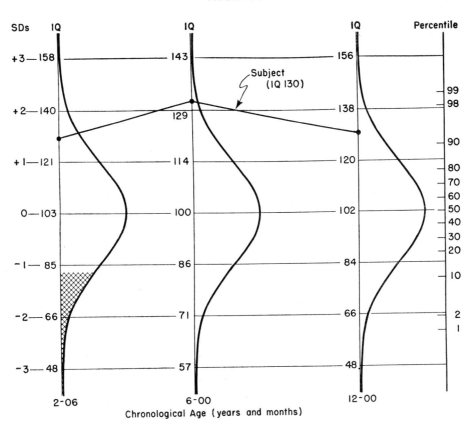

Theoretical distribution of conventional IQs at three ages on the 1937 Stanford-Binet scale

The cross-hatched area in the distribution of IQs at CA 2–06 indicates that values below 80 cannot be obtained with the Stanford-Binet for this age group.

at 2 years–6 months, and at 6 and 12 years, in terms of smoothed means and standard deviations for these ages. The scores of a subject with an IQ constant at 130 at each of the three ages are shown on this figure and furnish another concrete illustration of the effects of age changes in variability. The same

DIQ

conventional IQ does not necessarily indicate a constant position in the distribution. Conversely, the same relative standing may involve a varying conventional IQ, as illustrated by the horizontal lines in the figure.

In the case of the deviation IQ, there are no fluctuations in variability; that is, the standard deviation is the same at all ages, 16 DIQ points. Since the mean is also a constant for all levels between 2 and 18 years, the percentage of cases in a representative sample who fall above or below a given IQ is always the same.

Referring again to Figure 18 the reader will note that more subjects obtain a DIQ of 100 than any other score and that the number of individuals obtaining a given score decreases the more it deviates from 100. If this is the case, a given difference between percentiles includes a larger DIQ range the further it is from the median. For example, subjects who fall between the 50th and 60th percentiles have DIQs between 100 and 104, while the DIQs of those falling between the 85th and 95th percentiles range between 117 and 126. Thus, the individuals included in a given percentile range near the median are more alike in ability than are those included in the same range near the extremes of the distribution. The distribution of percentiles relative to the normal probability curve is given in Figure 18 and of percentage of cases within a selected DIQ range in Figure 19.

Subjects are sometimes assigned to an ability group (genius, superior, normal, dull, and feebleminded) on the basis of their mental test performance. One of the best known of these classificatory systems is that which Terman presented in 1916 (52). This scheme, modified so as to be applicable to the DIQ distribution, is included in Figure 18, together with the percentage of cases who obtain scores within a given IQ range. Because it is sometimes forgotten that the boundary lines between such groups is purely arbitrary, a better procedure is to report the percentage of cases whose scores fall at or below the DIQ score in question. These percentages can be obtained from Table 10. This table was patterned after that of Pintner, Dragositz and Kushner in their supplementary guide (47) to the 1937 revision of the Stanford-Binet scale. In using Table 10, the reader should keep in mind that subjects with percentile scores close to the median are more alike in ability than a group with the same range of percentile scores near the extremes of the distribution.

RELATIVE STANDING AND LEVEL OF ACHIEVEMENT

Among other things, an adequate measure of intelligence is necessary for evaluating an individual child's ability in relation to his parents' expectations; for judging whether or not he is achieving the scholastic level which can be reasonably expected of him; and for estimating whether the educational program is meeting his needs.

From the time that the child is born, through high school and into adult life, the parents are likely to have certain, definite ideas as to what the child should achieve. Often these notions do not depend on a realistic evaluation of the child's ability. The expectations may be based on experience the parents have had with children who possess greater or lesser ability than their own

TABLE 10

Deviation IQ Percentile Chart*

Subjects with a deviation IQ as extreme as:			Number per sample size specified:
164	or	36	3 out of 100,000
160	or	40	9 out of 100,000
156	or	44	2 out of 10,000
152	or	48	6 out of 10,000
148	or	52	1 out of 1,000
144	or	56	3 out of 1,000
140	or	60	6 out of 1,000
136	or	64	1 out of 100

DIQ	Percentile rank	DIQ	Percentile rank
135	99	100	50
134	98	99	48
133	98	98	45
132	98	97	43
131	97	96	40
130	97	95	38
129	96	94	35
128	96	93	33
127	95	92	31
126	95	91	29
125	94	90	27
124	93	89	25
123	93	88	23
122	92	87	21
121	90	86	19
120	89	85	17
119	88	84	16
118	87	83	15
117	85	82	13
116	84	81	12
115	83	80	11
114	81	79	10
113	79	78	8
112	77	77	7
111	75	76	7
110	73	75	6
109	71	74	5
108	69	73	5
107	67	72	4
106	65	71	4
105	62	70	3
104	60	69	3
103	57	68	2
102	55	67	2
101	52	66	2
		65	1

*The values in this table are based on the assumption of a normal distribution of DIQs in the general population.

73 ACHIEVEMENT LEVEL

child, may have as a source the parents' unfulfilled goals and aspirations, or may be based more on the parents' experience with an adult's than with a child's world. Whether or not the parental expectations are in accord with a child's ability to achieve can be determined only if that child's intellectual standing relative to others of the same age is known.

When the expectations of the home are out of keeping with the child's ability, the major task is to help the parents accept the child as he is, whether this is below average, average, or superior in ability. Since in such instances the parents frequently have little accurate information as to what can reasonably be expected of a child possessing a given level of ability, it is important to provide them with such information as will assist them in revising unrealistic plans or expectations.

In the literature emphasis is frequently on over-expectations by parents. While there can be little doubt that over-expectations are more damaging than under-expectations to the normal, healthy development of a child, it seems likely that under-expectations also have undesirable consequences. They may easily lead to a child's being satisfied with achievements below his ability level. This is suggested in comparisons of academic achievements of individuals of the same ability level who come from homes differing in emphasis upon intellectual pursuits (4, 10). Thus, parents who expect too little of their children may need information and counsel as much as do those who expect too much.

In the school perhaps even more than in the home, a major problem is to evaluate a child's accomplishments in terms of capability. Too frequently the assessments of ability (or the effective utilization of these assessments) are restricted to children who are not making average (compared with their age group) progress in school or who present behavior problems. Some of the children referred for assessment because of below expected achievement are either emotionally disturbed or below normal in ability. However, among those referred one occasionally finds children of superior ability who are not emotionally disturbed. The subject matter of the school, rather than being beyond them, is information they have had for some time. Finding the classroom exercises boring they escape into fantasy and fail to pay attention or carry out the assignments. In these instances, motivating the child by giving either more difficult and creative assignments or advancing to a higher grade in which the pupils are more nearly comparable in ability may be all that is required to bring achievement into line with capabilities.

Among those children who are tested because of manifest behavior problems, one finds not only emotionally disturbed children but also those who use these means to express their frustration with the school program. This frustration may arise, in the case of retarded children, because of their inability to keep up with the class. In the case of children with superior ability it may be because the school program does not meet their intellectual requirements.

If a child of superior ability performs adequately in the class and reveals no manifest signs of dissatisfaction, it may be concluded that the child needs no special attention. However, this conclusion may be erroneous. The writer contends that such a child has as much right to an educational program geared to his ability level as the child whose achievement is below normal or whose frustration is manifest in behavior disturbances. This position is in accord with contemporary theory in education which holds that the child should advance at his own rate.

If a school is to meet the needs of individual pupils, its program must include the frequent reassessment of each child's level of ability. Such a program depends, of course, on adequate measures of relative standing; that is, on the availability of tests whose scores indicate the same relative standing at different levels or ages. The deviation IQs yielded by the Stanford-Binet and Wechsler scales are examples of scores which adequately indicate this. If available tests do not yield appropriate indications, scores can easily be converted into a convenient standard score scale (cf., p. 20).

MENTAL AGE SCORES

It is not sufficient in either the practical or research situation to deal only with measures of relative ability such as the deviation IQ. One must also have available a record of the number of items passed or a measure of this performance relative to other age groups, for example MA, so that one can ascertain whether or not there has been a change in performance from one testing to another. Suppose, for example, that a subject, who at 10 years of age obtained a DIQ of 100, on a Stanford-Binet scale shows an eight point drop by age 11, and an additional twelve point drop by 13 years; what has been the absolute change in his performance? One must have his mental age score at all three ages, 10–03, in order to know that in absolute terms there has been neither an increase nor a decrease.

A second example involves re-tests on two subjects differing considerably in brightness. Compare one, who gets a DIQ of 100 at 10 years and a DIQ of 76 at age 14, with another who at the same ages obtains DIQs of 140 and 110, respectively. At the first age they differed in DIQ by 40 points, but at 14 by 34 points. The first subject has shown neither an increase nor a decrease in number of items passed; at both testings, the mental age is 10 years–3 months. In contrast the second subject has shown a gain, an increase in mental age score from 14 years–6 months to 15 years–4 months. Thus while the subjects are more similar in relative standing in their age group at the second testing, they are further apart in terms of absolute ability. This is a consequence of a process evident from infancy to maturity — an increase with age in individual difference in mentality.

Mental ages of subjects are of practical value for two other reasons. One, investigations of mental development have determined a number of psychological correlates of particular levels. Two, the mental age designates the chronological age for which the obtained performance is average. This designation has particular merit in those areas in which environmental demands have been geared to the ability level characteristic of different age groups.

For example, attempts to teach children to read are generally not made until they are between the chronological ages of 6 and 7. It is ordinarily accepted that it is reasonable to expect children performing at the level of the average child of 6 years–6 months to acquire this skill (40, 57). Indicating this level by mental age would seem to be more meaningful and economical than specifying the DIQ level at various chronological ages. To express this same information in DIQ terms, one would have to note for each DIQ score the chronological age at which the task could profitably be introduced. For example, specifying for children with a DIQ of 90 a CA of a little over 7 years, for children with a DIQ of 80 a CA of 8 years to 8 years–6 months, for children with a DIQ of 75 a CA of 8 years–6 months to 9 years, and so on.

In the practical situation, clinical and educational psychologists frequently have to evaluate the demands placed on a child in terms of his ability to meet them. In many instances, as in the preceding example, this evaluation can be made more easily by reference to the age group of which the subject's performance is typical than by reference to the child's relative standing in his own age group. It is for this reason that Terman and Merrill retain the mental age score (54, 55).

Terman and Merrill adjusted the mental age scores of the 1937 Stanford-Binet so that their samples would obtain IQs somewhat above 100 (54). This was necessary because their standardization included somewhat inadequate samplings of the lower occupational classes. At most ages, however, the adjustments raised the mean IQs of their samples somewhat too high. Consequently, a mental age score obtained on the Stanford-Binet Scales characteristically indicates an age level slightly above the true age group for which the performance is typical. Corrected mental age scores for these scales are presented in Appendix A. They were derived by a method which controls these various sources of error and makes possible determination of the age group to which a subject's performance corresponds.

If the corrected mental age scores are used in computing children's IQs by the $\frac{MA}{CA}$ ratio, a mean IQ of 100 will be obtained at ages 2–00 through 13–00 for representative samples of the general population. Thus the use of the corrected mental age scores standardizes the meaning of an IQ of 100. However, *except at the mean,* Terman and Merrill's over adjustment accounts for a very small portion of the age changes in the meaning of the conventional IQ. The major portion is due to fluctuations in the magnitude of the standard deviations. Hence, conventional IQs are not satisfactory even when the corrected mental age scores are used as the dividend. Instead, the subject's performance should be expressed in DIQ terms. The DIQ transformation standardizes the meaning of the IQ at all levels for all ages from 2 to 18 years since it includes a correction for both factors.

The Mental Age Extension of the Stanford-Binet

Terman and Merrill note that ". . . mental ages above 13 years cease to have the same significance as at lower levels, since they are no longer equivalent to the median performances of unselected populations of the corresponding chronological ages" (54, p. 30). In the present study the applicability of the mental age concept is extended from 13 to 18 years;

that is, the average performance of age groups was determined for subjects between 13 and 18 years as well as for the earlier ages. These average performances are included in the table of corrected mental age scores in Appendix A.

Mental Age Groupings

It has been suggested at various times that the children within a given school class would constitute a more homogeneous educational group if the basis of their assignment were mental rather than chronological age. Results of studies investigating this possibility have not in general supported such a conclusion. One reason this is not the case is that the bright subjects at all ages grow at a more rapid rate mentally than the dull.

Suppose that one were to take all subjects with a mental age of 8–00, and group them. Some would be retarded in their mental development; that is, would have a mental age of 8–00 while chronologically they were 9–00, 10–00, 11–00, and 12–00. On the other hand, there would be bright subjects who had reached this mental level at a chronological age of 5–00 or 6–00. The retarded subjects would be growing at a relatively slow rate as compared with the bright children.

What would one find after the children had been in this group for a year? If they maintained their same relative positions, the slow growers would have developed less than a year in mental age while the rapid growers would have gained more than a year. As a result, they would no longer be in the same mental age classification. In the years that follow they would diverge even more, both in mental age and in educational capabilities. In view of the differential rate of growth of the bright and the dull, it is not surprising that grouping purely on the basis of mental age has not proved effective in classifying school children.

The suggestion has also been made that children of the same mental age are not educationally homogeneous because of qualitative differences between the bright and the dull which enable the bright to be more efficient in organizing and synthesizing difficult information provided by the environment. This issue has been investigated to some extent in studies seeking to determine (a) whether or not bright and dull subjects obtain the same mental age score by passing different items (37, 56), and (b) whether or not bright subjects have a relatively greater proficiency in tool subjects such as arithmetic and reading than children of the same mental age but of lesser ability relative to their age group (20, 21).

Practical Uses of Mental Age Scores

The deviation IQ is the most convenient way of evaluating a child's standing in his age group. However, to an untrained person, or to one unacquainted with the individual difference in the capabilities of children of a given age, a DIQ above or below 100 may only indicate the extent to which the child is above or below average. That is, to such an individual a given DIQ may indicate little or nothing about what can reasonably be expected of the child in question — whether or not in relation to his position in his age group he is under or over achieving, or whether or not the school program is suited to his level of ability.

Parents and laymen in general have a broader experience with children of different ages than with children of the same age, but with different levels of ability. Hence, in discussing with them a child's mental test score, it is frequently more meaningful to consider the age group for which the child's performance is typical than to emphasize the child's relative standing within his own age group. The merits of the former are illustrated in a conference which the writer had with a mother of a four-year old who obtained a deviation IQ of 147. In discussing with her the general level of performance on the test, the writer indicated that at this age the child was very bright, that relative to others of his CA, he did as well as the top two or three of a representative sample of a thousand children.

Naturally, the mother was pleased to know that her son had done so well on the test. However, she immediately mentioned her concern and that of her husband, a mathematician, over the child not being able to do simple arithmetical problems. She gave as an example a problem as difficult as that which occurs at Year IX in the Stanford-Binet — "If I were to buy four cents' worth of candy and should give the storekeeper ten cents, how much money would I get back?" (54, p. 105; 55, p. 94) It is obvious in this case that the parents, both of whom were professional people, had decidedly unrealistic ideas as to what should be expected of their son.

It would have been a tedious task to detail to the mother the kinds of problems which a four-year-old with a DIQ of 147 could be expected to deal with effectively. It was fairly easy to get her to recognize that his performance was characteristic of that of a six-year-old who was ready to enter the first grade, and that solving the types of problems she expected was beyond his level of ability, and only to be reasonably expected of children 8 or 9 years of age who already had successfully experienced several years of elementary school.

The reader will perhaps be a little more in sympathy with parents who expect average development from a retarded child than with the demanding parents in the preceding illustration. Consider as an example a four-year-old with a DIQ of 50, whose parents expect his behavior to be typical of his age group. As in the case of the bright child, it is probable that the parents of the retarded subject could more readily understand their child's level of ability in terms of the age group which this mental test performance is most like (two-year-olds) than if one attempted to give them information on the achievements of four-year-olds with Deviation IQs of 50.

9

PRACTICAL INTERPRETATIONS

OF THE STABILITY OF SCORES

ON INTELLIGENCE TESTS

Growth from birth to adulthood is characterized by change both in the structure of the organism and in its functions. When the determinants of change (whether they are inherent or are of environmental origin) are operating in different subjects at different ages, the members of a group will shift with age in their relative standing in the group. Thus, in an unselected sample of boys, the beginning age of the growth spurt is only slightly related to their relative standing at 11 years on physical attributes such as height. Consequently in the following three or four years there will be a number of very marked shifts in relative position in the group on these variables.

As in the case of physical development, subjects can be expected to change their relative position in their age group in intellectual development if given determiners of mental growth are operative in different subjects at different ages. Indeed, unless the changes in structure and function which constitute mental growth are perfectly correlated with ability level, the changes will be reflected in variations in relative standing and hence in age fluctuations in the magnitude of the DIQ. Earlier it was noted that gains in ability are associated with relative position — bright subjects generally making larger gains in ability than average subjects, and average subjects larger gains than individuals of relatively low ability. This association is, however, far from perfect. Consequently, the change in DIQ tends to increase with the length of the interval between tests. Changes in relative ability are not as accurately reflected in changes in the conventional as they are in the deviation IQ. In some instances changes in the conventional IQ suggest larger, and in other instances smaller, changes in relative ability than actually take place. Any change in the DIQ, on the other hand, indicates an unambiguous amount of change in the subject's standing in his age group, assuming a perfectly reliable test score at both ages.

THE PREDICTIVE VALUE OF MENTAL TESTS

There are a number of practical implications in the use of earlier test results to predict later performance. If future performance could be predicted in the early years, long-range plans could be developed to give a child the kind of experiences which would facilitate the maximum fulfillment of his capacities. Programs could be established to inform parents of the achievements which are appropriate to a child's ability level, not merely at the time of testing but also at later ages. Educational programs suited to different ability levels could be set up in the elementary grades. In reality, such actions are *not* possible because intelligence tests in the early years have little predictive value (cf. p. 96).

What are the reasons for the poor consistency of mental scores at these early ages? One factor is the change in the nature or composition of mental ability as children grow older. Many elements are involved in mental ability, and they do not all grow at the same rate. For example, verbal ability is a component of intelligence which is much more important in the school years than in early childhood. A child especially endowed with verbal ability will show mental scores at the chronological age of 6–00 which might not be predictable from the relatively nonverbal tests given in infancy.

The generalization that scores obtained at early ages are not as a rule effective predictors of performance in elementary school may lead some to consider that tests at these ages have no value. Such a conclusion is unwarranted since one is interested in the child's present status, as well as the status at later ages. In this connection, it should be recalled that intelligence is one of the few psychological characteristics of the individual that can with reasonable reliability be assessed from infancy to adulthood. Also, it is one of those unique traits for which the predictive value that relative standing at one age has for relative standing at a later age is known.

The discussion thus far has dealt with the predictive value of early tests for normal children. It should be pointed out that a considerable proportion of children with neurological defect are discovered in these early examinations, whether the defect arises from brain damage or a defect in the germ plasm. It is not always clear whether the diagnosis of a neurological defect is made on the basis of test performance, or whether it depends on other characteristics of the child which the examiner noted during the test administration. There are studies in progress in which the investigators are seeking objective criteria so that individuals with neurological defect can be discovered as early in life as possible. Until results from such studies are made available, it will not be possible to specify the extent to which the children's responses to the tests are diagnostic and the extent to which the examiner is depending upon other clues.

PREDICTING SCORES AT LATER AGES

Our most succinct measure of the extent to which subjects maintain their same relative standing in the group with age is the correlation coefficient, r. If certain assumptions are made, this measure of relationship, together with the means and standard deviations at the different ages, can be used to predict the future intellectual status of subjects from their earlier intelligence test scores.

The formula used in achieving this, the regression equation, is very simple when representative samples are involved and when the DIQ is used. One determines x, the negative or positive amount the subject's DIQ deviates from 100, and multiplies it by the correlation between scores for the two ages concerned to determine the most likely amount, y, which the subject will deviate from 100 on a second test: $y = rx$. The subject's predicted score is 100 plus y, the expected amount of deviation on the second test. Since this procedure merely yields the subject's most likely score, one would probably also wish to obtain an estimate of the accuracy of prediction, for example, the standard error of estimate. (The regression formula for use with conventional IQs is considerably more complex than the one provided above.)

Although tables of intercorrelations among tests given at different ages have been available for a number of years, as far as the writer knows, psychometrists have not attempted to use these relationships in predicting individual scores. One very practical reason for not attempting this is the amount of time entailed. While it would take very little time to predict a given subject's score at several later ages using the regression equation, a considerable amount of time would be involved when dealing with a number of cases. It would be necessary to calculate a predicted score for each individual DIQ as well as change values in the formula for every change in size of the appropriate correlation coefficient.

There are, however, a number of reasons which would make this procedure questionable. For example, in using the regression equation, one needs to have for the population from which a subject is drawn a good estimate of the means and standard deviations of the DIQs at the two ages involved as well as for the correlations between the scores. These are rarely available, and guesses as to the magnitude of these values may be seriously in error even when there is considerable information from samples which have been drawn from the community. Of the three required measures, it might be expected that there would be little disagreement concerning average level of ability for such a group. However, in contrast to such an expectation, the range of opinion with respect to this level may be considerable. Recently, for example, a number of psychologists discussing the average mental ability level of school children in the city in which they live *estimated* the mean conventional IQ in a range from 110 to 120. A ten point range in the estimates was present in spite of the availability of reports from the local schools, and, mental test data on a large survey sample and two longitudinal samples, all reasonably representative of the community. Considering that such a large amount of information is the exception rather than the rule, very diverse results could be expected from the use of the regression equation by different psychometrists if they supplied their own estimates of means, standard deviations and correlations.

Predicting the future performance of individual subjects is hazardous not only from a statistical standpoint, but also from a practical one. If predicted scores were included in case reports, individuals who have access to the records but who have little training in interpretation may tend to attach too much significance to the predicted scores even if they were accompanied by the standard error of estimate. Indeed, it is doubtful if naive individuals would find the standard error of estimate helpful in tempering in any way the prediction of single score IQs. Since persons lacking effectual statistical backgrounds do make decisions for tested subjects, the decisions might frequently have undesirable consequences if predicted scores were included.

Until we actually know the regional differences in the constants which are to be utilized in the regression equation, and until we can be sure that all persons who use the reports of psychometrists possess appropriate qualifications, it would seem preferable to use a procedure which will indicate something of the change which is likely to occur with age but will not imply a precise prediction of an individual's future performance.

AMOUNT OF CHANGE IN CONVENTIONAL AND DEVIATION IQS BETWEEN TESTS

Tables of change in IQ subsequent to tests given at each of nineteen different ages within the first 17 years of age are presented in Appendix E (Table .1–.19, pp. 209–227). The values in these tables show for the subjects of the Berkeley Growth Study the amount of change in conventional and deviation IQ which occurred between tests administered at the age specified in the heading and the age indicated in the left-hand margin. The changes in conventional IQ are presented in Part A of the tables, while the changes in deviation IQ are presented in Part B. At some ages the changes in the conventional IQ are small, suggesting less change in relative position than actually takes place. At other ages they are large, implying more change than actually occurs. These discrepancies are to a considerable extent the result of fluctuations with age in the size of the variabilities (SDs) of the conventional IQ. Because of these fluctuations, changes in conventional IQ should not be used in evaluating the stability of mental test performance.

The values presented in Part B of each of the tables in Appendix E, the deviation IQ changes, undoubtedly vary to some degree from those which would be obtained from a truly representative sample of subjects. However, it seems likely that they do not deviate to any great extent since they compare favorably with the IQ changes which Bradway found in retests of sub-groups of the 1937 standardization sample of the Stanford-Binet (see pages 25–28). In the absence of knowledge of DIQ changes on other samples it seems appropriate to use the values presented in these tables as estimates of measures of change which would be obtained from data on representative samples.

It is better to use the median, range, and quartile measures to describe the change in the DIQ with age than the mean and standard deviation, since the distributions of change are not normal. Using the median, one finds that 50 per cent of subjects change as little, or as much, as the value specified. Using Quartile I shows that 25 per cent of subjects change as little as the indicated value, or that 75 per cent change this amount or more. Quartile III, on the other hand, shows that 25 per cent of the subjects change as much or more than the specified value, and/or that 75 per cent of the subjects change this amount or less. The range, of course, is interpreted as indicating the limits within which the changes might be expected to fall for a representative sample of size N.

Consider a practical example of how the tables of change might be used. Suppose that a six-year-old subject obtained a deviation IQ on the Stanford-Binet of 120. How much is this child's DIQ likely to change by the time he or she finishes the sixth grade at age 12? From Table .12 of Appendix E (p. 222) one finds that 50 per cent of subjects change eight points or more during this period, that 25 per cent change three points or less, and that the 25 per cent whose DIQs are the least stable change thirteen or more points. The range of change is zero to forty-two points for a sample of approximately forty subjects.

If such information is included in an evaluation of an individual's test performance, it is unlikely that even a person with minimum training would use the original test score later in the subject's school life without qualification. The evaluation definitely indicates that the deviation IQ is not capricious. On the other hand, it shows that some subjects exhibit a considerable amount of change with age. Hence, it would be expected that at a later age the worker would refer the subject for another examination if a decision in any way depended upon the subject's mental test performance.

10

COMPUTATIONAL ILLUSTRATIONS

In this chapter specific examples of the application of the tables in Part III, the Appendices, are discussed. *These examples will be used to illustrate in a practical manner certain topics developed in preceding chapters.* The corrected mental ages for the Stanford-Binet scales (54, 55) are found in Appendix A. Tables for determining deviation IQs for these scales are found in Appendices B, C, and D. Because they are used most frequently in determining DIQs the tables in Appendix B appear first in this group. Tables of changes in conventional and deviation IQs subsequent to tests given at various ages from birth to seventeen years are presented in Appendix E.

DERIVING THE DEVIATION IQ

To determine a subject's deviation IQ for the Stanford-Binet scales, it is necessary to know (a) the subject's chronological age at the time of testing and either the subject's (b) mental age or (b') conventional IQ. Since a different procedure is followed when the mental age score is available from that used when only the conventional IQ is known, a separate section is devoted to each.

Given Chronological Age and Mental Age Score

The revised IQ tables, Appendix B, are comparable in form to those which Terman and Merrill present with the 1937 revision of the Stanford-Binet scale (54), and are, of course, the actual ones included in the manual for the 1960 revision (55). Each table applies to one year, or twelve months, of mental age; and three years, or thirty-six months, of chronological age. Each page's running foot, appearing at the lower left on the even-numbered and the lower right on the odd-numbered pages, is a quick locating convenience. The first part of the running foot indicates the year and month of mental age which

84

appears first in the table on that page. The second part designates the first year and month of chronological age to which the table applies. For example, the running foot for the first table, page 125, is **MA 2–0/CA 2–0**, and indicates that this page carries the table which applies to any mental age from 2–00 through 2–11 and to any chronological age from 2–00 through 4–11. Because no computations are required, in *most* instances the reader will find it more convenient to directly use these tables for deriving deviation IQs than to determine them by the procedures detailed in the other Appendices.

The first step in determining a DIQ is to locate by means of the running foot the tables applicable to the obtained mental age score. Then, find the table within this group which includes the subject's chronological age. Next, identify the obtained mental age score in years and months in the top line, or in total number of months in the bottom line. Go down (or up) the column headed by this value to the row which contains the subject's chronological age in years and months in the left-hand margin, or in total months in the right-hand margin, of the table. The number at the intersection of the row and column is the subject's deviation IQ.

Example 1. Suppose that a three-year-old subject is tested with one of the Stanford-Binet scales and obtains a mental age score of 3–00. What is the DIQ? What is the conventional IQ? In this, and in subsequent examples, the test results and questions considered will be indicated in the following form:

CA	MA	Corrected MA	Conventional IQ	Deviation IQ
3–00	3–00	?	?	?

First, the deviation IQ will be obtained by reference to Appendix B. The running foot, appearing at the bottom of page 128, is used first to locate the tables applicable to a mental age score of three years and second to identify the particular table within this group which includes DIQs for subjects three years of age. Locate in the left-hand margin of the table the subject's chronological age in years and months, 3–00, and then go across this row to the column headed by the mental age score in years and months, 3–00. The score at the intersection of this row and column, 96, is the subject's DIQ.

If the IQ is computed by the traditional $\frac{MA}{CA}$ ratio, an IQ score of 100 is obtained ($\frac{36}{36} \times 100$). What accounts for the difference between these two scores? Terman and Merrill point out in their manual for the 1937 revision that the mean IQ for a representative sample of three-year-olds *is not 100*, as is customarily assumed, but *is 104* (54, p. 36). *Thus, the child who obtains an IQ of 100 at CA 3–00 is actually four points below the average.* Since the deviation IQ was developed so that the mean DIQ at every age would be 100, this subject's score when transformed will necessarily fall below this value by the indicated amount.

It might also be pointed out that the child's chronological age and mental age are both 3–00. This suggests that the subject is performing at the average for his age group. However, as has already been indicated (and will be considered in detail in the next section), mental ages on the Stanford-Binet scales are somewhat too high on the average and suggest that a subject's performance is typical of an age group above that of which it is actually characteristic. For example, a mental age score of 3–00 is actually the average performance of subjects CA 2–11 (cf., Appendix A) and hence the latter is the age group to which the subject's performance actually corresponds.

Example 2. A child of nine years obtained a mental age score of 9 years–3 months on one of the Stanford-Binet scales:

CA	MA	Corrected MA	Conventional IQ	Deviation IQ
9–00	9–03	?	?	?

To determine the subject's deviation IQ, use the tables in Appendix B. Refer to those for individuals with a mental age score of 9–00 and a chronological age of 9–00. Find the subject's chronological age in years and months in the left-hand margin and go across this row to the column headed by the subject's mental age score in years and months. The score at this intersection, 100, is the subject's deviation IQ. This subject's conventional IQ, obtained by the ratio method, is 103. This is, according to Terman and Merrill, the score which would be expected of the average subject in a representative sample of nine-year-olds (Ibid., p. 36). Thus, the subject is scoring right at the average for his age group, and hence in DIQ values his score is 100. The mental age of 9–03 is at the average for nine-year-olds (cf., Appendix A), and hence his actual mental age (corrected MA score) is 9–00.

Example 3. Consider a child of age 2 years–8 months whose mental age score on the Stanford-Binet is 4 years–0 months:

CA	MA	Corrected MA	Conventional IQ	Deviation IQ
2–08	4–00	?	?	?

This subject's deviation IQ is obtained directly from Appendix B by referring to the table appropriate for subjects of this mental and chronological age (p. 133). In the left-hand margin locate the chronological age in years and months, 2–08, and then go across this row to the column headed by the mental age of 4–00. The value at this row-column intersection is the subject's deviation IQ, 141. If this subject's IQ is computed by the traditional $\frac{MA}{CA}$ ratio, the score will be 150.

The deviation IQ can be transformed into a standard score by subtracting 100, the mean DIQ at every age, and dividing the remainder by 16, the standard deviation at every age. The standard score can also be determined from a conventional IQ by using data from the standardization sample. Subtract from the conventional IQ the mean IQ for the proper age group as presented by Terman and Merrill (54, p. 36) or the **Mean** presented in Appendix C, and divide the remainder by the standard deviation for the age group (cf. Table 5, p. 19). In the case of the present subject the proper value of the mean is 104 and of the standard deviation, 18. The same standard score is obtained by either procedure, 2.6.

Example 4. Given a subject at CA 6–00 with a mental age score on one of the Stanford-Binet scales of 8–03:

CA	MA	Corrected MA	Conventional IQ	Deviation IQ
6–00	8–03	?	?	?

To find the subject's DIQ refer to Appendix B (p. 153). Go down the left-hand margin to a chronological age of 6–00 and across this row to the mental age column headed by 8–03. The value at this point, 142, is the subject's deviation IQ. The subject's conventional IQ, determined by means of the $\frac{MA}{CA}$ ratio, is 138.

As in the preceding example, the subject's standard score can be determined by subtracting 100 from the DIQ and dividing the remainder by 16. Or, it can be calculated by subtracting 100, the mean for a representative sample of children of six years, from the conventional IQ and dividing the remainder by 14.4, the standard deviation for six-year-olds. The result obtained by either procedure is a standard score of 2.6.

The reader will note that this subject obtains essentially the same standard score as that of the subject in Example 3, and that the DIQs are essentially the same in the two instances, respectively 141 and 142. However, the conventional IQs are quite different for these two subjects who have the same relative standing; an IQ of 150 for the two-year-old versus an IQ of 138 for the subject of six years. This comparison shows that two numerically different conventional IQs at different ages can indicate the same relative standing. In contrast, a given DIQ at all ages indicates the same relative standing.

Suppose that the scores presented in this and the preceding example were actually obtained on the same subject at the ages indicated, 2 years–8 months and 6 years–0 months. A comparison of the deviation IQs (and standard scores) indicates that at both ages the subject has the same relative standing in his age group. However, a comparison of his conventional IQs reveals a change of twelve IQ points. This comparison illustrates a point considered in an earlier chapter (p. 18) — change in conventional IQ does not always indicate a change in relative standing.

Example 5. Consider the case of a twelve-year-old who obtained a mental age score of 16–06:

CA	MA	Corrected MA	Conventional IQ	Deviation IQ
12–00	16–06	?	?	?

Refer to the appropriate table (p. 186). Find in the margin the chronological age and go across to the mental age column headed 16–06. The value at this point, DIQ of 132, is the subject's score. The conventional IQ, as obtained from *Measuring Intelligence* (54) is 138, the same value that the six-year-old obtained in the preceding example. However, a comparison of their standard score or deviation IQs shows that the six-year-old is considerably brighter, relative to his age group (DIQ of 142), than the twelve-year-old (DIQ of 132).

Suppose the test results presented in this and the preceding example were obtained on the same subject at 6–00 and 12–00. A comparison of DIQs indicates that the subject had changed considerably in relative standing (approximately two-thirds of a standard deviation), while a comparison of the conventional IQs indicates no change at all — a score of 138 at both ages. This illustrates another finding considered earlier (p. 18) — a subject can at some ages obtain the same conventional IQ even though there has been a considerable change in his standing in his age group.

Deriving Deviation IQs Not Included in Appendix B

The deviation IQs in Appendix B range from 30 through 170, that is, between plus and minus 4.4 standard deviations from the mean. Deviation IQs for the few individuals who fall outside this range can be determined by using the information presented in Appendices C and D.

To determine the deviation IQ for a subject when the value is not included in Appendix B, the procedure is as follows.

(a) Determine the subject's conventional IQ by the traditional $\dfrac{MA}{CA} \times 100$ formula.

(b) Find in Appendix C the values of the mean and K for the chronological age group.

(c) Subtract the mean from the derived conventional IQ, multiply the remainder by K, and add 100.

(If the derived conventional IQ is below the value in the column headed **IQ Lower Limit,** obtain K from Appendix D.)

Example 1. Suppose a child, tested at CA 6–07, obtains a mental age score of 11–04:

CA	MA	Corrected MA	Conventional IQ	Deviation IQ
6–07	11–04	?	?	?

Referring to Appendix B (p. 167) it is found that the DIQ is more than 170, therefore it must be determined by using Appendix C. Determine the conventional IQ by the ratio method, $\dfrac{MA}{CA} \times 100$:

$$\frac{136 \text{ (months)}}{79 \text{ (months)}} \times 100 = 172.$$

Subtract from this score of 172 the mean given in Appendix C for the age group. Multiply the remainder by the indicated constant (K) and add 100.

$$
\begin{aligned}
DIQ &= [(IQ - mean\ IQ) \times K] + 100 \\
&= [(172 - 100) \times 1.09] + 100 \\
&= (72 \times 1.09) + 100 \\
&= 78 + 100 \\
&= 178.
\end{aligned}
$$

Example 2. A child, 9 years–5 months of age, obtains a mental age score of 2 years–8 months:

CA	MA	Corrected MA	Conventional IQ	Deviation IQ
9–05	2–08	?	?	?

On turning to Appendix B one finds that the deviation IQ is not available for this subject; that is, it is below 30 and hence one must use Appendix C to obtain the score. Determine the conventional IQ by dividing the mental age by the chronological age and multiplying by 100:

$$\frac{32 \text{ months}}{113 \text{ months}} \times 100 = 28$$

Having obtained this value refer to Appendix C and find the constants for the proper chronological age. Since the IQ falls below the value indicated in the column head **IQ Lower Limit** (an IQ of 29), the value of K must be obtained from Appendix D. To find the constant in Appendix D, locate the subject's IQ in the left-hand margin of the table. Go across this row to the column appropriate to the chronological age in years. Since the chronological age is actually halfway between 9 and 10 years of age, the value of K will be halfway between those presented in these two columns, i.e., .955.

Having obtained the value of the mean from Appendix C and the value of K from Appendix D, compute the deviation IQ. Subtract the mean for the age group from the conventional IQ, multiply the negative remainder by K, and add 100:

$$
\begin{aligned}
\text{DIQ} &= [(\text{IQ} - \text{mean IQ}) \times \text{K} + 100 \\
&= [(28 - 103) \times .955] + 100 \\
&= (-75 \times .955) + 100 \\
&= -72 + 100 \\
&= 28.
\end{aligned}
$$

The value obtained in the last step is the subject's deviation IQ. Now in this instance, the finally obtained DIQ, 28, is numerically the same as the conventional IQ. However, the deviation IQ is to be compared with a mean DIQ of 100 for this age group, while the conventional IQ is to be compared with a mean of 103.

It should be noted in computing the conventional IQ that the actual chronological age is not used after 13 years, but instead a corrected age divisor (54, p. 31). These corrected CA divisors are included in Appendix C, and have to be used in determining conventional IQs when subjects are over 13 years of age.

Given Chronological Age and Conventional IQ

When the chronological age of a subject at the time of testing and the obtained conventional IQ are available either of two procedures can be used to determine the deviation IQ. One can (a) use the tables in Appendix C to transform the conventional IQ into a deviation IQ or (b) determine the subject's mental age score and use Appendix B as in the earlier examples. If the latter procedure is used, the subject's mental age score is determined by multiplying the conventional IQ by the CA at the time of testing (or by the corrected CA if the subject is over 13 years of age), and dividing the product by 100. Some practical applications of these procedures will now be considered.

Example 1. Given a subject, 6 years–06 months of age, who obtained a conventional IQ of 127 in the Stanford-Binet:

CA	MA	Corrected MA	Conventional IQ	Deviation IQ
6–06	?	?	127	?

The deviation IQ can be obtained by either of the above described procedures.

(a) Refer to Appendix C and find the values of the mean and K which apply to a chronological age of 6 years–06 months. Subtract the mean, 100, from the obtained conventional IQ of 127. Multiply the remainder by the value of K, 1.09, and add 100, the mean DIQ of a representative sample of subjects:

$$
\begin{aligned}
\text{DIQ} &= [(127 - 100) \times 1.09] + 100 \\
&= (27 \times 1.09) + 100 \\
&= 29 + 100 \\
&= 129, \text{ the subject's deviation IQ.}
\end{aligned}
$$

(b) Determine the subject's mental age in months by multiplying the conventional IQ by the chronological age in months, and divide the product by 100:

$$
\begin{aligned}
\text{MA (in months)} &= \frac{127 \times 78}{100} \\
&= 99.06.
\end{aligned}
$$

Refer in Appendix B to the page with the running foot MA 8–00/CA 4–00 (p. 153) which identifies this page as carrying the table of DIQs applicable to a mental age of 99 months (8 years–3 months) and a chronological age of 6–06. Locate 99 (months) in the bottom line of the table. Go up this column to the intersection of the CA row headed by 6–06 (with 78 in the CA total months column). The score at this intersection, 129, is the DIQ. Thus, an identical DIQ is obtained by either procedure.

Example 2. Consider a subject who is below average in ability; one who received a conventional IQ of 62 when tested with one of the Stanford-Binet scales at 12 years–6 months of age:

CA	MA	Corrected MA	Conventional IQ	Deviation IQ
12–06	?	?	62	?

Refer to Appendix C to find the value of the Mean and of K for a subject of this age, respectively 101 and .89. Subtract the mean from the conventional IQ, multiply the remainder by K, and add 100:

$$
\begin{aligned}
\text{DIQ} &= [(62 - 101) \times .89] + 100 \\
&= (-39 \times .89) + 100 \\
&= -35 + 100 \\
&= 65, \text{ the subject's DIQ.}
\end{aligned}
$$

Again, one could use the alternate procedure; that is, determine the mental age in months and read the DIQ directly from Appendix B. This procedure would yield an identical DIQ, 65.

Example 3. Suppose a subject tested at 5 years–6 months obtains a conventional IQ of 70:

CA	MA	Corrected MA	Conventional IQ	Deviation IQ
5–06	?	?	70	?

Appendix C gives the appropriate mean and K for a subject of this age as 100 and 1.12, respectively. Subtract the mean from the conventional IQ, multiply the remainder by K, and add 100:

$$
\begin{aligned}
\text{DIQ} &= [(70 - 100) \times 1.12] + 100 \\
&= (-30 \times 1.12) + 100 \\
&= -34 + 100 \\
&= 66, \text{ the subject's DIQ.}
\end{aligned}
$$

In this example, the identical DIQ, 66, would have been obtained if the mental age score had been calculated and the DIQ read directly from Appendix B.

This child's conventional IQ is 70, whereas that of the subject in Example 2 is 62. Consideration of these scores suggests that, relative to their age groups, the present child is brighter than the subject of Example 2. However, when their conventional IQs are both transformed into deviation IQs, one finds that they have essentially the same relative standing in their respective age groups, DIQs of 65 and 66 respectively!

Example 4. Given a child aged three with a conventional IQ of 175:

CA	MA	Corrected MA	Conventional IQ	Deviation IQ
3–00	?	?	175	?

With a conventional IQ above 170 (apparently more than 4 SDs above the mean, 100), it seems unlikely that one would be able to read a deviation IQ from Appendix B, so Appendix C is used to obtain the appropriate mean and K, 104 and .88, respectively. Subtract the mean from the conventional IQ, multiply the remainder by K, and add 100:

$$
\begin{aligned}
\text{DIQ} &= [(175 - 104) \times .88] + 100 \\
&= 162.
\end{aligned}
$$

Since the DIQ is below 170, it could have been obtained from Appendix B. However, it would not have saved time or effort, and at another age it probably would have been necessary to use the present procedure for such an extreme score.

Example 5. The last example in this series will consider a subject of low ability, a child who at age 11 obtains a conventional IQ of 25:

CA	MA	Corrected MA	Conventional IQ	Deviation IQ
11–00	?	?	25	?

Since the conventional IQ is below 30, it is unlikely that the deviation IQ is to be found in Appendix B. Consequently, the table in Appendix C is used. The mean conventional IQ for this age group is 102 according to these tables, but the value in the column headed **IQ Lower Limit** indicates that at this age the K value provided is not an appropriate constant for IQs below 30. Therefore, the value of K is determined from Appendix D. In Appendix D go down the left-hand margin of the table to the subject's conventional IQ, 25; then across this row to the column headed by the chronological age in years, 11–00. The value at this intersection, .93, is the appropriate value of K. To determine the deviation IQ, subtract the mean from the conventional IQ, multiply the remainder by K, and add 100:

$$
\begin{aligned}
\text{DIQ} &= [(25 - 102) \times .93] + 100 \\
&= (-77 \times .93) + 100 \\
&= -72 + 100 \\
&= 28, \text{ the subject's DIQ.}
\end{aligned}
$$

DERIVING CORRECTED MENTAL AGE SCORES

The purpose of the mental age, as stated by Terman and Merrill, is to tell ". . . that the ability of a given subject corresponds to the average ability of children of such and such an age" (54, p. 25). As was previously noted (pp. 48–49), the mental age scores earned on the Stanford-Binet scales slightly overestimate a subject's level of performance. For example, when a child obtains a mental age score of 9 years–3 months, that child is actually performing at the level of average nine-year-olds. Similarly, a subject of age three who obtains a mental age score of 3–00 is not performing at the age levels of average three-year-olds, but at the level of average children approximately 2 years–9 months of age.

The table of corrected mental ages provided in Appendix A will enable the reader to obtain an estimate of the age group for which an individual's performance is typical which is more precise than scores derived directly from the Stanford-Binet scales' administration. This table can also be used to determine the mental age score that a subject must obtain in order to reach the mean of his, or of any other, age group. In the latter case, the mental age score usually will exceed the chronological age in question since the Stanford-Binet scales, on the average, give a mental age score somewhat higher than the age of the group for which the performance is typical.

It should perhaps be noted again that this table includes the extension of the mental age concept from 13 to 18 years. That is, one can determine what age group a subject's performance represents if his mental age does not exceed 15 years–10 months (190 months), the average mental age score for subjects 18 years of age.

It may be well to again caution the reader not to utilize these corrected mental age scores for determining conventional IQs. The corrections reduce relatively little the change in the meaning of the IQ with age and hence they do not lessen the need for scores which indicate the same relative standing at different ages, that is, deviation IQs. It should also be noted that the actual mental age scores obtained in the Stanford-Binet testing should be used in determining DIQs. The corrected mental ages should *not* be used, since the corrections are already included in the construction of the tables in Appendices B, C, and D.

Some illustrations of the application of the table of corrected mental ages for the Stanford-Binet scales are now considered.

Example 1. Suppose a subject at ten years of age obtains a mental age score of ten years:

CA	MA	Corrected MA	Conventional IQ	Deviation IQ
10–00	10–00	?	——	——

The following procedure is used to determine the age group of which this performance is characteristic. Transform the mental age score of years and months into months only, that is, 120 months. Locate the nearest value to the subject's mental age score in the body of the table in Appendix A, namely, 120.4 months. The headings of the row and column which intersect at this point give in years and months, respectively, the chronological age group for which this mental age score is average, 9–09.

The question might also be raised as to what mental age score the subject would have to obtain in order to achieve at the average level of ten-year-olds. To determine this, find the value at which the row for year 10, and the column for 0 months intersect. This value is 123.6 months. Thus, if the subject were performing at the average level of ten-year-olds, he would have to obtain a mental age score of 10 years–4 months.

Example 2. Given a sixteen-year-old subject with a mental age score of 15 years. It would appear that the subject is a year retarded in mental development unless it is recalled that mental age scores after 13 years do not have the usual significance.

CA	MA	Corrected MA	Conventional IQ	Deviation IQ
16–00	15–00	?	——	——

Determine the actual age group for which this performance is typical. Transform the mental age score into months, 180. Find the closest numerical value in the body of the table of Appendix A, 180.0 months. The heading of the row, 15 years, and column, 6 months, gives the age group for which this performance is average. Thus, 15–06, is the corrected mental age.

Suppose that you wish to determine what mental age score this subject would have to obtain in order to perform at the average of his age group. Find his chronological age in years and months in the margins of the table — years in the left-hand margin and months in the column heading. The desired mental age score is given at the point at which row 16 and column 0 intersect. The value given there, 185.9, is the mental age in months (or in years and months, 15–06) which the subject would have to obtain if he were performing at the average level of other subjects his age.

USE OF THE TABLES OF CHANGE IN DIQ WITH AGE

The tables of change in IQ are presented in Appendix E. A separate table is provided for each of nineteen different ages within the first 17 years. Each table is made up of two sections, A, the change in conventional IQ, and B, the deviation IQ score change. The IQ changes presented in Section A are included so that other investigators can compare differences which they obtain between conventional IQs with those which were obtained on the Berkeley Growth Study sample. The tables for the conventional IQ should *not* be used for estimating amount of change in relative position with age because they confound actual change in position with change due (a) to variation in the composition of the tests with age and/or (b) to differences between tests. The particular tests used with these subjects at each of the nineteen ages considered are presented in Table 6 (p. 20).

The validity of the tables of change was discussed in detail in Part One (p. 25) especially with respect to the effect which the change in the instruments may have had on the changes in conventional and deviation IQ. The evidence presented there indicates that, with respect to the conventional IQ, quite different results can be expected when different instruments are involved. On the other hand the available evidence indicates that the change in instruments did not materially contribute to the changes in the DIQ. Therefore, *in estimating amount of change in relative position subsequent to a given testing one should use that section of the tables in Appendix E which presents results obtained with the DIQ, Section B.* For the most practical purposes the median, quartiles and range are preferable to the mean and standard deviation for reporting these estimates because of the anormal distribution of the DIQ changes.

In using the measures of DIQ change several considerations regarding the data on which they were based should be kept in mind: (a) in all instances the tests were individually administered; (b) the instruments used had been carefully developed over a period of years with particular attention to the problems of reliability and validity; (c) Dr. Bayley, who administered the tests, had had frequent contacts with the children since birth and was thus in a much better position than is usually the case to gauge when conditions were optimal for giving the tests; (d) concern in this study was with growth processes in a normal sample of children; and (e) the data were obtained with only three of the available measures of general ability (cf. Table 6, p. 20). Somewhat different results might have been obtained if instruments were employed which sampled somewhat different abilities.

When these tables are used in relation to the DIQs of children referred because of behavior problems or psychological disorders, it may be that the measures of change will underestimate the instability of mental test scores; hence they should be used with discretion. On the other hand, *there is considerable question as to whether one should attempt to use these tables with DIQs obtained with group tests, abbreviated scales, performance scales or inadequately standardized instruments.*

Example 1. Suppose a three-year-old obtains a DIQ of 100. How much will his score change by the time he is 6–00? (a) Turn in Appendix E to Table .9 (p. 219). (This table presents the amount of IQ change found in the Berkeley Growth Study subsequent to the test at 3 years.) (b) Find the second age, 6 years, in the left-hand margin of the table. (c) To determine the amount of change in relative position between these two ages, go across the row to Part B.

First consider the value in the column headed **Median,** 11 points. This value indicates that 50 per cent of the Berkeley Growth Study subjects changed 11 points or less between their tests at CA 3–00 and at CA 6–00. In some instances the change was in terms of an increase in DIQ while in others it was in terms of a decrease. That is, the median given is the average change demonstrated by these subjects regardless of whether it was in a positive or negative direction.

The value given in the column headed **Quartile 1** indicates that 25 per cent of the subjects showed an increase or decrease of as little as 6 points; conversely, that 75 per cent of the subjects changed this much or more.

The column headed **Quartile 3** shows that 25 per cent of the subjects showed an increase or decrease in DIQ of at least 23 points; conversely, that 75 per cent changed this much or less.

As given in the next column, the range of DIQ changes for the subjects in the Berkeley Growth Study fell between 0 and 39 points in either a positive or negative direction.

Depending on exigencies of the situation, the reader may wish to use one or several of these alternative ways of estimating the stability of DIQ with age. In a case report on the subject in this example, it probably would be sufficient to note that there is considerable variation among individuals in amount of change between tests given at 3 and 6 years of age, that the average change of 11 points is our best guess of how much the subject's DIQ will increase or decrease during this interval, and in the case of an individual child there may be no change at all or a gain or loss of as much as 39 points.

Example 2. Consider a child of three months with a DIQ of 110. How much would his score be expected to change by the time he has finished elementary school, that is, by the time he is approximately 12 years of age? (a) In Appendix E find the appropriate table for subjects tested at three months, Table .2. (b) Go down the left-hand margin of the table to 12 years, and across this row to Part B.

The value in the column headed **Median** is the average amount of change, 26 points. From the next two columns we find that 25 per cent of the subjects change 18 points or less, and at the other extreme, that 25 per cent change 45 points or more. The column headed **Range** indicates that during this interval at least one subject changed as little as one point and that at least one changed as much as 81 points.

It might be informative to compare the average change in deviation IQ between 3 months and 12 years with that obtained with the conventional IQ. The medians are 26 and 39, respectively. Thus if the median for the conventional IQ had been used, the conclusion would probably have been drawn that there is greater change in relative position between tests than actually occurred. If the deviation IQ changes are used, the psychometrist is not faced with the problem of evaluating when the change in score reflects actual change in position and when it is totally or in part an artifact of the construction of the test and of the methods of scoring.

11

APPLICATION TO TYPICAL

PROBLEMS IN PROFESSIONAL

PRACTICE

PRE-ADOPTION TESTINGS

Mental measurements are frequently obtained on infants who are to be placed in adoption homes. Reasons for the testings include the desire to match the child and adoptive parents on mental as well as physical characteristics, and to avoid later problems which might arise from the placement of children with neurological defects. In this section attention focuses on the question as to whether mental test scores obtained in infancy can effectively serve the "matching" function.

Consider a child tested at 1 year. An inspection of Table .5 of Appendix E shows that by the time the child enters school (age 6), it is likely that he will have changed considerably in ability relative to his age group. The average change in DIQ for this age interval is 24 points, i.e., one-and-a-half standard deviations. (The average change by 6 years is even greater when subjects are tested before 1 year.) When the average amount of change is so great, it is obvious that a child who at one year receives a DIQ as low as 75 may be scoring within the normal range of 88–112 by the time he enters first grade. Indeed, since during this interval 25 per cent of children change as much as 44 points, it is evident that no attempt should be made to use DIQs obtained at such an early age as a basis for making statements concerning the mental status of the child at some future date when he is in elementary or secondary school. In terms of our present testing methods, the only exception to the statement would be in cases of poor test performance due to organic injury or other neurological defects. Any attempt to match potential adoptive parents and children on mental ability should be guided by the principle that in general the older the child is at the time of a test, the more predictive his score will be for a given time interval. For example, for a five year interval one finds from Appendix E that the median DIQ change is 24 points between 1 and 6 years, 10 points between the ages of 3 and 8, and 6 points between tests given at 12 and 17 years.

The increase in stability of mental test performance with age can also be illustrated by considering at different ages the time interval required for a given amount of average change. For example, the length of time it takes subjects at different ages to develop an average change of 11 DIQ points. This amount of change occurs in two years from 2 to 4, in three years from age 4 to 7, and in slightly more than 11 years from age 6 to just over 17.

The adoption agency usually does not wish to predict a child's ability at a given age but rather the average level which he will manifest throughout childhood and adolescence. The fluctuations in relative ability are so large in the early years that one would probably not wish to include tests at these ages in determining the child's average level of ability. However, intelligence test scores are sufficiently stable during the elementary and secondary grades that one may wish to speak of a child's *general level of ability,* defined in terms of the average DIQ during these years.

One may wish to accept the child's performance at school age on an individually administered test such as the Stanford-Binet (or the average of several if they are available) as an estimate of his general level of ability. How much a single assessment is likely to differ from test scores which would be obtained at a later age can be estimated from Appendix E. For illustrative purposes consider changes subsequent to tests at 6 and 11 years. The average change in the year following six-year-tests is 8 DIQ points. Only a slightly greater amount of average change (10 DIQ points) is shown in an interval over twice as long, that is from 6 to 17 years. The average DIQ change in the one year period following tests at 11 years is only half that shown in the same time interval for six-year tests. However, the amount of change from 11 to 17 is about the same as for the six-year period 6 to 12.

From this example it may seem that the deviation IQ has sufficient stability throughout the school years that one would wish to speak of a general level of ability. However, even for school ages, this concept should be used with considerable discretion — approximately a quarter of subjects tested with a Stanford-Binet scale at year 6 subsequently show a change of one to two standard deviations (16 to 32 DIQ points) by the time they finish school, and changes of more than one SD are shown by some subjects tested as late as age 11.

If an adoption agency wishes to predict a child's general level of ability, what are the best predictors? Correlations obtained on data from the Berkeley Growth Study indicate that if the child is under 3 years, the agency would do well to consider using the true parents' ability as the basis for making the prediction. [Where mental test scores of the parents are not available, a possible substitute is the parents' education (years of schooling).] If the child is 3 or 4 years of age, the best prediction can be obtained from a combination of the subject's performance on an individual test and an estimate of the true parents' ability. If the child is 5 years or older, his test performance by itself is the best predictor; that is, knowledge of the parents' ability as measured by educational status does not improve the prediction. Thus if the adoption agency wishes the child during the school years to be well matched with the adoptive parents in terms of mental ability, assuming normal development, it will use the available information on the true parents rather than the child during the first two or three years, both variables between 3–00 and 5–00, and the child's own performance if he is to be placed for adoption after the age of 5–00.

EDUCATIONAL APPLICATIONS

It is frequently maintained that the primary function of assessments of ability in educational institutions is to facilitate the grouping of individuals of comparable ability. Actually, the purpose should be to provide an objective basis for modifying the school program so that it will better meet the needs of individual children. Grouping helps in the attainment of this goal to the extent that it facilitates the development of a more integrated and stimulating program in the classroom. However, individual differences in various kinds of ability are usually quite evident even in groups which are relatively homogeneous in level of general intelligence. Therefore, flexibility in the educational program is essential even when grouping is employed if some children are not to be left behind and others needlessly held back.

The developments in the present work have very definite implications for the assignment of individuals to educational programs whether they are in school, correctional homes, or in other public and private institutions.

Classification in the School Years

If there are large numbers of pupils exceeding a given conventional IQ, say 120, it is more likely that a special program for superior students will be initiated than if the number is small. Thus, a school system might decide that such a program should be developed for those students with conventional IQ of 116 or above at each grade where 20 per cent of the group exceeded this level. If the 1937 Stanford-Binet scale were used and if at each age the children were representative of the general population, only 13 per cent of the children at year 6 would exceed a conventional IQ of 116 as compared with 22 per cent at year 12.

Use of the conventional IQ together with the assumption that a given IQ score has the same significance at different ages leads to the conclusion that in this school there is a larger proportion of children of superior intelligence around the age of 12 years than around the age of 6. Such an erroneous conclusion would not arise when scores are used which have the same relative significance at all ages, that is, deviation IQs or other standard scores based on population norms. As has been noted, the deviation IQ standardizes individual differences in ability at different ages in the sense that at all ages a given DIQ score indicates the same relative standing and/or percentile rank.

For practical purposes subjects are sometimes classified as *superior, normal,* or *inferior* on the basis of conventional or deviation IQs. Once they have been assigned to such categories, it is easy to forget that differences in ability are greater within a given group than they are between individuals on either side of a group boundary line. Consider subjects of *very* superior intelligence with DIQs between 125 and 130. They are more similar in ability to individuals of superior intelligence whose DIQs are between 120 and 124, than they are to a second group, who like themselves are classified as very superior but whose DIQs are between 140 and 145. If this fact is recognized when educational programs are developed for different ability groups, the differences in programs will be thought of in quantitative terms, rather than involving different *kinds* of education for different *types* of children. In addition, the differences between programs for subjects on either side of a boundary line will be less than the differences within the program for either ability group. Such a dovetailing of programs is essential since children often shift from one ability group to another.

The average child in the early school years has a somewhat greater tendency to move in or out of a given ability group than a child in the middle school years. When ability groups are abitrarily defined in terms of a 12-point range, as in Figure 1, it can be expected through age 8 that approximately half of a given group will within a year move into a different group (see Appendix E, Tables .12–.14). The proportion of subjects who move into a different ability group decreases from 8 to 17 years; however, even by the age of 14 there is considerable mobility.

The individual differences in mental growth in the school years, reflected in the tables of DIQ change, make periodic reassessments of children's ability necessary. They also indicate the importance of providing for a smooth transition to an easier or more difficult program when the reassessments show reliable evidence of a change in the child's rate of mental growth. If this is to be achieved, the difference in the programs for ability groups must consist chiefly in breadth of application of concepts and rate of increase in difficulty of the tasks. If such is the case, a subject in an accelerated phase of mental development will not be handicapped by lack of basic background content on being moved into a more accelerated group, and a subject in a decelerated phase will not have to repeat earlier mastered skills on being moved into a less advanced group. Thus an individualization of the school program is essential, even when groupings on the basis of ability are made, if the needs of such pupils are to be met.

It has become traditional to have several different reading groups within a given class in the early grades, so that the difficulty of the reading material provided a child within a class depends on the skills he has mastered. Such a procedure is employed to a lesser extent with arithmetic and to little or no extent in a number of other subject areas at intermediate and upper grade levels. The results of the present study show that bright individuals tend at all ages to make larger yearly gains in ability than those made by less capable subjects and hence that individual differences in intelligence increases with age. Thus, results of the present study indicate that in the majority of subject areas there should be increased diversification of the educational program with age, both in terms of breadth of application of concepts and rate of increase in difficulty of tasks.

Skipping

A child who is advanced in mental development, may more closely resemble members of an older age group in ability to perform educational tasks than he does those of his own age level; however, in other aspects of maturity he may be much more like those of his own chronological age. In the past a considerable number of children who were advanced a half-grade or grade on the basis of their intellectual development subsequently showed difficulties in adjusting in areas in which they were less mature than their new classmates. Because of this, *skipping* has generally fallen into disfavor except in instances in which it is quite evident that the child is accelerated in all phases of development. Advancement may also present educational problems to the child if the school system has adopted a stock educational program rather than one directed towards meeting the needs of individual children. If a child is double promoted in such a system, he may be penalized because of the loss of basic training in a tool subject.

If a child of superior mental ability is advanced a grade in a school where the philosophy is practiced that a child should move forward at his own rate, he will incur no educational penalty. He already will have acquired more basic background in tool subjects than a considerable proportion of his classmates. In most instances it would undoubtedly be preferable to group children on the basis of ability rather than to advance the bright and retard the dull. However, this is often not feasible in small communities because the total number in a given ability group is too small. In some large school systems it may also be difficult because funds are not available for establishing an adequately diversified educational program. In such instances skipping is about the only alternative if the teacher is not to be burdened with the task of carrying out a program for individual children considerably beyond the range of the rest of the pupils in her class.

Another problem which must be considered if a child is to be advanced a grade is the likelihood that he will remain sufficiently accelerated in his mental development to be able to keep pace with his new classmates. Consider as an example, a child of seven years whose teacher feels that he should be advanced because of his facility in tool subjects. Suppose he is tested with a Stanford-Binet scale and obtains a DIQ of 132; that is, he is two standard deviations above the mean of his age group and his corrected mental age is 8 years–11 months. If he is advanced a grade, he will still be somewhat above the average of his new classmates if they are average eight year olds. If he maintains the same DIQ as he grows older, he will even further outdistance them. His corrected mental age will be 10 years–6 months when they are 9, 12 years–1 month when they are 10, 13 years–11 months when they are 11, and so on.

Children do, however, change considerably in relative ability in the early school years. The largest average change subsequent to 7 year tests, as given in Table .12 of Appendix E, is 9 points, and in no instances do more than 25 per cent of the subjects change more than 14 points. If it is assumed that half the latter group show a gain and half a loss, then only 12.5 per cent show a decrease of more than 14 points by 17 years of age.

If the subject in the illustration changed no more than the average child, one would expect that he would compete adequately in educational tasks with an average group of subjects a year older than he. Even if his DIQ dropped 14 points within the next year, his progress would probably be adequate. About one in eight times his DIQ could be expected to drop more than this amount and in some of these instances it might be necessary the next year to keep him in the grade to which he had been double-promoted. The question as to whether or not he should be advanced would seem to depend on such additional factors as his maturity in other developmental areas, his facility in tool subjects, and his probable reaction to being held back at a future date. In any case, it would probably be desirable to make it clear to both the child and his parents that for at least a year the advancement was provisional.

Hold-overs

When a child is not making adequate progress in school, the decision as to whether he will be advanced with his classmates or whether he will be kept in the same grade may depend to a considerable extent on his mental test performance. If his poor performance in school is not attributable to inferior intellect, advancing him with his age mates and giving whatever individual help is necessary to keep him from getting too far behind is often a preferable procedure to retarding him because of the stigma attached to being retarded in school and because in numerous other areas of development he is likely to be out of step with the younger and more immature children. When the subject is of low mental ability, somewhat different considerations are involved.

There is an increasing disadvantage with age in intellectual tasks for children of low ability. A bright child on the average makes larger gains in ability each year than the child of low ability and thus they will become increasingly different in their ability to achieve on intellectual tests. If a child of consistently low mental ability is advanced with his age peers, he will as he grows older find that it is increasingly difficult to compete successfully with them in intellectual tasks. Because the educational program is tied more basically to the normal progress of intellectual growth than the other areas of development, some degree of retardation is likely to be less frustrating for such a child than the continued experience of being faced with demands for achievement that he is unable to meet.

In the preceding paragraph we specified a child of *consistently low ability*. However, in the practical situation we cannot say with certainty whether a child who is low in ability at a given age will be consistently low in the future. Of course, children of low ability, like children at other ability levels, tend to maintain their same relative standing with age. For individually administered tests such as the Stanford-Binet, the tables in Appendix E can be used to estimate the amount a subject's DIQ will change subsequent to a test at a specified age.

Suppose a six-year-old child is tested at the end of the first grade because of inadequate school progress. He obtains a DIQ of 75 on the Stanford-Binet. According to Table .12 of Appendix E, 50 per cent of six-year-olds change 8 or more points in a year, and one-quarter of the subjects change 13 or more points in a negative or positive direction. Thus, the chances are only about one in eight that he will fall within the normal range after a year. If he maintains his same relative standing a year later or if he shows a gain of as much as 13 points, he will still be more like the first- than the second-grader in ability and probably in reading readiness. Since it is likely that with age the difference between his ability to achieve on intellectual tasks and that of the average child will increase, it may be preferable to retard him for a year at this level if special classes are not available, rather than to wait until a later age when retardation may be psychologically more damaging.

Working Below Capacity

Whether differences in achievement are explained in terms of ability or in terms of motivation and other psychological factors is determined in the practical situation by numerical differences in the ability scores. When the IQs of a group of subjects tend to be numerically homogeneous one is likely to account for achievement differences in terms of variables other than ability. On the other hand, when the IQs are numerically heterogeneous, it is more likely that one will attribute differences in achievement to ability differences. If the scores for a group of subjects consist of conventional IQs on the Stanford-Binet scale, they will tend to be homogeneous if obtained at 6 years and heterogenous if obtained at 12 years because of factors inherent in the construction of the test.

Suppose a six-year-old child obtains a conventional IQ of 114 on the Stanford-Binet. It is unlikely that a teacher will feel that he is under achieving to any great extent if his performance is average for six-year-olds. On the other hand, suppose a twelve-year-old obtains an IQ of 120. His teacher is likely to feel that he is underachieving considerably if his achievements are not above those of the average pupil. Still both have a DIQ of 116; that is, both have the same relative standing in their age groups.

Consider as another example two children tested with the Stanford-Binet — a six-year-old with a conventional IQ of 138 and a twelve-year-old with a conventional IQ of 149. The younger child appears to be about in the middle of the ability group termed *very superior* in Figure 18. Certainly, he cannot be classified as *near genius* or *genius*. The older subject might well be considered to fit into the latter category. Actually, both have the same relative standing in their age groups, deviation IQs of 142!

The preceding examples indicate that use of the conventional IQ can lead to erroneous conclusions as to the ability level of a subject and consequently as to whether or not he is working up to capacity. Such conclusions may not have too serious consequences for subjects of superior mental ability. However, they may have undesirable ones for subjects of inferior intellect. The tendency is to believe, for ages where the scores are numerically homogeneous, that the dull child is closer to the average than he actually is in terms of standard score or percentile ranks; and, at ages where the scores are numerically heterogeneous, to regard him as less capable than he is in standard or percentile score terms.

What has been said in the preceding paragraphs about conventional IQs does not hold in the case of deviation IQs. Since a given DIQ score has the same relative significance from 2 to 18 years, that is, refers to the same standard score at all ages, differences between two groups in the homogeneity of DIQs reflect differences in the variability of intelligence of the groups rather than characteristics of the tests such as the varying concentration of items of different levels of difficulty.

If levels of achievement were empirically tied to different points on the DIQ distribution, for each group it would be feasible to determine the probable level of attainment for a given DIQ (ability) range. A knowledge of these relationships would provide an objective basis for ascertaining at each age whether or not a child is working at capacity indicated by standard measures. Thus, it would be possible to determine which pupils are consistently over-achieving and which are consistently underachieving. A comparison of these groups could be expected to suggest variables other than ability which are of major importance both in specific and general areas of academic achievement.

APPLICATIONS TO COUNSELING

Counseling of Parents

A parent may request a mental examination of a child for a number of different reasons: normal interest in following the child's intellectual development, fear that the goals he has for the child will not be realized, concern about the child's behavior, or suggested referral by a professional person, to name some. While in many instances the major task of the counselor will be to help the parent accept the child as the child is (cf., p. 75–78), in others an objective report of the child's ability level may be all that is required.

A common assumption is that parents are more anxious about the development of the first-born than of subsequent children. Certainly this is to be expected, since few have experience on which they can base an evaluation of their first child's development. However, parents can become equally anxious when a later child appears to be growing at a slower rate or appears to be following a different pattern in his development from that shown by the older children in the family at a similar age.

An evaluation of the child's mental test performance may or may not confirm the parents' feelings with respect to the child's ability at the time. Regardless of which is the case, it is important that the parents be apprised of the child's general level of ability at the time of the test and that they be helped to accept the child as he is. (There is question as to whether the parents should be given the child's specific conventional or deviation IQ score. Some parents attribute too much significance to such scores and use them long after they are applicable.) It is equally important that the parents should recognize the extent to which the child's mental ability may change relative to others of his age in subsequent tests, and hence of the necessity of relatively frequent reassessments, especially at early ages.

Because of the parents' emotional involvement in the intellectual capacity of their offspring, in the case of superior children it may be psychologically advisable in some instances to lay more stress on the possible drop in performance with age than on the possible increase. In the case of the child of below average ability, it may be more important to stress the stability of scores with age, at the same time pointing out that occasionally fairly large changes do occur and hence that the child should be retested periodically.

Recently a mother, a professional woman from an upper middle-class home, referred her four-year-old for an intelligence test because she felt that he was retarded. The father, who had been reared in a lower socio-economic group, was a skilled tradesman, and, judging from his facility with language, considerably above average in intelligence. Mental test records available on the older children at 8 and 10 years indicated that they were of superior ability, with IQs approximately two standard deviations above the mean. The mother was obviously ambivalent toward the four-year-old, readily admitting that she feared he would be "like the father's relatives." It was also evident from talking with her that she hoped to see her own earlier professional goals (which she felt had been thwarted by marriage and almost immediate pregnancy) fulfilled in the achievement of her children. The task was to help the mother accept the youngest child as a normal four-year-old performing on an intelligence test at the average for his age. Possibly an even more important task was helping the mother gain satisfaction from seeing the youngster grow at his own rate, aiding him when possible to make the most of his potentialities. Reassessments were scheduled for 6 and 8 years.

The reader may consider that in this instance it would have been fairly safe to predict an increase in the child's score with age — the mother was highly intelligent, the father appeared to be considerably above average, and the siblings stood at approximately the 97th percentile in intelligence relative to others of their age. However, if this had been suggested to the mother, for the child it probably would have resulted in unwarranted pressure to achieve. A preferable alternative seemed to be the scheduling of later tests. In this way it would be possible to deal in the counseling situation with the changes which actually occurred.

Counseling of Children

Knowledge of the child's level of ability is desirable, if not necessary, in most counseling situations. Here, as in earlier sections, attention will be restricted to the most direct application of the findings of the present study.

A fourteen-year-old junior high school boy was recently referred for counseling. In the first meeting with the counselor he was generally moody and un-cooperative. While it was evident during this interview that he had strong intellectual interests, it was just as evident that he had little hopes of achieving goals in this area because of the insufficiency of environmental supports. Thus, he spoke of wanting to go to college but at the same time indicated that since his father was a day-laborer he was undoubtedly destined for a similar occupational level.

On consulting the records the counselor found that the boy had recently transferred from another area of the country. No results from group tests were available in his record, but a guidance report was included which indicated that he had obtained a conventional IQ of 132 on the Stanford-Binet at age 6. In discussing this case with the counselor the writer pointed out that a conventional IQ of 132 at age 6 represents a somewhat higher level of ability than the same score at other ages. Therefore, the score was transformed into a deviation IQ, 136. In order to provide an idea of the probable stability of mental ability scores from 6 to 14 years, reference was made to the tables of IQ change. According to the table (Appendix E, Table .12) 50 per cent of six-year-olds change six points or less by 14 years. However, since 25 per cent of six-year-olds change sixteen points or more by this age, the subject was referred for a retest with the Stanford-Binet.

The subject obtained a deviation IQ of 132 on the retest. Since seventy-five per cent of fourteen-year-olds change eight points or less in the next three years and since he seemed to have the necessary motivation, he was encouraged to take a college preparatory course. Further impetus was given his academic efforts by apprising him of the availability of college scholarships for superior achievement in high school work.

In this and other illustrations throughout Part Two, the tables of IQ change (Appendix E) have been used to indicate the stability and/or lack of stability of DIQs obtained at different ages. It should perhaps be pointed out again that these tables are based on a fairly small and select sample. Despite some evidence to the contrary, the changes presented may vary considerably from those that would be obtained from a representative sample of the general population at each of a large number of different ages. Certainly, tables of change based on normative samples would be highly desirable. However, their absence does not relieve the professional person using mental tests from indicating on the basis of available knowledge something of the change in score which is likely to occur by the time of a later assessment. In this connection the writer has taken the position that use of the present tables are preferable to pronouncements based on (a) theoretical biases as to the stability or instability of measures of relative ability and/or (b) an individual's memory as to the changes in DIQ between scores for a large number of different ages.

12

WECHSLER INTELLIGENCE SCALE

FOR CHILDREN

If the reader uses the *Wechsler Intelligence Scale for Children* (WISC) (59) in his work, he may wish to know if the findings of the present study are applicable to this scale.

MEASURES OF RELATIVE ABILITY

The IQ obtained with the WISC is a deviation, or standard score, IQ; that is, the standard deviation is the same at every age. In contrast to a standard deviation of 16, which was used in deriving deviation IQs for the Stanford-Binet scales, Wechsler uses a standard deviation of 15. Consequently, a child comparably bright on the two tests, assuming that they both have numerically the same mean, will receive a slightly higher DIQ on the Stanford-Binet than on the WISC, and a child comparably dull will obtain a little lower DIQ on the Stanford-Binet. To obtain in numerical terms the equivalent score on the WISC for a given DIQ on a Stanford-Binet scale, determine the number of IQ points the subject's score deviates from 100. Divide this value by 16, and subtract the result from the DIQ if it is greater than 100 or add it if the DIQ is less than 100. If one wishes to determine the equivalent DIQ for the Stanford-Binet of a WISC score, one adds (or subtracts) from it the quotient obtained by dividing by 15 the number of IQ points the subject's score is above (or below) 100.

COMPARABILITY OF THE WISC AND OF THE STANFORD-BINET

Since the WISC appears to measure somewhat different abilities than the Stanford-Binet, one would not necessarily expect subjects to get similar scores on these scales. In general, the correlations between scores on the two tests as reported in the literature vary between .60 and .90 with a median above .80. In these studies there appears to be a definite relationship between the heterogeneity of the groups and the size of the correlations. As the SDs of the groups approximate the SDs of the standardization samples, the correlations tend to approach in size the values of the reliability coefficients for the instruments. These findings suggest that the two tests measure the same functions to a considerable degree despite the evident differences in content.

Studies which have compared the WISC and 1937 Stanford-Binet for average and/or below average groups indicate that the results tend to be fairly similar (3, 15, 48). However, the disparity between scores on these tests for high ability groups is quite evident (19, 36, 61), differences as large as 17 points having been reported (58). It appears that the differences between mean scores for the various groups would be reduced if these data were reanalyzed after the Stanford-Binet scores were transformed into Deviation IQs.[13] However, it is unlikely that in the case of the high ability groups the transformation would account for all of the differences between mean scores. Whether the remaining differences are to be accounted for in terms (a) of the measuring of somewhat different functions, (b) of different weightings of different facets of intelligence in total scores on the two tests, or (c) of differences in standardization procedures, can only be ascertained in further investigations.

STABILITY OF IQS ON THE WISC

Little is known at present about the change with age for IQs obtained with the WISC. In fact, it is likely that a considerable period of time will elapse before there is as much information available on the stability of scores on this test as there is at present for scores on Stanford-Binet scales. Despite the hazard involved, it would probably be safer to utilize the tables of change in Appendix E to estimate the stability of scores on the WISC than it would be to depend on one's own biases and clinical hunches. If these tables were to be used with this scale until comparable tables have been prepared for it, in each instance the values presented in the body of the table should be reduced by $\frac{1}{16}$ because of the difference between SDs for the two instruments. If the value is 16 DIQ points it should be reduced to 15, if the value is 32 DIQ points, it should be reduced to 30, and so on.

MENTAL AGE SCORES FOR THE WISC

Wechsler recognizes that the IQ, derived by means of the $\frac{MA}{CA}$ ratio, does not have the same relative significance at different ages; therefore, in developing IQs for the WISC he abandons the ratio approach. While it is not possible

[13] The differences between IQs on the WISC and on the Stanford-Binet are usually positively correlated with IQ on the latter test. It is likely that this relationship is at least partially a function of (a) change in the size of the variability of Stanford-Binet IQs with age, and (b) the means at various ages being somewhat above 100. Hence a decrease in this relationship can be predicted when the DIQ transformation is utilized.

TABLE 11

Age Weights for WISC Raw Scores
Adapted from Wechsler (60)

AGE WEIGHT	Information	Comprehension	Arithmetic	Similarities	Vocabulary	Digit Span	Picture Completion	Picture Arrangement	Block Design	Object Assembly	Code A	Code B	Mazes	AGE WEIGHT
1	5	5	3	3	15	5	—	—	4	8	15–16	—	5	1
2	—	—	4	4	—	—	6	4	—	9	17–20	—	—	2
3	6	—	—	—	16	6	—	5	—	10	21–24	10 or less	6	3
4	7	6	5	5	17	—	—	6	—	11	25–27	11–12	7	4
5	—	7	—	—	18	7	7	7–9	5	12	28–31	13–16	8	5
6	8	8	6	6	19	—	—	10–11	—	13	32–33	17–20	9	6
7	—	9	—	—	20	—	—	12–13	6	14	33–34	—	10	7
8	9	—	7	—	21–22	8	8	14–16	—	15	35–36	21–22	11	8
9	—	10	—	7	23	—	—	17–19	7–8	16	37	23–24	12	9
10	10	—	8	—	24	—	—	20–21	9	17	38–39	25	13	10
11	11	11	—	—	25	—	9	22–23	10	18	40–41	26	14	11
12	—	—	—	8	26	—	—	24	11	—	—	27–28	—	12
13	—	—	—	—	27	—	—	25	12	19	42–43	29	15	13
14	12	—	—	—	28	9	10	26	13–14	20	44–45	30–32	—	14
15	—	—	—	—	29–30	—	—	—	15	—	—	33–34	—	15

TABLE 11 (Continued)

16	—	35	46	—	16–17	27	—	—	31	—	—	—	—
17	16	36–37	—	21–22	18–19	28	11	—	32–33	9	9	12	13
18	—	38–39	—	—	20	—	—	—	34	—	—	13	14
19	—	40	47	—	21–22	29	12	—	35	10	10	—	—
20	—	41	—	23	23–24	—	—	10	36–37	—	—	14	15
21	—	42–43	48	—	—	—	—	—	38	11	—	15	16
22	17	44	—	—	25–28	30	—	—	39	—	11	—	17
23	—	45–46	—	24	29	—	—	—	—	12	—	16	—
24	—	47	—	—	30	31	—	—	40–41	—	12	—	—
25	—	48	—	—	31	—	13	—	42	13	—	—	18
26	—	49	—	—	32	32	—	—	43	—	—	17	—
27	—	50–51	—	—	33	33	—	—	44	—	—	—	19
28	—	52–53	—	25	34	—	—	11	45	14	—	—	—
29	—	54	—	—	35	34	14	—	—	—	—	—	—
30	—	55	—	—	—	—	—	—	46	—	—	—	—
31	—	56	—	26	36–37	35	—	—	47	—	—	—	—
32	18	57	—	—	38–39	36	—	—	48	—	—	—	20
33	—	—	—	—	—	—	—	—	49	—	—	—	—

(in a practical sense) to determine from the WISC manual (59) the age group which a subject's performance is most like, it is possible to approximate the age group by utilizing procedures subsequently set forth by Wechsler (60). Because these procedures are presented in a technical journal and are not readily available to all workers who utilize this scale, tables similar to those he presents are provided in the present work in order to facilitate the derivation of mental ages for this test.

To determine the age group which a subject's performance is most like (a) find the subject's raw score for a given sub-scale in the appropriate row in Table 11 as indicated by the side-heading. The heading of the column in which the value falls gives the **Age Weight.** (b) After determining the age weight for the subject's performance on each sub-test, add them together. (c) Determine the subject's average age weight; that is, divide the total age weight by the number of sub-tests included. (d) Multiply the result by 10. (e) Find in the body of Table 12 the numerical value closest to this result. The heading of the row and column in which this value falls gives the age group for which the subject's performance is average.

Example: Consider a subject 12 years–6 months of age whose performance is as indicated in the **Raw Score** column. In this example each step indicated above is designated by the appropriate letter in parentheses.

Subtest	Raw Score	(a) Age weight
Information	10	11
Comprehension	11	14
Arithmetic	9	17
Similarities	7	11
Vocabulary	33	17
(Digit Span)	9	14
Picture completion	12	20
Picture arrangement	22	11
Block design	12	13
Object assembly	20	14
Coding (Code B)	24	9
(Mazes)	17	23
		(b) 174

(c) $\frac{174}{12} = 14.50$ (All 12 sub-tests were administered; hence the divisor is 12.)

(d) $14.50 \times 10 = 145.00$

(e) Entering Table 12 with the test age weight of 145 one finds that the age group which the subject's performance is most like is 9 years–8 months.

Using the procedure described one can, of course, determine for any combination of sub-tests the age group for which performance in the selected areas is average. However, if concern is with only one sub-test, one need only determine from Table 11 the age weight for the raw score in question, multiply it by 10, and find the age group for which this value is average by referring to Table 12.

TABLE 12

Mental Age Equivalents for WISC Age Weights

Adapted from Wechsler (60)

YEARS	MONTHS											
	00	01	02	03	04	05	06	07	08	09	10	11
4	—	—	—	—	—	—	—	—	—	—	—	—
5	—	—	10	12.5	15	17.5	20	22.5	25	27.5	30	32.5
6	35	37.5	40	42.5	45	47.5	50	52.5	55	57.5	60	62.5
7	65	67.5	70	72.5	75	77.5	80	82.5	85	87.5	90	92.5
8	95	97.5	100	102.5	105	107.5	110	112.5	115	117.5	120	122.5
9	125	127.5	130	132.5	135	137.5	140	142.5	145	147.5	150	152.5
10	155	157.5	160	162.5	165	167.5	170	172.5	175	177.5	180	182.5
11	185	187.5	190	192.5	195	197.5	200	202.5	205	207.5	210	212.5
12	215	217.5	220	222.5	225	227.5	230	232.5	235	237.5	240	242.5
13	245	247.5	250	252.5	255	257.5	260	262.5	265	267.5	270	272.5
14	275	277.5	280	282.5	285	287.5	290	292.5	295	297.5	300	302.5
15	305	307.5	310	312.5	315	317.5	—	—	—	—	—	—

13

SUMMARY

In Part One of this work the findings of the study were considered in terms of their methodological and theoretical soundness. In Part Two the same findings were presented from the standpoint of their practical implications and use.

The study from which the findings were obtained is primarily dependent on two samples, the subjects of the Berkeley Growth Study and the subjects used in the 1937 standardization of the Stanford-Binet Scale. The Berkeley Growth Study is one of the longitudinal investigations conducted at the Institute of Child Welfare (now Institute of Human Development), University of California. Of the 61 children initially enrolled in the study at the time of birth, approximately 40 remained in the study through the age of 18 years. While the number of subjects was not large, results obtained from the data collected are of exceptional importance because at this time it is one of the rare studies in which the members of the sample have been followed in their mental development from such an early age to adulthood and on whom results are available in the literature.

The BGS data were analyzed to determine the amount of change in conventional IQs (computed by the traditional $\frac{MA}{CA}$ ratio, between tests administered at 20 different ages within the first 17 years). The tendencies which are apparent in these tables of IQ change are the same as those which various investigators have found in the correlations between tests administered at different ages to the same subjects. When the interval between tests is held constant, amount of change decreases with age of the earlier of the two tests, and, as the interval between tests increases, IQ changes increase. Since IQ change depends on both variables, studies which report change in score for subjects heterogeneous with respect either to age of initial test or to interval between tests are of limited practical value.

The changes in conventional IQ between tests were compared with the correlations obtained between them. This comparison indicates that the IQ changes do not vary systematically with the correlations between scores.

112

(Thus, a given numerical change in conventional IQ does not denote the same amount of change in relative position at different ages.) Two possible explanations were considered; namely, that this is to be accounted for in terms of age changes in the mean IQ of the group and/or in terms of systematic age changes in the variabilities, a possibility suggested by earlier investigators. To test the latter hypothesis the IQs were transformed into deviation IQs (DIQs), defined as a mental test standard score times 16, plus 100. The changes obtained between the deviation IQs were much more consistent with those expected on the basis of the correlations than were the changes between conventional IQs. When DIQ scores were used, the age changes in means from 2 to 17 years did not materially contribute to the score changes except at age 5.

A number of investigators have recognized that the age variations in size of the Stanford-Binet 1937 standard deviations are too great to be accounted for in terms of chance fluctuations. From his analysis of the standardization data McNemar concluded that the most extreme of these fluctuations are probably to be accounted for by an uneven concentration of easy and difficult items at different ages, and he suggested that corrections be applied at those ages at which the variations were most extreme. The procedure of correcting only the most extreme variations assumes that the fluctuations in standard deviations at the adjacent ages (which generally tend to be in the same direction) are to be accepted as random variations. This assumption appears questionable since subjects at ages adjacent to those with marked variations are also tested with these items, and thus their standard deviations will tend to be similarly affected. Rather, it appears reasonable to assume that the obtained standard deviations, smoothed to rule out small errors in sampling, represent the best estimates of the true standard deviations for the test. This conclusion, drawn on the basis of a re-evaluation of findings available on the standardization data, was supported by results obtained with data on the superior BGS sample at those ages at which the 1937 revision of the Stanford-Binet was administered.

The analysis of data on the BGS sample involved transforming the subjects' IQ scores into deviation IQs. This entailed, in the case of the 1937 revision of the Stanford-Binet scale, using as the best estimate of the true standard deviations of conventional IQs the smoothed values of standard deviations for the standardization samples, and using the mean conventional IQs which would have been obtained for representative samples at the various ages. It was necessary to use the latter values rather than the means obtained on the standardization samples (or an arbitrary value of 100) because mental age scores of the Stanford-Binet scales tend at all ages except Year VI to give mean conventional IQs slightly above 100 for representative samples. As compared with results obtained with the conventional IQ, the fluctuations in the means for this superior group were reduced by half when the deviation IQs were used. Thus, a considerable proportion of the variation in the means appears to be the result of age changes in the variabilities of the test. (The fluctuations in means were also much smaller than when the corrections suggested by McNemar were used.) In addition, the changes in conventional IQs between tests were compared with the changes in deviation IQs. The comparison indicated that part of the changes in the conventional IQs is artifactual;

that is, in part they are due to fluctuations with age in the magnitude of the standard deviation.

These findings indicate that deviation IQs are needed in order to take account of the age changes in variability for the Stanford-Binet scales. Consequently, revised IQ tables were established for these scales. Tables for converting conventional IQs into DIQs are presented in Appendices C and D. Tables for computing DIQs from a knowledge of MA and CA are presented in Appendix B. Because mental growth, as measured by the Stanford-Binet scales, continues at least until age 18, the new IQ tables include DIQs for ages 16 to 18, as well as for the earlier ages. The tables presented in Appendices B and C are basically those which are included in the manual for the 1960 revision of the Stanford-Binet scale (55).

Mental age scores on the Stanford-Binet scales at most ages between 2 and 13 overestimate the age level for which a given performance is average, and after 13 years they no longer serve this function. The table of corrected mental ages in Appendix A avoids these problems and enables one to determine the age group between 2 and 18 years for which a given mental age score is average.

The BGS data were also analyzed with respect to hypotheses accounting for the consistency of intelligence test performance with age; for example, Anderson's hypothesis that growth subsequent to a given assessment is unrelated to relative position. The results indicate that, when difficulty of the items is taken into consideration, the more intelligent subjects as of age 6 make larger yearly mental ability gains at all ages after the first year than the less intelligent.

References

1. Aborn, M., and Derner, G. F., "IQ variability in relation to age on the Revised Stanford-Binet," *J. Consult. Psychol.*, 1951, 15, 231–235.
2. Allan, Mary E., and Young, Florence M., "The constancy of the intelligence quotient as indicated by retests of 130 children," *J. Appl. Psychol.*, 1943, 27, 41–60.
3. Altus, Grace T., "A note on the validity of the Wechsler Intelligence Scale for Children," *J. Consult. Psychol.*, 1952, 16, 231.
4. Ames, Viola, "Factors related to high school achievement," *J. Educ. Psychol.*, 1943, 34, 229–236.
5. Anderson, J. E., "The limitations of infant and preschool tests in the measurement of intelligence," *J. Psychol.*, 1939, 8, 351–379.
6. Bayley, Nancy, "Mental growth during the first three years. A developmental study of 61 children by repeated tests," *Genet. Psychol. Monogr.*, 1933, 14, 1–92.
7. Bayley, Nancy. *The California First-Year Mental Scale.* Berkeley: University of California Press, 1933.
8. Bayley, Nancy, "Consistency and variability in the growth of intelligence from birth to eighteen years," *J. Genet. Psychol.*, 1949, 75, 165–196.
9. Bayley, Nancy, "On the growth of intelligence," *Amer. Psychologist*, 1955, 10, 805–818.
10. Bishton, R., "A study of some factors related to achievement of intellectually superior eighth grade children," *J. Educ. Res.*, 1957, 51, 203–207.
11. Bradway, Katherine P., "IQ constancy in the revised Stanford-Binet from the preschool to the junior high school level," *J. Genet. Psychol.*, 1944, 65, 197–217.

12. Bradway, Katherine P., Thompson, Clare W., and Cravens, R. B., "Preschool IQs after twenty-five years," *J. Educ. Psychol.*, 1958, 49, 278–281.
13. Brown, F., "The significance of the IQ variability in relation to age on the Revised Stanford-Binet scale," *J. Genet. Psychol.*, 1943, 63, 177–181.
14. Clarke, A. D. B., and Clarke, A. M., "How constant is the IQ?," *Lancet*, 1953, 265, 877–880.
15. Cohen, B. D., and Collier, Mary J., "A Note on the WISC and other tests of children six to eight years old," *J. Consult. Psychol.*, 1952, 16, 226–227.
16. Conrad, H. S., Freeman, F. N., and Jones, H. E., "Differential mental growth," *Yearb. Nat. Soc. Stud. Educ.*, 1944, 43 (I), 164–184.
17. Ebert, Elizabeth, and Simmons, Katherine. The Brush Foundation study of child growth and development. "I. Psychometric tests," *Monogr., Soc. Res. Child Developm.*, 1943, 8, No. 2, 1–113.
18. Elwood, Mary I., "Changes in Stanford-Binet IQ of retarded six-year-olds," *J. Consult. Psychol.*, 1952, 16, 217–219.
19. Frandsen, A. N., and Higginson, J. B., "The Stanford-Binet and the Wechsler Intelligence Scale of Children," *J. Consult. Psychol.*, 1951, 15, 236–238.
20. Gates, A. I., "The necessary mental age for beginning reading," *Elem. Sch. J.*, 1937, 37, 497–508.
21. Gates, A. I. and Russell, D. H., "The effects of delaying beginning reading a half year in the case of underprivileged pupils with IQ's 75–95," *J. Educ. Res.*, 1939, 32, 321–328.
22. Goodenough, Florence L., "Studies of the 1937 revision of the Stanford-Binet Scale. I. Variability of the IQ at successive age-levels," *J. Educ. Psychol.*, 1942, 33, 241–251.
23. Goodenough, Florence L., *Mental testing — Its history, principles and applications*. New York: Rinehart, 1949.
24. Hildreth, Gertrude H., "Stanford-Binet retests of 441 school children," *Ped. Sem.*, 1926, 33, 365–386.
25. Hirt, Zoe I., "Another study of retests with the 1916 Stanford-Binet Scale," *J. Genet, Psychol.*, 1945, 66, 83–105.
26. Hofstaetter, P. R., "The changing composition of 'intelligence': A study in T-technique," *J. Genet. Psychol.*, 1954, 85, 159–164.
27. Hofstaetter, P. R., and O'Connor, J. P., "Anderson's overlap-hypothesis and the discontinuities of growth," *J. Genet. Psychol.*, 1956, 88, 95–106.
28. Honzik, Marjorie P., "The constancy of mental test performance during the preschool period," *J. Genet. Psychol.*, 1938, 52, 285–302.
29. Honzik, Marjorie P., Macfarlane, Jean W., and Allen, Lucille, "The stability of mental test performance between two and eighteen years," *J. Exp. Educ.*, 1938, 17, 309–324.
30. Jaffa, Adele S., *The California Preschool Mental Scale: Form A*. Berkeley: University of California Press, 1934.
31. Jones, H. E., "The environment and mental development," in L. Carmichael (Ed.), *Manual of child psychology*. (2nd Ed.) New York: Wiley, 1954.
32. Jones, H. E., "Trends in mental abilities." (Paper read at Amer. Psychol. Assoc., San Francisco, September, 1955.)

33. Jones, H. E., and Bayley, Nancy, "The Berkeley Growth Study," *Child Develpm.*, 1941, 12, 167–173.
34. Jones, H. E., and Conrad, H. S., "The growth and decline of intelligence: A study of a homogeneous group between the ages of ten and sixty," *Genet. Psychol.*, Monogr., 1933, 13, No. 3, 223–298.
35. Jones, H. E., and Conrad, H. S., "Mental development in adolescence," *Yearb. Nat. Soc. Stud. Educ.*, 1944, 43(I), 146–163.
36. Krugman, Judith I., Justman, J., Wrightstone, J. W., and Krugman, M., "Pupil functioning on the Stanford-Binet and the Wechsler Intelligence Scale for children," *J. consult. Psychol.*, 1951, 15, 475–483.
37. Laycock, S. R., and Clark, S., "The comparative performance of a group of old-dull and young-bright children on some items of the Revised Stanford-Binet Scale of intelligence, Form L.," *J. Educ. Psychol.*, 1942, 33, 1–12.
38. Mann, C. W., and Mann, Helene P., "An analysis of the results obtained by retesting juvenile delinquents," *J. Psychol.*, 1939, 8, 133–141.
39. McNemar, Q., *The revision of the Stanford-Binet Scale: An analysis of the standardization data.* Boston: Houghton Mifflin, 1942.
40. Morphett, M. V., and Washburne, C., "When should children begin to read?," *Elem. Sch. J.*, 1931, 31, 496–503.
41. Pinneau, S. R., "Changes in performance on intelligence tests from one month to eighteen years." (Paper read at West. Psychol. Assoc., Seattle, June, 1953.)
42. Pinneau, S. R., "Rate of mental maturing as related to level of intelligence." (Paper read at Amer. Psychol. Assoc., San Francisco, September, 1955.)
43. Pinneau, S. R., "The infantile disorders of hospitalism and anaclitic depression," *Psychol. Bull.*, 1955, 52, 429–452.
44. Pinneau, S. R., and Jones, H. E., "Mental development in infancy and childhood and mental abilities in adult life," *Rev. Educ. Res.*, 1955, 25, 415–437.
45. Pinneau, S. R., and Jones, H. E., "Development of mental abilities," *Rev. Educ. Res.*, 1958, 28, 392–400.
46. Pinneau, S. R., "Pinneau Revised IQ Tables," L. M. Terman and Maud A. Merrill, *Stanford-Binet Intelligence Scale: Manual for the Third Revision Form L-M.* Boston: Houghton Mifflin, 1960, Part III.
47. Pintner, R., Dragositz, Anna, and Kushner, Rose, "Supplementary guide for the Revised Stanford-Binet Scale (Form L)," *Appl. Psychol. Monogr.*, 1944, No. 3., 1–135.
48. Sandercock, Marian G., and Butler, A. J., "An analysis of the performance of mental defectives on the Wechsler Intelligence Scale for Children," *Amer. J. Ment. Def.*, 1952, 57, 100–105.
49. Sloan, W., and Harmon, H. H., "Constancy of IQ in mental defectives," *J. Genet. Psychol.*, 1947, 71, 177–185.
50. Sontag, L. W., Baker, C. T., Nelson, Virginia L., "Mental growth and personality development: A longitudinal study," *Monogr. Soc. Res. Child Develpm.*, 1958, 23, 1–143, No. 2 (Whole no. 68).
51. Spaulding, Patricia J., "Retest results on the Stanford L with mental defectives," *Amer. J. Ment. Def.*, 1946, 51, 35–42.

52. Terman, L. M., *The Measurement of Intelligence.* Boston: Houghton Mifflin, 1916.
53. Terman, L. M., *The Stanford Revision and Extension of Binet-Simon Scale for measuring intelligence.* Baltimore: Warwick and York, 1917.
54. Terman, L. M., and Merrill, Maud A., *Measuring Intelligence. A guide to the administration of the new revised Stanford-Binet Tests of intelligence.* Boston: Houghton Mifflin, 1937.
55. Terman, L. M., and Merrill, Maud A., *Stanford-Binet Intelligence Scale. Manual for the Third Revision Form L-M.* Boston: Houghton Mifflin, 1960.
56. Thompson, Clare W., and Magaret, Ann, "Differential test responses of normals and mental defectives," *J. Abnorm. Soc. Psychol.,* 1947, 42, 285–293.
57. Thompson, C. G., *Child psychology: growth trends in psychological adjustment.* Boston: Houghton Mifflin, 1952.
58. Triggs, Frances O., and Cartee, J., "Pre-school pupil performance on the Stanford-Binet and the Wechsler Intelligence Scale for Children," *J. Clin. Psychol.,* 1953, 9: 27–29.
59. Wechsler, D., *The Wechsler Intelligence Scale for Children.* New York: Psychological Corp., 1949.
60. Wechsler, D., "Equivalent test and mental ages for the WISC," *J. consult. Psychol.,* 1951, 15, 381–384.
61. Weider, A., Noller, P. A., and Schramm, T. A., "The Wechsler Intelligence Scale for Children and the Revised Stanford-Binet," *J. consult. Psychol.,* 1951, 15, 330–333.

PART THREE

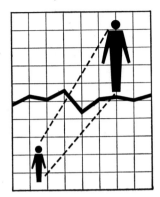

Appendices

Corrected Mental Age Scores for the Stanford-Binet Scales

Mental age scores on the Stanford-Binet scales in most instances indicate an age level higher than that for which they are average. Consequently, to be average for a particular chronological age group, a subject must obtain a mental age score slightly in excess of the age in question. Furthermore, mental age scores on these scales after age 13 do not refer to the age group for which performance is typical.

The accompanying table makes it possible to (a) obtain a relatively precise estimate of the age group for which a subject's performance is typical and (b) relate a subject's mental age score to the average performance of subjects from age 2 to 18.

To determine the age group for which a subject's performance is average:

(1) transform the obtained mental age score into total number of months;

(2) locate the closest value to this score in the body of the table; and,

(3) read the age group for which this performance is average in the left-hand margin and top line, respectively, of the table.

APPENDIX A

Stanford-Binet Mean Mental Age Scores in Months, Corresponding to Specified Chronological Ages: 1937 Standardization Sample

Interpretation: On the Stanford-Binet scales, a mental age of 24.5 months is the mean MA to be expected from an unselected national sample of native-born white children of chronological age 2 years–0 months; a mental age of 25.6 months is to be expected at 2 years–1 month; and so on.

MONTHS

YEARS	0	1	2	3	4	5	6	7	8	9	10	11
2	24.5	25.6	26.7	27.7	28.8	29.9	31.0	32.0	33.2	34.2	35.3	36.4
3	37.5	38.4	39.3	40.2	41.2	42.0	42.9	43.9	44.9	45.9	46.8	47.8
4	48.8	49.7	50.6	51.6	52.6	53.5	54.4	55.4	56.4	57.3	58.3	59.3
5	60.2	61.2	62.2	63.1	64.1	65.1	66.0	67.0	67.9	68.9	69.9	70.9
6	71.9	72.9	74.0	75.0	76.1	77.2	78.2	79.3	80.4	81.4	82.5	83.6
7	84.7	85.8	86.9	88.0	89.1	90.2	91.3	92.4	93.5	94.6	95.7	96.8
8	97.9	98.9	100.1	101.2	102.2	103.3	104.4	105.5	106.6	107.6	108.8	109.8
9	110.9	111.9	113.1	114.1	115.1	116.2	117.2	118.3	119.4	120.4	121.5	122.6
10	123.6	124.5	125.5	126.4	127.4	128.4	129.3	130.2	131.2	132.1	133.0	134.0
11	134.9	135.9	136.8	137.7	138.7	139.7	140.6	141.5	142.5	143.5	144.4	145.3
12	146.3	147.2	148.2	149.1	150.1	151.1	152.0	152.8	153.8	154.8	155.7	156.6
13	157.6	158.6	158.6	159.7	160.8	160.8	161.9	162.9	162.9	163.9	165.0	165.1
14	166.1	167.1	167.1	168.2	169.2	169.2	170.2	171.2	171.2	172.2	173.2	173.2
15	174.2	175.6	175.8	177.1	178.5	178.7	180.0	181.4	181.6	183.0	184.4	184.6
16	185.9	186.0	186.1	186.2	186.2	186.3	186.4	186.5	186.6	186.6	186.7	186.9
17	187.0	187.2	187.4	187.5	187.7	188.0	188.2	188.4	188.6	188.9	189.1	189.3
18	189.5											

APPENDIX B

Deviation IQ Tables for the Stanford-Binet
Intelligence Scales (55, pp. 254–335)

The tables in Appendix B enable one to derive a deviation IQ from a mental age score obtained on the 1937 revision of the Stanford-Binet, Form L or Form M (54); or the 1960 revision of the scales, Form L–M (55).

To obtain a deviation IQ from these tables, first find the tables appropriate to the mental age score by reference to the first part of the *running foot* which appears at the lower left of even-numbered and the lower right of odd-numbered pages. (The first half of the running foot is the first month of the year of mental age to which a table applies.) Next, locate within this group of tables the particular one applicable to the chronological age of the subject at the time of testing, by referring to the second part of the running foot. (The second half of the running foot indicates the first year and month of chronological age to which a table applies. Three chronological years, or thirty-six months, are covered by each table. Then, locate on the top line of the table in years and months, or in the bottom line in total months, the particular mental age score. Finally, go down (or up) the column in which this value falls to the row which contains the chronological age (a) in years and months in the left-hand margin and (b) in total months in the right-hand margin of the table. The value at the intersection of the row and column is the deviation IQ (DIQ) for the MA and CA in question.

Consult Appendices C and D to obtain DIQs for extreme $\frac{MA}{CA}$ combinations for which values do not appear in these tables.

It was pointed out earlier (p. 76) that the mental age scores obtained on the Stanford-Binet scales tend, at all ages except 6, to be a fraction of a year too high. The required mental age corrections are built into these revised IQ tables so that, as precisely as possible, any difference between DIQs obtained on different occasions will reflect only changes in relative position. Because of these corrections, the reader will find that in the tables a mental age score numerically equivalent to a given chronological age will, at most ages, yield a deviation IQ slightly below 100.

	2-0	2-1	2-2	2-3	2-4	2-5	2-6	2-7	2-8	2-9	2-10	2-11	TOTAL MONTHS
2-00	98	102	106	110	114	118	122	127	131	135	139	143	24
2-01	94	98	102	105	109	113	117	121	125	129	132	136	25
2-02	90	94	98	101	105	108	112	116	119	123	127	130	26
2-03	87	91	94	98	101	104	108	111	115	118	122	125	27
2-04	84	88	91	94	97	101	104	107	110	114	117	120	28
2-05	82	85	88	91	94	97	100	103	106	110	112	116	29
2-06	80	83	86	89	91	94	97	100	103	106	109	112	30
2-07	77	80	83	86	89	91	94	97	100	103	106	108	31
2-08	75	78	81	83	86	89	91	94	97	100	102	105	32
2-09	73	76	78	81	84	86	89	92	94	97	99	102	33
2-10	71	74	76	79	81	84	86	89	92	94	97	99	34
2-11	69	71	74	76	79	81	84	87	89	92	94	97	35
3-00	67	70	72	74	77	79	82	84	87	89	92	94	36
3-01	66	68	70	73	75	77	80	82	85	87	89	92	37
3-02	64	66	69	71	73	76	78	80	83	85	88	90	38
3-03	62	65	67	69	72	74	76	79	81	83	86	88	39
3-04	61	63	66	68	70	73	75	77	79	82	84	86	40
3-05	60	62	64	66	69	71	73	75	78	80	82	84	41
3-06	58	61	63	65	67	69	72	74	76	78	80	83	42
3-07	57	59	61	63	66	68	70	72	74	76	79	81	43
3-08	55	57	60	62	64	66	68	70	72	75	77	79	44
3-09	54	56	58	60	62	64	67	69	71	73	75	77	45
3-10	52	54	57	59	61	63	65	67	69	71	73	75	46
3-11	51	53	55	57	59	61	63	65	67	70	72	74	47
4-00	50	52	54	56	58	60	62	64	66	68	70	72	48
4-01	48	50	52	54	56	58	60	62	64	66	68	70	49
4-02	47	49	51	53	55	57	59	61	63	65	67	69	50
4-03	46	47	49	51	53	55	57	59	61	63	65	67	51
4-04	44	46	48	50	52	54	56	58	60	62	64	66	52
4-05	43	45	47	49	51	53	55	57	58	60	62	64	53
4-06	42	44	46	47	49	51	53	55	57	59	61	63	54
4-07	40	42	44	46	48	50	52	54	56	58	59	61	55
4-08	39	41	43	45	47	49	50	52	54	56	58	60	56
4-09	38	40	42	44	45	47	49	51	53	55	57	58	57
4-10	37	39	40	42	44	46	48	50	52	53	55	57	58
4-11	35	37	39	41	43	45	46	48	50	52	54	56	59
TOTAL MONTHS	24	25	26	27	28	29	30	31	32	33	34	35	

YEARS / MONTHS

CHRONOLOGICAL AGE

MA 2–0 / CA 2–0

MENTAL AGE

YEARS MONTHS	2-0	2-1	2-2	2-3	2-4	2-5	2-6	2-7	2-8	2-9	2-10	2-11	TOTAL MONTHS
5-00	34	36	38	40	42	43	45	47	49	51	52	54	60
5-01	33	35	37	39	41	42	44	46	48	49	51	53	61
5-02	32	34	36	38	39	41	43	45	46	48	50	52	62
5-03	31	33	35	37	38	40	42	44	45	47	49	51	63
5-04	30	32	34	36	37	39	41	43	44	46	48	50	64
5-05		31	33	35	36	38	40	41	43	45	47	48	65
5-06		30	32	34	35	37	39	40	42	44	46	47	66
5-07		30	31	33	35	36	38	40	41	43	45	46	67
5-08			31	33	34	36	38	39	41	42	44	46	68
5-09			30	32	34	35	37	39	40	42	43	45	69
5-10			30	32	33	35	36	38	40	41	43	44	70
5-11				31	33	34	36	37	39	41	42	44	71
6-00				31	32	34	35	37	38	40	41	43	72
6-01				30	32	33	35	36	38	39	41	42	73
6-02				30	31	33	34	36	37	39	40	42	74
6-03				30	31	32	34	35	37	38	40	41	75
6-04					31	32	33	35	36	38	39	41	76
6-05					30	32	33	34	36	37	39	40	77
6-06					30	31	33	34	35	37	38	40	78
6-07						31	32	34	35	36	38	39	79
6-08						30	32	33	35	36	37	39	80
6-09						30	32	33	34	36	37	38	81
6-10						30	31	32	34	35	36	38	82
6-11						30	31	32	33	35	36	37	83
7-00								32	33	34	36	37	84
7-01								31	33	34	35	36	85
7-02								31	32	34	35	36	86
7-03								31	32	33	35	36	87
7-04								31	32	33	34	35	88
7-05								30	32	33	34	35	89
7-06								30	31	33	34	35	90
7-07								30	31	32	33	35	91
7-08								30	31	32	33	34	92
7-09								30	31	32	33	34	93
7-10									31	32	33	34	94
7-11									30	31	32	34	95
TOTAL MONTHS	24	25	26	27	28	29	30	31	32	33	34	35	

CHRONOLOGICAL AGE

MENTAL AGE

YEARS MONTHS	2-0	2-1	2-2	2-3	2-4	2-5	2-6	2-7	2-8	2-9	2-10	2-11	
8-00									30	31	32	33	96
8-01									30	31	32	33	97
8-02									30	31	32	33	98
8-03									30	31	32	33	99
8-04										30	31	32	100
8-05										30	31	32	101
8-06										**30**	31	32	102
8-07										30	31	32	103
8-08										30	31	32	104
8-09										30	31	32	105
8-10											30	31	106
8-11											30	31	107
9-00											**30**	31	108
9-01											30	31	109
9-02											30	31	110
9-03											30	31	111
9-04											30	31	112
9-05											30	31	113
9-06											**30**	31	114
9-07											30	30	115
9-08											30	30	116
9-09											30	30	117
9-10												30	118
9-11												30	119
10-00												**30**	120
10-01												30	121
10-02												30	122
10-03													123
10-04													124
10-05													125
10-06													126
10-07													127
10-08													128
10-09													129
10-10													130
10-11													131
	24	25	26	27	28	29	30	31	32	33	34	35	TOTAL MONTHS

CHRONOLOGICAL AGE

MA 2-0 / CA 8-0

YEARS → MONTHS	3 0	3 1	3 2	3 3	3 4	3 5	3 6	3 7	3 8	3 9	3 10	3 11	TOTAL MONTHS
2–00	147	151	155	160	164	168	172						24
2–01	140	144	148	152	156	160	164	167	171				25
2–02	134	138	141	145	148	152	156	160	163	167	170		26
2–03	128	132	135	139	142	146	149	152	156	159	163	166	27
2–04	123	126	130	133	136	140	143	146	149	152	156	159	28
2–05	119	122	125	128	131	134	137	140	143	146	149	152	29
2–06	115	117	120	123	126	129	132	135	138	141	143	146	30
2–07	111	114	117	120	122	125	128	131	134	136	139	142	31
2–08	108	111	113	116	119	121	124	127	130	132	135	138	32
2–09	105	107	110	113	115	118	121	123	126	129	131	134	33
2–10	102	104	107	110	112	115	117	120	122	125	128	130	34
2–11	99	102	104	107	109	112	114	117	119	122	124	127	35
3–00	96	99	101	104	106	109	111	114	116	118	121	123	36
3–01	94	97	99	101	104	106	109	111	113	116	118	121	37
3–02	92	95	97	99	102	104	106	109	111	113	116	118	38
3–03	90	93	95	97	99	102	104	106	109	111	113	116	39
3–04	88	91	93	95	98	100	102	104	107	109	111	113	40
3–05	87	89	91	93	96	98	100	102	104	107	109	111	41
3–06	85	87	89	91	94	96	98	100	102	105	107	109	42
3–07	83	85	87	89	92	94	96	98	100	102	105	107	43
3–08	81	83	85	87	90	92	94	96	98	100	102	105	44
3–09	79	81	83	86	88	90	92	94	96	98	100	102	45
3–10	77	80	82	84	86	88	90	92	94	96	98	100	46
3–11	76	78	80	82	84	86	88	90	92	94	96	98	47
4–00	74	76	78	80	82	84	86	88	90	92	94	96	48
4–01	72	74	76	78	80	82	84	86	88	90	93	95	49
4–02	71	73	75	77	79	81	83	85	87	89	91	93	50
4–03	69	71	73	75	77	79	81	83	85	87	89	91	51
4–04	68	70	72	74	75	77	79	81	83	85	87	89	52
4–05	66	68	70	72	74	76	78	80	82	84	86	88	53
4–06	65	67	69	70	72	74	76	78	80	82	84	86	54
4–07	63	65	67	69	71	73	75	77	78	80	82	84	55
4–08	62	64	65	67	69	71	73	75	77	79	81	82	56
4–09	60	62	64	66	68	70	71	73	75	77	79	81	57
4–10	59	61	63	64	66	68	70	72	74	76	77	79	58
4–11	57	59	61	63	65	67	68	70	72	74	76	78	59
TOTAL MONTHS	36	37	38	39	40	41	42	43	44	45	46	47	

CHRONOLOGICAL AGE

MA 3–0 / CA 2–0

MENTAL AGE

YEARS / MONTHS	3‑0	3‑1	3‑2	3‑3	3‑4	3‑5	3‑6	3‑7	3‑8	3‑9	3‑10	3‑11	TOTAL MONTHS
5‑00	56	58	60	62	63	65	67	69	71	72	74	76	60
5‑01	55	57	58	60	62	64	66	67	69	71	73	75	61
5‑02	54	55	57	59	61	62	64	66	68	70	71	73	62
5‑03	52	54	56	58	59	61	63	65	66	68	70	72	63
5‑04	51	53	55	56	58	60	62	63	65	67	69	70	64
5‑05	50	52	53	55	57	59	60	62	64	66	67	69	65
5‑06	49	51	52	54	56	57	59	61	63	64	66	68	66
5‑07	48	50	51	53	55	57	58	60	62	63	65	67	67
5‑08	47	49	51	52	54	56	57	59	61	62	64	66	68
5‑09	47	48	50	52	53	55	56	58	60	61	63	64	69
5‑10	46	47	49	51	52	54	55	57	59	60	62	63	70
5‑11	45	47	48	50	52	53	55	56	58	59	61	63	71
6‑00	45	46	48	49	51	52	54	55	57	58	60	62	72
6‑01	44	45	47	48	50	51	53	55	56	58	59	61	73
6‑02	43	45	46	48	49	51	52	54	55	57	58	60	74
6‑03	43	44	46	47	49	50	52	53	54	56	57	59	75
6‑04	42	44	45	46	48	49	51	52	54	55	57	58	76
6‑05	42	43	44	46	47	49	50	51	53	54	56	57	77
6‑06	41	42	44	45	47	48	49	51	52	54	55	56	78
6‑07	40	42	43	45	46	47	49	50	51	53	54	56	79
6‑08	40	41	43	44	45	47	48	49	51	52	53	55	80
6‑09	40	41	42	44	45	46	48	49	50	52	53	54	81
6‑10	39	40	42	43	44	46	47	48	50	51	52	53	82
6‑11	39	40	41	42	44	45	46	48	49	50	52	53	83
7‑00	38	39	41	42	43	45	46	47	48	50	51	52	84
7‑01	38	39	40	42	43	44	45	47	48	49	50	52	85
7‑02	37	39	40	41	42	44	45	46	47	48	50	51	86
7‑03	37	38	39	41	42	43	44	45	47	48	49	50	87
7‑04	37	38	39	40	41	43	44	45	46	47	49	50	88
7‑05	36	38	39	40	41	42	43	45	46	47	48	49	89
7‑06	36	37	38	39	41	42	43	44	45	46	48	49	90
7‑07	36	37	38	39	40	41	43	44	45	46	47	48	91
7‑08	35	37	38	39	40	41	42	43	44	46	47	48	92
7‑09	35	36	37	38	40	41	42	43	44	45	46	47	93
7‑10	35	36	37	38	39	40	41	43	44	45	46	47	94
7‑11	35	36	37	38	39	40	41	42	43	44	45	46	95
TOTAL MONTHS	36	37	38	39	40	41	42	43	44	45	46	47	

CHRONOLOGICAL AGE

MA 3–0 / CA 5–0

MENTAL AGE

YEARS → MONTHS ↓	3-0	3-1	3-2	3-3	3-4	3-5	3-6	3-7	3-8	3-9	3-10	3-11	TOTAL MONTHS
8–00	34	35	37	38	39	40	41	42	43	44	45	46	96
8–01	34	35	36	37	38	39	40	42	43	44	45	46	97
8–02	34	35	36	37	38	39	40	41	42	43	44	45	98
8–03	34	35	36	37	38	39	40	41	42	43	44	45	99
8–04	33	34	35	36	37	38	39	40	42	43	44	45	100
8–05	33	34	35	36	37	38	39	40	41	42	43	44	101
8–06	33	34	35	36	37	38	39	40	41	42	43	44	102
8–07	33	34	35	36	37	38	39	40	41	42	42	43	103
8–08	33	34	34	35	36	37	38	39	40	41	42	43	104
8–09	32	33	34	35	36	37	38	39	40	41	42	43	105
8–10	32	33	34	35	36	37	38	39	40	41	42	42	106
8–11	32	33	34	35	36	37	38	39	39	40	41	42	107
9–00	32	33	34	35	36	36	37	38	39	40	41	42	108
9–01	32	33	34	35	35	36	37	38	39	40	41	42	109
9–02	32	33	33	34	35	36	37	38	39	40	41	41	110
9–03	32	32	33	34	35	36	37	38	39	39	40	41	111
9–04	32	32	33	34	35	36	37	38	38	39	40	41	112
9–05	32	32	33	34	35	36	37	38	38	39	40	41	113
9–06	31	32	33	34	35	36	37	37	38	39	40	41	114
9–07	31	32	33	34	35	35	36	37	38	39	40	40	115
9–08	31	32	33	34	35	35	36	37	38	39	40	40	116
9–09	31	32	33	34	34	35	36	37	38	39	39	40	117
9–10	31	32	33	34	34	35	36	37	38	38	39	40	118
9–11	31	32	33	33	34	35	36	37	37	38	39	40	119
10–00	31	32	33	33	34	35	36	37	37	38	39	40	120
10–01	31	32	33	33	34	35	36	37	37	38	39	40	121
10–02	31	32	33	34	34	35	36	37	37	38	39	40	122
10–03	31	32	33	34	34	35	36	37	37	38	39	40	123
10–04	31	32	33	34	34	35	36	37	37	38	39	40	124
10–05	31	32	33	34	34	35	36	37	37	38	39	40	125
10–06	31	32	33	34	34	35	36	37	37	38	39	40	126
10–07	32	32	33	34	35	35	36	37	37	38	39	40	127
10–08	32	32	33	34	35	35	36	37	37	38	39	40	128
10–09	32	33	33	34	35	35	36	37	37	38	39	40	129
10–10	32	33	33	34	35	36	36	37	38	38	39	40	130
10–11	32	33	33	34	35	36	36	37	38	38	39	40	131
TOTAL MONTHS	36	37	38	39	40	41	42	43	44	45	46	47	

CHRONOLOGICAL AGE

MA 3–0 / CA 8–0

YEARS MONTHS	3 0	3 1	3 2	3 3	3 4	3 5	3 6	3 7	3 8	3 9	3 10	3 11	
11–00	32	33	34	34	35	36	36	37	38	38	39	40	132
11–01	32	33	33	34	35	36	36	37	38	38	39	40	133
11–02	32	33	34	34	35	36	36	37	38	38	39	40	134
11–03	32	33	34	34	35	36	36	37	38	38	39	40	135
11–04	32	33	33	34	35	35	36	37	37	38	39	39	136
11–05	32	33	33	34	35	35	36	37	37	38	39	39	137
11–06	32	33	33	34	35	35	36	37	37	38	39	39	138
11–07	32	33	34	34	35	35	36	37	37	38	39	39	139
11–08	32	33	34	34	35	35	36	37	37	38	39	39	140
11–09	32	33	34	34	35	35	36	37	37	38	39	39	141
11–10	32	33	34	34	35	35	36	37	37	38	39	39	142
11–11	32	33	34	34	35	35	36	37	37	38	39	39	143
12–00	32	33	34	34	35	35	36	37	37	38	38	39	144
12–01	32	33	33	34	35	35	36	36	37	38	38	39	145
12–02	32	33	33	34	34	35	36	36	37	37	38	39	146
12–03	32	33	33	34	34	35	36	36	37	37	38	39	147
12–04	32	32	33	34	34	35	35	36	37	37	38	38	148
12–05	32	32	33	33	34	35	35	36	36	37	38	38	149
12–06	32	32	33	33	34	35	35	36	36	37	37	38	150
12–07	32	32	33	33	34	34	35	36	36	37	37	38	151
12–08	31	32	32	33	34	34	35	35	36	37	37	38	152
12–09	31	32	32	33	33	34	35	35	36	36	37	38	153
12–10	31	32	32	33	33	34	35	35	36	36	37	37	154
12–11	31	32	32	33	33	34	34	35	36	36	37	37	155
13–00	31	31	32	33	33	34	34	35	35	36	37	37	156
13–01	31	31	32	32	33	33	34	35	35	36	36	37	157
13–02	31	31	32	32	33	33	34	35	35	36	36	37	158
13–03	30	31	31	32	32	33	34	34	35	35	36	36	159
13–04	30	31	31	32	32	33	33	34	34	35	36	36	160
13–05	30	30	31	32	32	33	33	34	34	35	36	36	161
13–06		30	31	31	32	32	33	34	34	35	35	36	162
13–07		30	31	31	32	32	33	33	34	34	35	36	163
13–08			30	31	32	32	33	33	34	34	35	35	164
13–09			30	31	31	32	32	33	34	34	35	35	165
13–10			30	30	31	32	32	33	33	34	34	35	166
13–11				30	31	31	32	33	33	34	34	35	167
	36	37	38	39	40	41	42	43	44	45	46	47	TOTAL MONTHS

CHRONOLOGICAL AGE

MA 3–0 / CA 11–0

MENTAL AGE

YEARS MONTHS	3-0	3-1	3-2	3-3	3-4	3-5	3-6	3-7	3-8	3-9	3-10	3-11	TOTAL MONTHS
14–00				30	31	31	32	32	33	33	34	35	168
14–01				30	30	31	32	32	33	33	34	34	169
14–02					30	31	31	32	33	33	34	34	170
14–03					30	31	31	32	32	33	33	34	171
14–04						30	31	32	32	33	33	34	172
14–05						30	31	31	32	32	33	34	173
14–06						30	31	31	32	32	33	33	174
14–07							30	31	31	32	33	33	175
14–08							30	31	31	32	32	33	176
14–09							30	31	31	32	32	33	177
14–10								30	31	31	32	33	178
14–11								30	31	31	32	32	179
15–00								30	30	31	32	32	180
15–01									30	31	31	32	181
15–02										30	31	31	182
15–03											30	31	183
15–04												30	184
15–05													185
15–06													186
15–07													187
15–08													188
15–09													189
15–10													190
15–11													191
16–00													192
	36	37	38	39	40	41	42	43	44	45	46	47	TOTAL MONTHS

CHRONOLOGICAL AGE

CHRONOLOGICAL AGE YEARS / MONTHS	4 0	4 1	4 2	4 3	4 4	4 5	4 6	4 7	4 8	4 9	4 10	4 11	TOTAL MONTHS
2–00													24
2–01													25
2–02													26
2–03	170												27
2–04	162	166	169	172									28
2–05	155	158	162	165	168	171							29
2–06	149	152	155	158	161	164	167	170					30
2–07	145	148	150	153	156	159	162	164	167	170			31
2–08	141	143	146	149	151	154	157	160	162	165	168	170	32
2–09	137	139	142	144	147	150	152	155	158	160	163	166	33
2–10	133	135	138	141	143	146	148	151	153	156	159	161	34
2–11	129	132	134	137	139	142	144	147	149	152	154	157	35
3–00	126	128	131	133	136	138	140	143	145	148	150	153	36
3–01	123	125	128	130	133	135	137	140	142	145	147	149	37
3–02	120	123	125	128	130	132	135	137	139	142	144	146	38
3–03	118	120	123	125	127	130	132	134	136	139	141	143	39
3–04	116	118	120	123	125	127	129	132	134	136	138	141	40
3–05	113	116	118	120	122	125	127	129	131	134	136	138	41
3–06	111	113	116	118	120	122	124	127	129	131	133	135	42
3–07	109	111	113	115	118	120	122	124	126	128	131	133	43
3–08	107	109	111	113	115	117	120	122	124	126	128	130	44
3–09	105	107	109	111	113	115	117	119	121	124	126	128	45
3–10	102	105	107	109	111	113	115	117	119	121	123	125	46
3–11	100	103	105	107	109	111	113	115	117	119	121	123	47
4–00	98	101	103	105	107	109	111	113	115	117	119	121	48
4–01	97	99	101	103	105	107	109	111	113	115	117	119	49
4–02	95	97	99	101	103	105	107	109	111	113	115	117	50
4–03	93	95	97	99	101	103	105	107	109	111	113	115	51
4–04	91	93	95	97	99	101	103	105	107	109	111	113	52
4–05	89	91	93	95	97	99	101	103	105	107	109	111	53
4–06	88	90	92	93	95	97	99	101	103	105	107	109	54
4–07	86	88	90	92	94	96	97	99	101	103	105	107	55
4–08	84	86	88	90	92	94	96	97	99	101	103	105	56
4–09	83	85	86	88	90	92	94	96	98	99	101	103	57
4–10	81	83	85	87	88	90	92	94	96	98	100	101	58
4–11	79	81	83	85	87	89	90	92	94	96	98	100	59
TOTAL MONTHS	48	49	50	51	52	53	54	55	56	57	58	59	

MA 4–0 / CA 2–0

YEARS → MONTHS ↓	4 0	4 1	4 2	4 3	4 4	4 5	4 6	4 7	4 8	4 9	4 10	4 11	
5–00	78	80	81	83	85	87	89	91	92	94	96	98	60
5–01	76	78	80	82	84	85	87	89	91	93	94	96	61
5–02	75	77	78	80	82	84	86	87	89	91	93	94	62
5–03	73	75	77	79	81	82	84	86	88	89	91	93	63
5–04	72	74	76	77	79	81	83	84	86	88	90	91	64
5–05	71	72	74	76	78	79	81	83	84	86	88	90	65
5–06	69	71	73	75	76	78	80	81	83	85	86	88	66
5–07	68	70	72	73	75	77	78	80	82	83	85	87	67
5–08	67	69	70	72	74	75	77	79	80	82	84	85	68
5–09	66	68	69	71	73	74	76	77	79	81	82	84	69
5–10	65	67	68	70	71	73	75	76	78	79	81	83	70
5–11	64	66	67	69	70	72	74	75	77	78	80	81	71
6–00	63	65	66	68	69	71	72	74	76	77	79	80	72
6–01	62	64	65	67	68	70	71	73	74	76	77	79	73
6–02	61	63	64	66	67	69	70	72	73	75	76	78	74
6–03	60	62	63	65	66	68	69	71	72	74	75	77	75
6–04	59	61	62	64	65	67	68	70	71	72	74	75	76
6–05	59	60	61	63	64	66	67	69	70	71	73	74	77
6–06	58	59	61	62	63	65	66	68	69	70	72	73	78
6–07	57	58	60	61	62	64	65	67	68	69	71	72	79
6–08	56	58	59	60	62	63	64	66	67	68	70	71	80
6–09	56	57	58	60	61	62	64	65	66	68	69	70	81
6–10	55	56	57	59	60	61	63	64	65	67	68	69	82
6–11	54	55	57	58	59	61	62	63	64	66	67	68	83
7–00	53	55	56	57	59	60	61	62	64	65	66	67	84
7–01	53	54	55	57	58	59	60	62	63	64	65	67	85
7–02	52	53	55	56	57	58	60	61	62	63	64	66	86
7–03	52	53	54	55	56	58	59	60	61	62	64	65	87
7–04	51	52	53	55	56	57	58	59	61	62	63	64	88
7–05	50	52	53	54	55	56	58	59	60	61	62	63	89
7–06	50	51	52	53	55	56	57	58	59	60	62	63	90
7–07	49	51	52	53	54	55	56	57	59	60	61	62	91
7–08	49	50	51	52	53	55	56	57	58	59	60	61	92
7–09	48	50	51	52	53	54	55	56	57	58	60	61	93
7–10	48	49	50	51	52	53	55	56	57	58	59	60	94
7–11	48	49	50	51	52	53	54	55	56	57	58	59	95
	48	49	50	51	52	53	54	55	56	57	58	59	TOTAL MONTHS

CHRONOLOGICAL AGE

YEARS → MONTHS ↓	4 0	4 1	4 2	4 3	4 4	4 5	4 6	4 7	4 8	4 9	4 10	4 11	TOTAL MONTHS
8–00	47	48	49	50	51	52	53	55	56	57	58	59	96
8–01	47	48	49	50	51	52	53	54	55	56	57	58	97
8–02	46	47	48	49	50	51	52	54	55	56	57	58	98
8–03	46	47	48	49	50	51	52	53	54	55	56	57	99
8–04	46	47	48	49	50	51	52	53	54	55	56	57	100
8–05	45	46	47	48	49	50	51	52	53	54	55	56	101
8–06	45	46	47	48	49	50	51	52	53	54	55	56	102
8–07	44	45	46	47	48	49	50	51	52	53	54	55	103
8–08	44	45	46	47	48	49	50	51	52	53	54	55	104
8–09	44	45	46	47	48	48	49	50	51	52	53	54	105
8–10	43	44	45	46	47	48	49	50	51	52	53	54	106
8–11	43	44	45	46	47	47	49	50	51	51	52	53	107
9–00	43	44	45	46	46	47	48	49	50	51	52	53	108
9–01	43	44	44	45	46	47	48	49	50	51	52	52	109
9–02	42	43	44	45	46	47	48	49	49	50	51	52	110
9–03	42	43	44	45	46	46	47	48	49	50	51	52	111
9–04	42	43	44	44	45	46	47	48	49	50	51	51	112
9–05	42	43	43	44	45	46	47	48	49	49	50	51	113
9–06	42	42	43	44	45	46	47	48	48	49	50	51	114
9–07	41	42	43	44	45	46	46	47	48	49	50	51	115
9–08	41	42	43	44	44	45	46	47	48	49	49	50	116
9–09	41	42	43	43	44	45	46	47	48	48	49	50	117
9–10	41	42	42	43	44	45	46	46	47	48	49	50	118
9–11	41	41	42	43	44	45	45	46	47	48	49	49	119
10–00	41	41	42	43	44	44	45	46	47	48	48	49	120
10–01	40	41	42	43	44	44	45	46	47	47	48	49	121
10–02	40	41	42	43	44	44	45	46	47	47	48	49	122
10–03	40	41	42	43	43	44	45	46	46	47	48	49	123
10–04	40	41	42	43	43	44	45	46	46	47	48	49	124
10–05	40	41	42	43	43	44	45	46	46	47	48	48	125
10–06	40	41	42	43	43	44	45	45	46	47	48	48	126
10–07	40	41	42	43	43	44	45	45	46	47	48	48	127
10–08	40	41	42	42	43	44	45	45	46	47	47	48	128
10–09	40	41	42	42	43	44	45	45	46	47	47	48	129
10–10	40	41	42	43	43	44	45	45	46	47	47	48	130
10–11	40	41	42	42	43	44	45	45	46	47	47	48	131
TOTAL MONTHS	48	49	50	51	52	53	54	55	56	57	58	59	

CHRONOLOGICAL AGE

MA 4–0 / CA 8–0

MENTAL AGE

YEARS MONTHS	4 0	4 1	4 2	4 3	4 4	4 5	4 6	4 7	4 8	4 9	4 10	4 11	
11–00	40	41	42	42	43	44	45	45	46	47	47	48	132
11–01	40	41	42	42	43	44	44	45	46	46	47	48	133
11–02	40	41	42	42	43	44	44	45	46	46	47	48	134
11–03	40	41	42	42	43	44	44	45	46	46	47	48	135
11–04	40	41	41	42	43	43	44	45	45	46	47	47	136
11–05	40	41	41	42	43	43	44	45	45	46	47	47	137
11–06	40	41	41	42	43	43	44	45	45	46	46	47	138
11–07	40	41	41	42	43	43	44	44	45	46	46	47	139
11–08	40	41	41	42	42	43	44	44	45	46	46	47	140
11–09	40	40	41	42	42	43	44	44	45	45	46	47	141
11–10	40	40	41	42	42	43	44	44	45	45	46	47	142
11–11	40	40	41	42	42	43	43	44	45	45	46	47	143
12–00	40	40	41	42	42	43	43	44	45	45	46	46	144
12–01	39	40	41	41	42	43	43	44	44	45	46	46	145
12–02	39	40	41	41	42	42	43	44	44	45	45	46	146
12–03	39	40	40	41	42	42	43	43	44	45	45	46	147
12–04	39	40	40	41	41	42	43	43	44	44	45	46	148
12–05	39	39	40	41	41	42	42	43	44	44	45	45	149
12–06	39	39	40	40	41	42	42	43	43	44	45	45	150
12–07	39	39	40	40	41	41	42	43	43	44	44	45	151
12–08	38	39	39	40	41	41	42	42	43	44	44	45	152
12–09	38	39	39	40	40	41	42	42	43	43	44	44	153
12–10	38	39	39	40	40	41	41	42	43	43	44	44	154
12–11	38	38	39	40	40	41	41	42	42	43	44	44	155
13–00	38	38	39	39	40	41	41	42	42	43	43	44	156
13–01	37	38	39	39	40	40	41	41	42	43	43	44	157
13–02	37	38	38	39	40	40	41	41	42	42	43	44	158
13–03	37	38	38	39	39	40	40	41	41	42	43	43	159
13–04	37	37	38	38	39	40	40	41	41	42	42	43	160
13–05	37	37	38	38	39	39	40	41	41	42	42	43	161
13–06	36	37	37	38	39	39	40	40	41	41	42	42	162
13–07	36	37	37	38	38	39	39	40	41	41	42	42	163
13–08	36	37	37	38	38	39	39	40	40	41	42	42	164
13–09	36	36	37	37	38	39	39	40	40	41	41	42	165
13–10	35	36	37	37	38	38	39	39	40	40	41	42	166
13–11	35	36	36	37	38	38	39	39	40	40	41	41	167
TOTAL MONTHS	48	49	50	51	52	53	54	55	56	57	58	59	

CHRONOLOGICAL AGE

MA 4–0 / CA 11–0

MENTAL AGE

CHRONOLOGICAL AGE (YEARS MONTHS)	4‑0	4‑1	4‑2	4‑3	4‑4	4‑5	4‑6	4‑7	4‑8	4‑9	4‑10	4‑11	TOTAL MONTHS
14–00	35	36	36	37	37	38	38	39	39	40	41	41	168
14–01	35	35	36	36	37	38	38	39	39	40	40	41	169
14–02	35	35	36	36	37	37	38	39	39	40	40	41	170
14–03	34	35	36	36	37	37	38	38	39	39	40	40	171
14–04	34	35	35	36	36	37	37	38	39	39	40	40	172
14–05	34	35	35	36	36	37	37	38	38	39	40	40	173
14–06	34	34	35	35	36	37	37	38	38	39	39	40	174
14–07	34	34	35	35	36	36	37	37	38	38	39	40	175
14–08	33	34	35	35	36	36	37	37	38	38	39	39	176
14–09	33	34	34	35	35	36	36	37	38	38	39	39	177
14–10	33	34	34	35	35	36	36	37	37	38	38	39	178
14–11	33	33	34	35	35	36	36	37	37	38	38	39	179
15–00	33	33	34	34	35	35	36	36	37	37	38	39	180
15–01	32	33	33	34	34	35	35	36	36	37	37	38	181
15–02	32	32	33	33	34	35	35	36	36	37	37	38	182
15–03	31	32	32	33	33	34	35	35	36	36	37	37	183
15–04	31	31	32	32	33	33	34	34	35	36	36	37	184
15–05	31	31	32	32	33	33	34	34	35	35	36	36	185
15–06		31	31	32	32	33	33	34	34	35	35	36	186
15–07			30	31	32	32	33	33	34	34	35	35	187
15–08				31	31	32	32	33	33	34	34	35	188
15–09					31	31	32	32	33	33	34	34	189
15–10						31	31	32	32	33	33	34	190
14–11						30	31	32	32	33	33	34	191
16–00 } 16–02							30	31	31	32	32	33	{ 192 194
16–03 } 16–07								30	30	31	31	32	{ 195 199
16–08 } 17–00										30	30	31	{ 200 204
17–01 } 17–05												30	{ 205 209
17–06 } 17–10													{ 210 214
17–11 } 18–00													{ 215 216
TOTAL MONTHS	48	49	50	51	52	53	54	55	56	57	58	59	

MA 4–0 / CA 14–0

YEARS → MONTHS → / CHRONOLOGICAL AGE	5 0	5 1	5 2	5 3	5 4	5 5	5 6	5 7	5 8	5 9	5 10	5 11	TOTAL MONTHS
2–00													24
2–01													25
2–02													26
2–03													27
2–04													28
2–05													29
2–06													30
2–07													31
2–08													32
2–09	168	171											33
2–10	164	166	169	171									34
2–11	159	162	164	167	169								35
3–00	155	158	160	162	165	167	170						36
3–01	152	154	157	159	161	164	166	169	171				37
3–02	149	151	153	156	158	160	163	165	167	170			38
3–03	146	148	150	153	155	157	160	162	164	167	169	171	39
3–04	143	145	147	150	152	154	157	159	161	163	166	168	40
3–05	140	142	145	147	149	151	154	156	158	160	163	165	41
3–06	138	140	142	144	146	149	151	153	155	157	160	162	42
3–07	135	137	139	141	144	146	148	150	152	154	157	159	43
3–08	132	135	137	139	141	143	145	147	150	152	154	156	44
3–09	130	132	134	136	138	141	143	145	147	149	151	153	45
3–10	128	130	132	134	136	138	140	142	144	146	148	150	46
3–11	125	127	129	131	133	136	138	140	142	144	146	148	47
4–00	123	125	127	129	131	133	135	137	139	141	143	145	48
4–01	121	123	125	127	129	131	133	135	137	139	141	143	49
4–02	119	121	123	125	127	129	131	133	135	137	139	141	50
4–03	117	119	121	123	125	126	128	130	132	134	136	138	51
4–04	115	117	118	120	122	124	126	128	130	132	134	136	52
4–05	113	115	117	118	120	122	124	126	128	130	132	134	53
4–06	111	113	115	116	118	120	122	124	126	128	130	132	54
4–07	109	111	113	114	116	118	120	122	124	126	128	130	55
4–08	107	109	111	112	114	116	118	120	122	124	126	128	56
4–09	105	107	109	111	112	114	116	118	120	122	124	125	57
4–10	103	105	107	109	111	112	114	116	118	120	122	123	58
4–11	101	103	105	107	109	110	112	114	116	118	120	121	59
TOTAL MONTHS	60	61	62	63	64	65	66	67	68	69	70	71	

MA 5–0 / CA 2–0

138

CHRONOLOGICAL AGE (YEARS–MONTHS)	5-0	5-1	5-2	5-3	5-4	5-5	5-6	5-7	5-8	5-9	5-10	5-11	TOTAL MONTHS
5–00	100	101	103	105	107	109	110	112	114	116	118	120	60
5–01	98	100	102	103	105	107	109	110	112	114	116	118	61
5–02	96	98	100	101	103	105	107	109	110	112	114	116	62
5–03	95	96	98	100	102	103	105	107	109	110	112	114	63
5–04	93	95	96	98	100	102	103	105	107	109	110	112	64
5–05	91	93	95	96	98	100	102	103	105	107	109	110	65
5–06	90	92	93	95	97	98	100	102	103	105	107	109	66
5–07	88	90	92	93	95	97	98	100	102	103	105	107	67
5–08	87	89	90	92	94	95	97	99	100	102	103	105	68
5–09	86	87	89	90	92	94	95	97	99	100	102	103	69
5–10	84	86	87	89	91	92	94	95	97	99	100	102	70
5–11	83	85	86	88	89	91	92	94	96	97	99	100	71
6–00	82	83	85	86	88	89	91	93	94	96	97	99	72
6–01	80	82	83	85	86	88	90	91	93	94	96	97	73
6–02	79	81	82	84	85	87	88	90	91	93	94	96	74
6–03	78	79	81	82	84	85	87	88	90	91	93	94	75
6–04	77	78	80	81	83	84	85	87	88	90	91	93	76
6–05	76	77	78	80	81	83	84	86	87	88	90	91	77
6–06	75	76	77	79	80	82	83	84	86	87	89	90	78
6–07	73	75	76	78	79	80	82	83	84	86	87	89	79
6–08	72	74	75	76	78	79	81	82	83	85	86	87	80
6–09	72	73	74	76	77	78	80	81	82	84	85	86	81
6–10	71	72	73	74	76	77	78	80	81	82	84	85	82
6–11	70	71	72	73	75	76	77	79	80	81	83	84	83
7–00	69	70	71	72	74	75	76	78	79	80	81	83	84
7–01	68	69	70	72	73	74	75	77	78	79	80	82	85
7–02	67	68	69	71	72	73	74	76	77	78	79	80	86
7–03	66	67	69	70	71	72	73	75	76	77	78	79	87
7–04	65	67	68	69	70	71	73	74	75	76	77	78	88
7–05	65	66	67	68	69	70	72	73	74	75	76	78	89
7–06	64	65	66	67	68	70	71	72	73	74	75	77	90
7–07	63	64	65	67	68	69	70	71	72	73	75	76	91
7–08	62	64	65	66	67	68	69	70	71	73	74	75	92
7–09	62	63	64	65	66	67	68	70	71	72	73	74	93
7–10	61	62	63	64	65	67	68	69	70	71	72	73	94
7–11	60	62	63	64	65	66	67	68	69	70	71	72	95
TOTAL MONTHS	60	61	62	63	64	65	66	67	68	69	70	71	

MA 5–0 / CA 5–0

YEARS MONTHS	5 0	5 1	5 2	5 3	5 4	5 5	5 6	5 7	5 8	5 9	5 10	5 11	
8–00	60	61	62	63	64	65	66	67	68	69	70	71	96
8–01	59	60	61	62	63	65	66	67	68	69	70	71	97
8–02	59	60	61	62	63	64	65	66	67	68	69	70	98
8–03	58	59	60	61	62	63	64	65	66	67	68	69	99
8–04	58	59	60	61	62	63	64	65	66	67	68	69	100
8–05	57	58	59	60	61	62	63	64	65	66	67	68	101
8–06	57	58	59	60	60	61	62	63	64	65	66	67	102
8–07	56	57	58	59	60	61	62	63	64	65	66	67	103
8–08	56	56	57	58	59	60	61	62	63	64	65	66	104
8–09	55	56	57	58	59	60	61	62	63	64	65	65	105
8–10	55	56	56	57	58	59	60	61	62	63	64	65	106
8–11	54	55	56	57	58	59	60	61	62	63	63	64	107
9–00	54	55	56	56	57	58	59	60	61	62	63	64	108
9–01	53	54	55	56	57	58	59	60	61	61	62	63	109
9–02	53	54	55	56	57	57	58	59	60	61	62	63	110
9–03	53	53	54	55	56	57	58	59	60	61	61	62	111
9–04	52	53	54	55	56	57	57	58	59	60	61	62	112
9–05	52	53	54	55	55	56	57	58	59	60	61	61	113
9–06	52	53	53	54	55	56	57	58	58	59	60	61	114
9–07	51	52	53	54	55	56	56	57	58	59	60	61	115
9–08	51	52	53	54	54	55	56	57	58	58	59	60	116
9–09	51	52	52	53	54	55	56	57	57	58	59	60	117
9–10	50	51	52	53	54	54	55	56	57	58	59	59	118
9–11	50	51	52	53	53	54	55	56	57	57	58	59	119
10–00	50	51	52	52	53	54	55	55	56	57	58	59	120
10–01	50	51	51	52	53	54	54	55	56	57	58	58	121
10–02	50	50	51	52	53	53	54	55	56	57	57	58	122
10–03	50	50	51	52	53	53	54	55	56	56	57	58	123
10–04	49	50	51	52	52	53	54	55	55	56	57	58	124
10–05	49	50	51	51	52	53	54	54	55	56	57	57	125
10–06	49	50	51	51	52	53	54	54	55	56	56	57	126
10–07	49	50	51	51	52	53	53	54	55	56	56	57	127
10–08	49	50	50	51	52	53	53	54	55	55	56	57	128
10–09	49	50	50	51	52	52	53	54	55	55	56	57	129
10–10	49	50	50	51	52	52	53	54	54	55	56	57	130
10–11	49	49	50	51	51	52	53	54	54	55	56	56	131
	60	61	62	63	64	65	66	67	68	69	70	71	TOTAL MONTHS

CHRONOLOGICAL AGE

YEARS MONTHS	5 0	5 1	5 2	5 3	5 4	5 5	5 6	5 7	5 8	5 9	5 10	5 11	
11–00	49	49	50	51	51	52	53	53	54	55	56	56	132
11–01	48	49	50	50	51	52	53	53	54	55	55	56	133
11–02	48	49	50	50	51	52	52	53	54	54	55	56	134
11–03	48	49	50	50	51	52	52	53	54	54	55	56	135
11–04	48	49	49	50	51	51	52	53	53	54	55	55	136
11–05	48	48	49	50	50	51	52	52	53	54	54	55	137
11–06	48	48	49	50	50	51	52	52	53	54	54	55	138
11–07	48	48	49	50	50	51	52	52	53	53	54	55	139
11–08	48	48	49	49	50	51	51	52	53	53	54	55	140
11–09	47	48	49	49	50	51	51	52	52	53	54	54	141
11–10	47	48	49	49	50	50	51	52	52	53	54	54	142
11–11	47	48	48	49	50	50	51	52	52	53	53	54	143
12–00	47	48	48	49	50	50	51	51	52	53	53	54	144
12–01	47	47	48	49	49	50	50	51	52	52	53	54	145
12–02	47	47	48	48	49	50	50	51	51	52	53	53	146
12–03	46	47	48	48	49	49	50	51	51	52	52	53	147
12–04	46	47	47	48	49	49	50	50	51	52	52	53	148
12–05	46	46	47	48	48	49	49	50	51	51	52	52	149
12–06	46	46	47	48	48	49	49	50	50	51	52	52	150
12–07	46	46	47	47	48	49	49	50	50	51	51	52	151
12–08	45	46	46	47	48	48	49	49	50	51	51	52	152
12–09	45	46	46	47	47	48	49	49	50	50	51	51	153
12–10	45	46	46	47	47	48	48	49	50	50	51	51	154
12–11	45	45	46	46	47	48	48	49	49	50	50	51	155
13–00	45	45	46	46	47	47	48	48	49	50	50	51	156
13–01	44	45	45	46	46	47	48	48	49	49	50	50	157
13–02	44	45	45	46	46	47	48	48	49	49	50	50	158
13–03	44	44	45	45	46	47	47	48	48	49	49	50	159
13–04	43	44	45	45	46	46	47	47	48	49	49	50	160
13–05	43	44	45	45	46	46	47	47	48	48	49	50	161
13–06	43	44	44	45	45	46	46	47	48	48	49	49	162
13–07	43	43	44	44	45	46	46	47	47	48	48	49	163
13–08	43	43	44	44	45	45	46	47	47	48	48	49	164
13–09	42	43	44	44	45	45	46	46	47	47	48	49	165
13–10	42	43	43	44	44	45	45	46	47	47	48	48	166
13–11	42	42	43	44	44	45	45	46	46	47	47	48	167
	60	61	62	63	64	65	66	67	68	69	70	71	TOTAL MONTHS

CHRONOLOGICAL AGE

141

MA 5–0 / CA 11–0

MENTAL AGE

YEARS MONTHS	5 0	5 1	5 2	5 3	5 4	5 5	5 6	5 7	5 8	5 9	5 10	5 11	
14–00	42	42	43	43	44	44	45	46	46	47	47	48	168
14–01	41	42	43	43	44	44	45	45	46	46	47	47	169
14–02	41	42	42	43	43	44	45	45	46	46	47	47	170
14–03	41	42	42	43	43	44	44	45	45	46	46	47	171
14–04	41	41	42	42	43	43	44	45	45	46	46	47	172
14–05	41	41	42	42	43	43	44	44	45	46	46	47	173
14–06	40	41	41	42	43	43	44	44	44	45	46	46	174
14–07	40	41	41	42	42	43	43	44	44	45	45	46	175
14–08	40	41	41	42	42	43	43	44	44	45	45	46	176
14–09	40	40	41	41	42	42	43	43	44	45	45	46	177
14–10	39	40	41	41	42	42	43	43	44	44	45	45	178
14–11	39	40	40	41	41	42	43	43	44	44	45	45	179
15–00	39	40	40	41	41	42	42	43	43	44	44	45	180
15–01	39	39	40	40	41	41	42	42	43	43	44	44	181
15–02	38	39	39	40	40	41	41	42	43	43	44	44	182
15–03	38	38	39	39	40	40	41	41	42	42	43	44	183
15–04	37	38	38	39	39	40	40	41	41	42	42	43	184
15–05	37	37	38	39	39	40	40	41	41	42	42	43	185
15–06	36	37	37	38	38	39	40	40	41	41	42	42	186
15–07	36	36	37	37	38	38	39	39	40	41	41	42	187
15–08	36	36	37	37	38	38	39	39	40	40	41	41	188
15–09	35	35	36	37	37	38	38	39	39	40	40	41	189
15–10	34	35	35	36	36	37	38	38	39	39	40	40	190
15–11	34	35	35	36	36	37	37	38	38	39	39	40	191
16–00 16–02	33	34	34	35	35	36	37	37	38	38	39	39	192 194
16–03 16–07	32	33	33	34	34	35	36	36	37	37	38	38	195 199
16–08 17–00	31	32	32	33	33	34	35	35	36	36	37	37	200 204
17–01 17–05	30	31	31	32	32	33	34	34	35	35	36	36	205 209
17–06 17–10		30	30	31	31	32	33	33	34	34	35	35	210 214
17–11 18–00				30	31	31	32	32	33	33	34	34	215 216
	60	61	62	63	64	65	66	67	68	69	70	71	TOTAL MONTHS

CHRONOLOGICAL AGE

MENTAL AGE

YEARS → MONTHS ↓	6-0	6-1	6-2	6-3	6-4	6-5	6-6	6-7	6-8	6-9	6-10	6-11	TOTAL MONTHS
2-00													24
2-01													25
2-02													26
2-03													27
2-04													28
2-05													29
2-06													30
2-07													31
2-08													32
2-09													33
2-10													34
2-11													35
3-00													36
3-01													37
3-02													38
3-03													39
3-04	170												40
3-05	167	169											41
3-06	164	166	168	171									42
3-07	161	163	165	167	170								43
3-08	158	160	162	165	167	169	171						44
3-09	155	157	160	162	164	166	168	170					45
3-10	153	155	157	159	161	163	165	167	169				46
3-11	150	152	154	156	158	160	162	164	167	169	171		47
4-00	147	149	152	154	156	158	160	162	164	166	168	170	48
4-01	145	147	149	151	153	155	157	159	161	163	165	167	49
4-02	143	145	147	149	151	153	155	157	159	161	163	165	50
4-03	140	142	144	146	148	150	152	154	156	158	160	162	51
4-04	138	140	142	144	146	148	150	152	154	156	158	159	52
4-05	136	138	140	142	144	146	148	149	151	153	155	157	53
4-06	134	136	138	139	141	143	145	147	149	151	153	155	54
4-07	132	133	135	137	139	141	143	145	147	149	151	152	55
4-08	129	131	133	135	137	139	141	143	144	146	148	150	56
4-09	127	129	131	133	135	137	139	140	142	144	146	148	57
4-10	125	127	129	131	133	135	136	138	140	142	144	146	58
4-11	123	125	127	129	131	132	134	136	138	140	142	143	59
TOTAL MONTHS	72	73	74	75	76	77	78	79	80	81	82	83	

CHRONOLOGICAL AGE

143

MA 6-0 / CA 2-0

YEARS MONTHS	6 0	6 1	6 2	6 3	6 4	6 5	6 6	6 7	6 8	6 9	6 10	6 11	
5–00	121	123	125	127	129	130	132	134	136	138	140	141	60
5–01	119	121	123	125	127	128	130	132	134	136	137	139	61
5–02	117	119	121	123	125	126	128	130	132	133	135	137	62
5–03	116	117	119	121	123	124	126	128	130	131	133	135	63
5–04	114	116	117	119	121	123	124	126	128	129	131	133	64
5–05	112	114	115	117	119	121	122	124	126	127	129	131	65
5–06	110	112	114	115	117	119	120	122	124	126	127	129	66
5–07	108	110	112	113	115	117	118	120	122	123	125	127	67
5–08	107	108	110	112	113	115	117	118	120	122	123	125	68
5–09	105	107	108	110	112	113	115	116	118	120	121	123	69
5–10	103	105	107	108	110	111	113	115	116	118	119	121	70
5–11	102	103	105	107	108	110	111	113	114	116	118	119	71
6–00	100	102	103	105	106	108	110	111	113	114	116	117	72
6–01	99	100	102	103	105	106	108	109	111	112	114	115	73
6–02	97	99	100	102	103	105	106	108	109	111	112	113	74
6–03	96	97	99	100	102	103	104	106	107	109	110	112	75
6–04	94	96	97	98	100	101	103	104	106	107	109	110	76
6–05	93	94	96	97	98	100	101	103	104	106	107	108	77
6–06	91	93	94	96	97	98	100	101	103	104	105	107	78
6–07	90	91	93	94	95	97	98	100	101	102	104	105	79
6–08	89	90	91	93	94	95	97	98	100	101	102	104	80
6–09	88	89	90	92	93	94	96	97	98	100	101	102	81
6–10	86	88	89	90	92	93	94	95	97	98	99	101	82
6–11	85	86	88	89	90	92	93	94	95	97	98	99	83
7–00	84	85	86	88	89	90	92	93	94	95	97	98	84
7–01	83	84	85	87	88	89	90	92	93	94	95	97	85
7–02	82	83	84	85	87	88	89	90	92	93	94	95	86
7–03	81	82	83	84	86	87	88	89	90	92	93	94	87
7–04	80	81	82	83	84	86	87	88	89	90	92	93	88
7–05	79	80	81	82	83	85	86	87	88	89	90	92	89
7–06	78	79	80	81	82	84	85	86	87	88	89	90	90
7–07	77	78	79	80	81	83	84	85	86	87	88	89	91
7–08	76	77	78	79	80	82	83	84	85	86	87	88	92
7–09	75	76	77	78	79	81	82	83	84	85	86	87	93
7–10	74	75	76	77	79	80	81	82	83	84	85	86	94
7–11	73	74	76	77	78	79	80	81	82	83	84	85	95
	72	73	74	75	76	77	78	79	80	81	82	83	TOTAL MONTHS

CHRONOLOGICAL AGE

MA 6–0 / CA 5–0

144

YEARS MONTHS	6 0	6 1	6 2	6 3	6 4	6 5	6 6	6 7	6 8	6 9	6 10	6 11	
8–00	73	74	75	76	77	78	79	80	81	82	83	84	96
8–01	72	73	74	75	76	77	78	79	80	81	82	83	97
8–02	71	72	73	74	75	76	77	78	79	80	81	82	98
8–03	70	71	72	73	74	75	76	77	78	79	80	82	99
8–04	70	71	72	73	74	75	76	77	78	79	80	81	100
8–05	69	70	71	72	73	74	75	76	77	78	79	80	101
8–06	68	69	70	71	72	73	74	75	76	77	78	79	102
8–07	68	69	70	71	72	72	73	74	75	76	77	78	103
8–08	67	68	69	70	71	72	73	74	75	76	77	77	104
8–09	66	67	68	69	70	71	72	73	74	75	76	77	105
8–10	66	67	68	69	70	70	71	72	73	74	75	76	106
8–11	65	66	67	68	69	70	71	72	73	74	74	75	107
9–00	65	66	66	67	68	69	70	71	72	73	74	75	108
9–01	64	65	66	67	68	69	70	70	71	72	73	74	109
9–02	64	64	65	66	67	68	69	70	71	72	72	73	110
9–03	63	64	65	66	67	68	68	69	70	71	72	73	111
9–04	63	64	64	65	66	67	68	69	70	70	71	72	112
9–05	62	63	64	65	66	67	67	68	69	70	71	72	113
9–06	62	63	64	64	65	66	67	68	69	69	70	71	114
9–07	61	62	63	64	65	66	66	67	68	69	70	71	115
9–08	61	62	63	63	64	65	66	67	68	68	69	70	116
9–09	61	61	62	63	64	65	65	66	67	68	69	70	117
9–10	60	61	62	63	63	64	65	66	67	67	68	69	118
9–11	60	61	61	62	63	64	65	65	66	67	68	69	119
10–00	59	60	61	62	63	63	64	65	66	67	67	68	120
10–01	59	60	61	62	62	63	64	65	65	66	67	68	121
10–02	59	60	60	61	62	63	63	64	65	66	67	67	122
10–03	59	59	60	61	62	62	63	64	65	66	66	67	123
10–04	58	59	60	61	61	62	63	64	64	65	66	67	124
10–05	58	59	60	60	61	62	63	63	64	65	66	66	125
10–06	58	59	59	60	61	62	62	63	64	65	65	66	126
10–07	58	59	59	60	61	61	62	63	64	64	65	66	127
10–08	58	58	59	60	60	61	62	63	63	64	65	65	128
10–09	57	58	59	59	60	61	62	62	63	64	64	65	129
10–10	57	58	59	59	60	61	61	62	63	64	64	65	130
10–11	57	58	58	59	60	60	61	62	63	63	64	65	131
	72	73	74	75	76	77	78	79	80	81	82	83	TOTAL MONTHS

MA 6–0 / CA 8–0

YEARS	6	6	6	6	6	6	6	6	6	6	6	6	
MONTHS	0	1	2	3	4	5	6	7	8	9	10	11	
11–00	57	58	58	59	60	60	61	62	62	63	64	64	132
11–01	57	57	58	59	59	60	61	61	62	63	63	64	133
11–02	56	57	58	58	59	60	60	61	62	62	63	64	134
11–03	56	57	58	58	59	60	60	61	62	62	63	64	135
11–04	56	57	57	58	59	59	60	61	61	62	63	63	136
11–05	56	56	57	58	58	59	60	60	61	62	62	63	137
11–06	56	56	57	57	58	59	59	60	61	61	62	63	138
11–07	55	56	57	57	58	59	59	60	61	61	62	62	139
11–08	55	56	56	57	58	58	59	60	60	61	62	62	140
11–09	55	56	56	57	57	58	59	59	60	61	61	62	141
11–10	55	55	56	57	57	58	59	59	60	60	61	62	142
11–11	55	55	56	56	57	58	58	59	60	60	61	61	143
12–00	54	55	56	56	57	58	58	59	59	60	61	61	144
12–01	54	55	55	56	57	57	58	58	59	60	60	61	145
12–02	54	54	55	56	56	57	57	58	59	59	60	61	146
12–03	54	54	55	55	56	57	57	58	58	59	60	60	147
12–04	53	54	55	55	56	56	57	58	58	59	59	60	148
12–05	53	54	54	55	55	56	57	57	58	58	59	60	149
12–06	53	53	54	55	55	56	56	57	58	58	59	59	150
12–07	53	53	54	54	55	56	56	57	57	58	58	59	151
12–08	52	53	53	54	55	55	56	56	57	58	58	59	152
12–09	52	53	53	54	54	55	56	56	57	57	58	58	153
12–10	52	52	53	54	54	55	55	56	56	57	58	58	154
12–11	52	52	53	53	54	54	55	56	56	57	57	58	155
13–00	51	52	52	53	54	54	55	55	56	56	57	58	156
13–01	51	52	52	53	53	54	54	55	56	56	57	57	157
13–02	51	52	52	53	53	54	54	55	56	56	57	57	158
13–03	51	51	52	52	53	53	54	54	55	56	56	57	159
13–04	50	51	51	52	52	53	54	54	55	55	56	56	160
13–05	50	51	51	52	52	53	54	54	55	55	56	56	161
13–06	50	50	51	51	52	53	53	54	54	55	55	56	162
13–07	49	50	51	51	52	52	53	53	54	54	55	56	163
13–08	49	50	50	51	52	52	53	53	54	54	55	56	164
13–09	49	50	50	51	51	52	52	53	54	54	55	55	165
13–10	49	49	50	50	51	51	52	53	53	54	54	55	166
13–11	49	49	50	50	51	51	52	52	53	54	54	55	167
TOTAL MONTHS	72	73	74	75	76	77	78	79	80	81	82	83	

CHRONOLOGICAL AGE

MENTAL AGE

YEARS MONTHS	6 0	6 1	6 2	6 3	6 4	6 5	6 6	6 7	6 8	6 9	6 10	6 11	
14–00	48	49	49	50	50	51	52	52	53	53	54	54	168
14–01	48	49	49	50	50	51	51	52	52	53	53	54	169
14–02	48	48	49	50	50	51	51	52	52	53	53	54	170
14–03	48	48	49	49	50	50	51	51	52	52	53	54	171
14–04	47	48	48	49	49	50	51	51	52	52	53	53	172
14–05	47	48	48	49	49	50	50	51	52	52	53	53	173
14–06	47	47	48	48	49	50	50	51	51	52	52	53	174
14–07	47	47	48	48	49	49	50	50	51	51	52	53	175
14–08	46	47	48	48	49	49	50	50	51	51	52	52	176
14–09	46	47	47	48	48	49	49	50	50	51	52	52	177
14–10	46	46	47	47	48	49	49	50	50	51	51	52	178
14–11	46	46	47	47	48	48	49	50	50	51	51	52	179
15–00	45	46	47	47	48	48	49	49	50	50	51	51	180
15–01	45	45	46	46	47	48	48	49	49	50	50	51	181
15–02	45	45	46	46	47	47	48	48	49	49	50	51	182
15–03	44	45	45	46	46	47	47	48	48	49	49	50	183
15–04	44	44	45	45	46	46	47	47	48	48	49	49	184
15–05	43	44	44	45	45	46	46	47	48	48	49	49	185
15–06	43	43	44	44	45	45	46	46	47	47	48	49	186
15–07	42	43	43	44	44	45	45	46	46	47	47	48	187
15–08	42	42	43	43	44	45	45	46	46	47	47	48	188
15–09	41	42	42	43	43	44	44	45	46	46	47	47	189
15–10	41	41	42	42	43	43	44	44	45	45	46	47	190
15–11	41	41	42	42	43	43	44	44	45	45	46	46	191
16–00 } 16–02	40	40	41	41	42	43	43	44	44	45	45	46	{ 192 194
16–03 } 16–07	39	40	40	41	41	42	42	43	43	44	44	45	{ 195 199
16–08 } 17–00	38	39	39	40	40	41	41	42	42	43	43	44	{ 200 204
17–01 } 17–05	37	38	38	39	39	40	40	41	41	42	42	43	{ 205 209
17–06 } 17–10	36	37	37	38	38	39	39	40	40	41	41	42	{ 210 214
17–11 } 18–00	35	36	36	37	37	38	38	39	39	40	41	41	{ 215 216
	72	73	74	75	76	77	78	79	80	81	82	83	TOTAL MONTHS

CHRONOLOGICAL AGE

MA 6–0 / CA 14–0

MENTAL AGE

YEARS MONTHS	7 0	7 1	7 2	7 3	7 4	7 5	7 6	7 7	7 8	7 9	7 10	7 11	
2–00													24
2–01													25
2–02													26
2–03													27
2–04													28
2–05													29
2–06													30
2–07													31
2–08													32
2–09													33
2–10													34
2–11													35
3–00													36
3–01													37
3–02													38
3–03													39
3–04													40
3–05													41
3–06													42
3–07													43
3–08													44
3–09													45
3–10													46
3–11													47
4–00													48
4–01	169												49
4–02	167	169	171										50
4–03	164	166	168	170									51
4–04	161	163	165	167	169								52
4–05	159	161	163	165	167	169	171						53
4–06	157	159	161	162	164	166	168	170					54
4–07	154	156	158	160	162	164	166	168	170				55
4–08	152	154	156	158	159	161	163	165	167	169	171		56
4–09	150	152	153	155	157	159	161	163	165	166	168	170	57
4–10	147	149	151	153	155	157	159	160	162	164	166	168	58
4–11	145	147	149	151	153	154	156	158	160	162	164	165	59
TOTAL MONTHS	84	85	86	87	88	89	90	91	92	93	94	95	

CHRONOLOGICAL AGE

MA 7–0 / CA 2–0

148

YEARS⟍ MONTHS	7 0	7 1	7 2	7 3	7 4	7 5	7 6	7 7	7 8	7 9	7 10	7 11	
5-00	143	145	147	149	150	152	154	156	158	159	161	163	60
5-01	141	143	145	146	148	150	152	154	155	157	159	161	61
5-02	139	141	142	144	146	148	149	151	153	155	156	158	62
5-03	137	138	140	142	144	145	147	149	151	152	154	156	63
5-04	135	136	138	140	142	143	145	147	149	150	152	154	64
5-05	133	134	136	138	139	141	143	145	146	148	150	152	65
5-06	131	132	134	136	138	139	141	143	144	146	148	149	66
5-07	129	130	132	134	135	137	139	140	142	144	145	147	67
5-08	127	128	130	131	133	135	136	138	140	141	143	145	68
5-09	124	126	128	129	131	133	134	136	137	139	141	142	69
5-10	123	124	126	127	129	130	132	134	135	137	138	140	70
5-11	121	122	124	125	127	129	130	132	133	135	136	138	71
6-00	119	120	122	123	125	127	128	130	131	133	134	136	72
6-01	117	118	120	121	123	124	126	128	129	131	132	134	73
6-02	115	116	118	119	121	122	124	125	127	128	130	131	74
6-03	113	115	116	118	119	121	122	124	125	126	128	129	75
6-04	112	113	114	116	117	119	120	122	123	125	126	127	76
6-05	110	111	113	114	115	117	118	120	121	123	124	125	77
6-06	108	110	111	112	114	115	117	118	119	121	122	123	78
6-07	106	108	109	111	112	113	115	116	117	119	120	122	79
6-08	105	106	108	109	110	112	113	114	116	117	118	120	80
6-09	104	105	106	107	109	110	111	113	114	115	117	118	81
6-10	102	103	105	106	107	109	110	111	113	114	115	116	82
6-11	101	102	103	104	106	107	108	110	111	112	114	115	83
7-00	99	100	102	103	104	106	107	108	109	111	112	113	84
7-01	98	99	100	102	103	104	105	107	108	109	110	112	85
7-02	97	98	99	100	101	103	104	105	106	108	109	110	86
7-03	95	96	98	99	100	101	103	104	105	106	107	109	87
7-04	94	95	96	98	99	100	101	102	104	105	106	107	88
7-05	93	94	95	96	98	99	100	101	102	103	105	106	89
7-06	92	93	94	95	96	97	99	100	101	102	103	104	90
7-07	90	92	93	94	95	96	97	98	100	101	102	103	91
7-08	89	91	92	93	94	95	96	97	98	100	101	102	92
7-09	88	89	91	92	93	94	95	96	97	98	99	101	93
7-10	87	88	89	91	92	93	94	95	96	97	98	99	94
7-11	86	87	88	89	91	92	93	94	95	96	97	98	95
	84	85	86	87	88	89	90	91	92	93	94	95	TOTAL MONTHS

CHRONOLOGICAL AGE

149

MA 7–0 / CA 5–0

YEARS MONTHS	7 0	7 1	7 2	7 3	7 4	7 5	7 6	7 7	7 8	7 9	7 10	7 11	
8–00	85	86	87	88	90	91	92	93	94	95	96	97	96
8–01	84	85	86	88	89	90	91	92	93	94	95	96	97
8–02	83	84	86	87	88	89	90	91	92	93	94	95	98
8–03	83	84	85	86	87	88	89	90	91	92	93	94	99
8–04	82	83	84	85	86	87	88	89	90	91	92	93	100
8–05	81	82	83	84	85	86	87	88	89	90	91	92	101
8–06	80	81	82	83	84	85	86	87	88	89	90	91	102
8–07	79	80	81	82	83	84	85	86	87	88	89	90	103
8–08	78	79	80	81	82	83	84	85	86	87	88	89	104
8–09	78	79	80	81	82	82	83	84	85	86	87	88	105
8–10	77	78	79	80	81	82	83	83	84	85	86	87	106
8–11	76	77	78	79	80	81	82	83	84	85	86	86	107
9–00	76	76	77	78	79	80	81	82	83	84	85	86	108
9–01	75	76	77	78	79	79	80	81	82	83	84	85	109
9–02	74	75	76	77	78	79	80	80	81	82	83	84	110
9–03	74	75	75	76	77	78	79	80	81	82	82	83	111
9–04	73	74	75	76	77	77	78	79	80	81	82	83	112
9–05	73	73	74	75	76	77	78	79	79	80	81	82	113
9–06	72	73	74	75	75	76	77	78	79	80	80	81	114
9–07	71	72	73	74	75	76	76	77	78	79	80	81	115
9–08	71	72	73	73	74	75	76	77	77	78	79	80	116
9–09	70	71	72	73	74	74	75	76	77	78	79	79	117
9–10	70	71	71	72	73	74	75	75	76	77	78	79	118
9–11	69	70	71	72	73	73	74	75	76	76	77	78	119
10–00	69	70	70	71	72	73	74	74	75	76	77	78	120
10–01	69	69	70	71	72	72	73	74	75	76	76	77	121
10–02	68	69	70	70	71	72	73	73	74	75	76	77	122
10–03	68	69	69	70	71	72	72	73	74	75	75	76	123
10–04	67	68	69	70	70	71	72	73	73	74	75	76	124
10–05	67	68	69	69	70	71	72	72	73	74	75	75	125
10–06	67	68	68	69	70	70	71	72	73	73	74	75	126
10–07	67	67	68	69	69	70	71	72	72	73	74	75	127
10–08	66	67	68	68	69	70	70	71	72	73	73	74	128
10–09	66	67	67	68	69	69	70	71	72	72	73	74	129
10–10	66	66	67	68	68	69	70	71	71	72	73	73	130
10–11	65	66	67	67	68	69	70	70	71	72	72	73	131
TOTAL MONTHS	84	85	86	87	88	89	90	91	92	93	94	95	

CHRONOLOGICAL AGE

YEARS MONTHS	7 0	7 1	7 2	7 3	7 4	7 5	7 6	7 7	7 8	7 9	7 10	7 11	
11–00	65	66	66	67	68	69	69	70	71	71	72	73	132
11–01	65	65	66	67	67	68	69	70	70	71	72	72	133
11–02	64	65	66	67	67	68	69	69	70	71	71	72	134
11–03	64	65	66	66	67	68	68	69	70	70	71	72	135
11–04	64	65	65	66	67	67	68	69	69	70	70	71	136
11–05	64	64	65	66	66	67	67	68	69	69	70	71	137
11–06	63	64	65	65	66	67	67	68	69	69	70	70	138
11–07	63	64	64	65	66	66	67	68	68	69	70	70	139
11–08	63	63	64	65	65	66	67	67	68	69	69	70	140
11–09	63	63	64	64	65	66	66	67	68	68	69	69	141
11–10	62	63	64	64	65	65	66	67	67	68	69	69	142
11–11	62	63	63	64	65	65	66	66	67	68	68	69	143
12–00	62	62	63	64	64	65	65	66	67	67	68	69	144
12–01	61	62	63	63	64	64	65	66	66	67	68	68	145
12–02	61	62	62	63	64	64	65	65	66	67	67	68	146
12–03	61	61	62	63	63	64	64	65	66	66	67	67	147
12–04	61	61	62	62	63	64	64	65	65	66	67	67	148
12–05	60	61	61	62	63	63	64	64	65	66	66	67	149
12–06	60	60	61	62	62	63	63	64	65	65	66	66	150
12–07	60	60	61	61	62	63	63	64	64	65	66	66	151
12–08	59	60	60	61	62	62	63	63	64	65	65	66	152
12–09	59	60	60	61	61	62	62	63	64	64	65	65	153
12–10	59	59	60	60	61	62	62	63	63	64	65	65	154
12–11	58	59	60	60	61	61	62	62	63	64	64	65	155
13–00	58	59	59	60	60	61	62	62	63	63	64	64	156
13–01	58	58	59	60	60	61	61	62	62	63	63	64	157
13–02	58	58	59	59	60	61	61	62	62	63	63	64	158
13–03	57	58	58	59	60	60	61	61	62	62	63	63	159
13–04	57	57	58	59	59	60	60	61	61	62	63	63	160
13–05	57	57	58	59	59	60	60	61	61	62	63	63	161
13–06	56	57	58	58	59	59	60	60	61	61	62	63	162
13–07	56	57	57	58	58	59	59	60	61	61	62	62	163
13–08	56	57	57	58	58	59	59	60	61	61	62	62	164
13–09	56	56	57	57	58	58	59	60	60	61	61	62	165
13–10	55	56	56	57	58	58	59	59	60	60	61	61	166
13–11	55	56	56	57	57	58	59	59	60	60	61	61	167
	84	85	86	87	88	89	90	91	92	93	94	95	TOTAL MONTHS

CHRONOLOGICAL AGE

MA 7–0 / CA 11–0

YEARS MONTHS	7 0	7 1	7 2	7 3	7 4	7 5	7 6	7 7	7 8	7 9	7 10	7 11	
14–00	55	55	56	57	57	58	58	59	59	60	60	61	168
14–01	55	55	56	56	57	57	58	58	59	59	60	61	169
14–02	54	55	56	56	57	57	58	58	59	59	60	60	170
14–03	54	55	55	56	56	57	57	58	58	59	60	60	171
14–04	54	54	55	55	56	57	57	58	58	59	59	60	172
14–05	54	54	55	55	56	56	57	57	58	59	59	60	173
14–06	53	54	54	55	56	56	57	57	58	58	59	59	174
14–07	53	54	54	55	55	56	56	57	57	58	58	59	175
14–08	53	53	54	55	55	56	56	57	57	58	58	59	176
14–09	53	53	54	54	55	55	56	56	57	57	58	59	177
14–10	52	53	53	54	54	55	56	56	57	57	58	58	178
14–11	52	53	53	54	54	55	55	56	56	57	58	58	179
15–00	52	52	53	53	54	55	55	56	56	57	57	58	180
15–01	51	52	52	53	53	54	54	55	56	56	57	57	181
15–02	51	52	52	53	53	54	54	55	55	56	56	57	182
15–03	50	51	52	52	53	53	54	54	55	55	56	56	183
15–04	50	50	51	51	52	53	53	54	54	55	55	56	184
15–05	50	50	51	51	52	52	53	53	54	54	55	56	185
15–06	49	50	50	51	51	52	52	53	53	54	54	55	186
15–07	48	49	50	50	51	51	52	52	53	53	54	54	187
15–08	48	49	49	50	50	51	51	52	53	53	54	54	188
15–09	48	48	49	49	50	50	51	51	52	52	53	53	189
15–10	47	48	48	49	49	50	50	51	51	52	52	53	190
15–11	47	47	48	48	49	49	50	51	51	52	52	53	191
16–00 } 16–02	46	47	47	48	48	49	49	50	50	51	51	52	{ 192 194
16–03 } 16–07	45	46	46	47	47	48	48	49	49	50	50	51	{ 195 199
16–08 } 17–00	44	45	45	46	46	47	47	48	48	49	49	50	{ 200 204
17–01 } 17–05	43	44	44	45	45	46	46	47	47	48	48	49	{ 205 209
17–06 } 17–10	42	43	43	44	44	45	45	46	46	47	47	48	{ 210 214
17–11 } 18–00	42	42	43	43	44	44	45	46	46	47	47	48	{ 215 216
	84	85	86	87	88	89	90	91	92	93	94	95	TOTAL MONTHS

CHRONOLOGICAL AGE

MENTAL AGE

YEARS / MONTHS	8 0	8 1	8 2	8 3	8 4	8 5	8 6	8 7	8 8	8 9	8 10	8 11	
4–00													48
4–01													49
4–02													50
4–03													51
4–04													52
4–05													53
4–06													54
4–07													55
4–08													56
4–09													57
4–10	170												58
4–11	167	169	171										59
5–00	165	167	169	170									60
5–01	162	164	166	168	170								61
5–02	160	162	164	165	167	169	171						62
5–03	158	160	161	163	165	167	168	170					63
5–04	156	157	159	161	162	164	166	168	169				64
5–05	153	155	157	158	160	162	164	165	167	169	170		65
5–06	151	153	155	156	158	160	161	163	165	166	168	170	66
5–07	149	150	152	154	155	157	159	160	162	164	165	167	67
5–08	146	148	150	151	153	155	156	158	160	161	163	164	68
5–09	144	146	147	149	150	152	154	155	157	159	160	162	69
5–10	142	143	145	146	148	150	151	153	154	156	158	159	70
5–11	140	141	143	144	146	147	149	151	152	154	155	157	71
6–00	137	139	140	142	144	145	147	148	150	151	153	154	72
6–01	135	137	138	140	141	143	144	146	147	149	150	152	73
6–02	133	134	136	137	139	140	142	143	145	146	148	149	74
6–03	131	132	134	135	137	138	140	141	143	144	146	147	75
6–04	129	130	132	133	135	136	138	139	140	142	143	145	76
6–05	127	128	130	131	133	134	135	137	138	140	141	142	77
6–06	125	126	128	129	130	132	133	135	136	137	139	140	78
6–07	123	124	126	127	129	130	131	133	134	135	137	138	79
6–08	121	123	124	125	127	128	129	131	132	133	135	136	80
6–09	119	121	122	123	125	126	127	129	130	131	133	134	81
6–10	118	119	120	122	123	124	126	127	128	130	131	132	82
6–11	116	117	119	120	121	123	124	125	126	128	129	130	83
TOTAL MONTHS	96	97	98	99	100	101	102	103	104	105	106	107	

CHRONOLOGICAL AGE

153

MA 8–0 / CA 4–0

YEARS MONTHS	8 0	8 1	8 2	8 3	8 4	8 5	8 6	8 7	8 8	8 9	8 10	8 11	
7–00	114	116	117	118	120	121	122	123	125	126	127	128	84
7–01	113	114	115	117	118	119	120	122	123	124	125	127	85
7–02	111	113	114	115	116	117	119	120	121	122	124	125	86
7–03	110	111	112	113	115	116	117	118	120	121	122	123	87
7–04	108	110	111	112	113	114	115	117	118	119	120	121	88
7–05	107	108	109	110	112	113	114	115	116	118	119	120	89
7–06	106	107	108	109	110	111	112	114	115	116	117	118	90
7–07	104	105	106	108	109	110	111	112	113	114	116	117	91
7–08	103	104	105	106	107	109	110	111	112	113	114	115	92
7–09	102	103	104	105	106	107	108	109	110	112	113	114	93
7–10	100	101	103	104	105	106	107	108	109	110	111	112	94
7–11	99	100	101	102	103	105	106	107	108	109	110	111	95
8–00	98	99	100	101	102	103	104	105	106	108	109	110	96
8–01	97	98	99	100	101	102	103	104	105	106	107	108	97
8–02	96	97	98	99	100	101	102	103	104	105	106	107	98
8–03	95	96	97	98	99	100	101	102	103	104	105	106	99
8–04	94	95	96	97	98	99	100	101	102	103	104	105	100
8–05	93	94	95	96	97	98	99	100	101	102	103	104	101
8–06	92	93	94	95	96	97	98	99	100	101	102	103	102
8–07	91	92	93	94	95	96	97	98	99	100	101	102	103
8–08	90	91	92	93	94	95	96	97	98	99	99	100	104
8–09	89	90	91	92	93	94	95	96	97	98	99	99	105
8–10	88	89	90	91	92	93	94	95	96	97	97	98	106
8–11	87	88	89	90	91	92	93	94	95	96	97	97	107
9–00	86	87	88	89	90	91	92	93	94	95	96	96	108
9–01	86	87	88	88	89	90	91	92	93	94	95	96	109
9–02	85	86	87	88	88	89	90	91	92	93	94	95	110
9–03	84	85	86	87	88	89	89	90	91	92	93	94	111
9–04	83	84	85	86	87	88	89	90	90	91	92	93	112
9–05	83	84	85	85	86	87	88	89	90	91	91	92	113
9–06	82	83	84	85	86	86	87	88	89	90	91	91	114
9–07	81	82	83	84	85	86	86	87	88	89	90	91	115
9–08	81	82	82	83	84	85	86	87	87	88	89	90	116
9–09	80	81	82	83	83	84	85	86	87	87	88	89	117
9–10	79	80	81	82	83	83	84	85	86	87	88	88	118
9–11	79	80	80	81	82	83	84	84	85	86	87	88	119
	96	97	98	99	100	101	102	103	104	105	106	107	TOTAL MONTHS

CHRONOLOGICAL AGE

YEARS / MONTHS	8 0	8 1	8 2	8 3	8 4	8 5	8 6	8 7	8 8	8 9	8 10	8 11	
10–00	78	79	80	81	81	82	83	84	85	85	86	87	120
10–01	78	79	79	80	81	82	83	83	84	85	86	86	121
10–02	77	78	79	80	80	81	82	83	83	84	85	86	122
10–03	77	78	78	79	80	81	81	82	83	84	85	85	123
10–04	76	77	78	79	79	80	81	82	83	83	84	85	124
10–05	76	77	77	78	79	80	80	81	82	83	83	84	125
10–06	76	76	77	78	79	79	80	81	81	82	83	84	126
10–07	75	76	77	77	78	79	80	80	81	82	82	83	127
10–08	75	75	76	77	78	78	79	80	81	81	82	83	128
10–09	74	75	76	77	77	78	79	79	80	81	82	82	129
10–10	74	75	75	76	77	78	78	79	80	80	81	82	130
10–11	74	74	75	76	76	77	78	79	79	80	81	81	131
11–00	73	74	75	75	76	77	77	78	79	80	80	81	132
11–01	73	74	74	75	76	76	77	78	78	79	80	80	133
11–02	73	73	74	75	75	76	77	77	78	79	79	80	134
11–03	72	73	74	74	75	76	76	77	78	78	79	80	135
11–04	72	72	73	74	74	75	76	76	77	78	78	79	136
11–05	71	72	73	73	74	75	75	76	77	77	78	79	137
11–06	71	72	72	73	74	74	75	76	76	77	78	78	138
11–07	71	71	72	73	73	74	75	75	76	77	77	78	139
11–08	70	71	72	72	73	74	74	75	76	76	77	77	140
11–09	70	71	71	72	73	73	74	74	75	76	76	77	141
11–10	70	70	71	72	72	73	74	74	75	75	76	77	142
11–11	70	70	71	71	72	73	73	74	74	75	76	76	143
12–00	69	70	70	71	72	72	73	73	74	75	75	76	144
12–01	69	69	70	71	71	72	72	73	74	74	75	75	145
12–02	68	69	70	70	71	71	72	73	73	74	74	75	146
12–03	68	69	69	70	71	71	72	72	73	74	74	75	147
12–04	68	68	69	70	70	71	71	72	72	73	74	74	148
12–05	67	68	68	69	70	70	71	71	72	73	73	74	149
12–06	67	68	68	69	69	70	71	71	72	72	73	73	150
12–07	67	67	68	68	69	70	70	71	71	72	73	73	151
12–08	66	67	67	68	69	69	70	70	71	72	72	73	152
12–09	66	67	67	68	68	69	69	70	71	71	72	72	153
12–10	66	66	67	67	68	69	69	70	70	71	71	72	154
12–11	65	66	67	67	68	68	69	69	70	71	71	72	155
TOTAL MONTHS	96	97	98	99	100	101	102	103	104	105	106	107	

CHRONOLOGICAL AGE

MA 8–0 / CA 10–0

YEARS MONTHS	8 0	8 1	8 2	8 3	8 4	8 5	8 6	8 7	8 8	8 9	8 10	8 11	
13–00	65	66	66	67	67	68	68	69	70	70	71	71	156
13–01	65	65	66	66	67	67	68	69	69	70	70	71	157
13–02	65	65	66	66	67	67	68	69	69	70	70	71	158
13–03	64	65	65	66	66	67	67	68	69	69	70	70	159
13–04	64	64	65	65	66	66	67	68	68	69	69	70	160
13–05	64	64	65	65	66	66	67	68	68	69	69	70	161
13–06	63	64	64	65	65	66	67	67	68	68	69	69	162
13–07	63	63	64	64	65	66	66	67	67	68	68	69	163
13–08	63	63	64	64	65	66	66	67	67	68	68	69	164
13–09	62	63	63	64	65	65	66	66	67	67	68	68	165
13–10	62	63	63	64	64	65	65	66	66	67	67	68	166
13–11	62	62	63	63	64	65	65	66	66	67	67	68	167
14–00	61	62	63	63	64	64	65	65	66	66	67	68	168
14–01	61	62	62	63	63	64	64	65	65	66	67	67	169
14–02	61	62	62	63	63	64	64	65	65	66	67	67	170
14–03	61	61	62	62	63	63	64	64	65	66	66	67	171
14–04	60	61	61	62	62	63	64	64	65	65	66	66	172
14–05	60	61	61	62	62	63	63	64	65	65	66	66	173
14–06	60	60	61	61	62	63	63	64	64	65	65	66	174
14–07	60	60	61	61	62	62	63	63	64	64	65	65	175
14–08	59	60	60	61	62	62	63	63	64	64	65	65	176
14–09	59	60	60	61	61	62	62	63	63	64	64	65	177
14–10	59	59	60	60	61	61	62	62	63	64	64	65	178
14–11	59	59	60	60	61	61	62	62	63	63	64	65	179
15–00	58	59	59	60	60	61	61	62	63	63	64	64	180
15–01	58	58	59	59	60	60	61	61	62	62	63	64	181
15–02	57	58	59	59	60	60	61	61	62	62	63	63	182
15–03	57	57	58	58	59	60	60	61	61	62	62	63	183
15–04	56	57	57	58	58	59	59	60	60	61	62	62	184
15–05	56	57	57	58	58	59	59	60	60	61	61	62	185
15–06	55	56	57	57	58	58	59	59	60	60	61	61	186
15–07	55	55	56	56	57	57	58	59	59	60	60	61	187
15–08	55	55	56	56	57	57	58	58	59	59	60	60	188
15–09	54	55	55	56	56	57	57	58	58	59	59	60	189
15–10	53	54	54	55	56	56	57	57	58	58	59	59	190
15–11	53	54	54	55	55	56	56	57	57	58	58	59	191
	96	97	98	99	100	101	102	103	104	105	106	107	TOTAL MONTHS

CHRONOLOGICAL AGE

MENTAL AGE

YEARS MONTHS	8 0	8 1	8 2	8 3	8 4	8 5	8 6	8 7	8 8	8 9	8 10	8 11	
16–00 16–02	52	53	53	54	55	55	56	56	57	57	58	58	192 194
16–03 16–07	51	52	52	53	54	54	55	55	56	56	57	57	195 199
16–08 17–00	50	51	51	52	53	53	54	54	55	55	56	56	200 204
17–01 17–05	49	50	50	51	52	52	53	53	54	54	55	55	205 209
17–06 17–10	48	49	49	50	51	51	52	52	53	53	54	54	210 214
17–11 18–00	48	49	49	50	51	51	52	52	53	53	54	54	215 216
	96	97	98	99	100	101	102	103	104	105	106	107	TOTAL MONTHS

CHRONOLOGICAL AGE

MA 8–0 / CA 16–0

YEARS MONTHS	9 0	9 1	9 2	9 3	9 4	9 5	9 6	9 7	9 8	9 9	9 10	9 11	
4–00													48
4–01													49
4–02													50
4–03													51
4–04													52
4–05													53
4–06													54
4–07													55
4–08													56
4–09													57
4–10													58
4–11													59
5–00													60
5–01													61
5–02													62
5–03													63
5–04													64
5–05													65
5–06													66
5–07	169	170											67
5–08	166	168	169										68
5–09	163	165	167	168	170								69
5–10	161	162	164	166	167	169	170						70
5–11	158	160	162	163	165	166	168	169					71
6–00	156	158	159	161	162	164	165	167	168	170			72
6–01	153	155	156	158	159	161	162	164	166	167	169	170	73
6–02	151	152	154	155	157	158	160	161	163	164	166	167	74
6–03	149	150	151	153	154	156	157	159	160	162	163	165	75
6–04	146	148	149	151	152	153	155	156	158	159	161	162	76
6–05	144	145	147	148	150	151	152	154	155	157	158	160	77
6–06	142	143	144	146	147	149	150	151	153	154	156	157	78
6–07	140	141	142	144	145	146	148	149	151	152	153	155	79
6–08	137	139	140	141	143	144	146	147	148	150	151	152	80
6–09	135	137	138	139	141	142	143	145	146	147	149	150	81
6–10	134	135	136	137	139	140	141	143	144	145	147	148	82
6–11	132	133	134	135	137	138	139	141	142	143	144	146	83
TOTAL MONTHS	108	109	110	111	112	113	114	115	116	117	118	119	

CHRONOLOGICAL AGE

MA 9–0 / CA 4–0

CHRONOLOGICAL AGE — YEARS MONTHS	9-0	9-1	9-2	9-3	9-4	9-5	9-6	9-7	9-8	9-9	9-10	9-11	
7-00	130	131	132	134	135	136	137	139	140	141	142	144	84
7-01	128	129	130	132	133	134	135	137	138	139	140	142	85
7-02	126	127	129	130	131	132	133	135	136	137	138	140	86
7-03	124	126	127	128	129	130	132	133	134	135	137	138	87
7-04	123	124	125	126	127	129	130	131	132	133	135	136	88
7-05	121	122	123	125	126	127	128	129	130	132	133	134	89
7-06	119	121	122	123	124	125	126	128	129	130	131	132	90
7-07	118	119	120	121	122	124	125	126	127	128	129	130	91
7-08	116	118	119	120	121	122	123	124	125	127	128	129	92
7-09	115	116	117	118	119	120	122	123	124	125	126	127	93
7-10	113	115	116	117	118	119	120	121	122	123	124	125	94
7-11	112	113	114	115	116	117	119	120	121	122	123	124	95
8-00	111	112	113	114	115	116	117	118	119	120	121	122	96
8-01	110	111	112	113	114	115	116	117	118	119	120	121	97
8-02	108	109	110	111	112	113	114	115	117	118	119	120	98
8-03	107	108	109	110	111	112	113	114	115	116	117	118	99
8-04	106	107	108	109	110	111	112	113	114	115	116	117	100
8-05	105	106	107	108	109	110	111	112	113	114	115	116	101
8-06	104	105	106	107	108	109	110	110	111	112	113	114	102
8-07	102	103	104	105	106	107	108	109	110	111	112	113	103
8-08	101	102	103	104	105	106	107	108	109	110	111	112	104
8-09	100	101	102	103	104	105	106	107	108	109	110	111	105
8-10	99	100	101	102	103	104	105	106	107	108	109	110	106
8-11	98	99	100	101	102	103	104	105	106	107	108	109	107
9-00	97	98	99	100	101	102	103	104	105	106	106	107	108
9-01	97	97	98	99	100	101	102	103	104	105	105	106	109
9-02	96	96	97	98	99	100	101	102	103	104	104	105	110
9-03	95	96	96	97	98	99	100	101	102	103	103	104	111
9-04	94	95	96	96	97	98	99	100	101	102	103	103	112
9-05	93	94	95	96	96	97	98	99	100	101	102	102	113
9-06	92	93	94	95	96	97	97	98	99	100	101	102	114
9-07	91	92	93	94	95	96	96	97	98	99	100	101	115
9-08	91	91	92	93	94	95	96	96	97	98	99	100	116
9-09	90	91	92	92	93	94	95	96	96	97	98	99	117
9-10	89	90	91	92	92	93	94	95	96	96	97	98	118
9-11	88	89	90	91	92	92	93	94	95	96	96	97	119
TOTAL MONTHS	108	109	110	111	112	113	114	115	116	117	118	119	

MA 9-0 / CA 7-0

YEARS MONTHS	9 0	9 1	9 2	9 3	9 4	9 5	9 6	9 7	9 8	9 9	9 10	9 11	
10–00	88	89	89	90	91	92	92	93	94	95	96	96	120
10–01	87	88	89	90	90	91	92	93	93	94	95	96	121
10–02	87	87	88	89	90	90	91	92	93	93	94	95	122
10–03	86	87	88	88	89	90	91	91	92	93	94	94	123
10–04	86	86	87	88	89	89	90	91	92	92	93	94	124
10–05	85	86	86	87	88	89	89	90	91	92	92	93	125
10–06	84	85	86	87	87	88	89	90	90	91	92	92	126
10–07	84	85	85	86	87	88	88	89	90	90	91	92	127
10–08	83	84	85	86	86	87	88	88	89	90	91	91	128
10–09	83	84	84	85	86	86	87	88	89	89	90	91	129
10–10	83	83	84	85	85	86	87	87	88	89	90	90	130
10–11	82	83	83	84	85	85	86	87	88	88	89	90	131
11–00	82	82	83	84	84	85	86	86	87	88	88	89	132
11–01	81	82	82	83	84	84	85	86	86	87	88	89	133
11–02	81	81	82	83	83	84	85	85	86	87	87	88	134
11–03	80	81	82	82	83	84	84	85	86	86	87	88	135
11–04	80	80	81	82	82	83	84	84	85	86	86	87	136
11–05	79	80	81	81	82	83	83	84	85	85	86	86	137
11–06	79	80	80	81	81	82	83	83	84	85	85	86	138
11–07	79	79	80	80	81	82	82	83	84	84	85	86	139
11–08	78	79	79	80	81	81	82	83	83	84	84	85	140
11–09	78	78	79	80	80	81	81	82	83	83	84	85	141
11–10	77	78	79	79	80	80	81	82	82	83	84	84	142
11–11	77	78	78	79	79	80	81	81	82	83	83	84	143
12–00	77	77	78	78	79	80	80	81	81	82	83	83	144
12–01	76	77	77	78	79	79	80	80	81	82	82	83	145
12–02	76	76	77	78	78	79	79	80	81	81	82	82	146
12–03	75	76	77	77	78	78	79	80	80	81	81	82	147
12–04	75	75	76	77	77	78	78	79	80	80	81	81	148
12–05	74	75	76	76	77	77	78	79	79	80	80	81	149
12–06	74	75	75	76	76	77	78	78	79	79	80	81	150
12–07	74	74	75	76	76	77	77	78	78	79	80	80	151
12–08	73	74	74	75	76	76	77	77	78	79	79	80	152
12–09	73	73	74	75	75	76	76	77	78	78	79	79	153
12–10	73	73	74	74	75	75	76	77	77	78	78	79	154
12–11	72	73	73	74	75	75	76	76	77	77	78	79	155
	108	109	110	111	112	113	114	115	116	117	118	119	TOTAL MONTHS

CHRONOLOGICAL AGE

MA 9–0 / CA 10–0

160

CHRONOLOGICAL AGE	YEARS → MONTHS ↓	9-0	9-1	9-2	9-3	9-4	9-5	9-6	9-7	9-8	9-9	9-10	9-11	TOTAL MONTHS
	13-00	72	72	73	74	74	75	75	76	76	77	78	78	156
	13-01	71	72	73	73	74	74	75	75	76	77	77	78	157
	13-02	71	72	73	73	74	74	75	75	76	76	77	78	158
	13-03	71	71	72	73	73	74	74	75	75	76	76	77	159
	13-04	70	71	72	72	73	73	74	74	75	75	76	77	160
	13-05	70	71	72	72	73	73	74	74	75	75	76	77	161
	13-06	70	70	71	72	72	73	73	74	74	75	75	76	162
	13-07	69	70	71	71	72	72	73	73	74	74	75	76	163
	13-08	69	70	71	71	72	72	73	73	74	74	75	76	164
	13-09	69	70	70	71	71	72	72	73	73	74	75	75	165
	13-10	69	69	70	70	71	71	72	72	73	74	74	75	166
	13-11	68	69	70	70	71	71	72	72	73	73	74	75	167
	14-00	68	69	69	70	70	71	71	72	72	73	74	74	168
	14-01	68	68	69	69	70	70	71	72	72	73	73	74	169
	14-02	68	68	69	69	70	70	71	71	72	73	73	74	170
	14-03	67	68	68	69	69	70	70	71	72	72	73	73	171
	14-04	67	67	68	68	69	70	70	71	71	72	72	73	172
	14-05	67	67	68	68	69	69	70	71	71	72	72	73	173
	14-06	66	67	67	68	69	69	70	70	71	71	72	72	174
	14-07	66	67	67	68	68	69	69	70	70	71	71	72	175
	14-08	66	66	67	68	68	69	69	70	70	71	71	72	176
	14-09	66	66	67	67	68	68	69	69	70	70	71	71	177
	14-10	65	66	66	67	67	68	68	69	69	70	70	71	178
	14-11	65	66	66	67	67	68	68	69	69	70	70	71	179
	15-00	65	65	66	66	67	67	68	68	69	69	70	71	180
	15-01	64	65	65	66	66	67	67	68	68	69	69	70	181
	15-02	64	64	65	65	66	67	67	68	68	69	69	70	182
	15-03	63	64	64	65	65	66	66	67	68	68	69	69	183
	15-04	63	63	64	64	65	65	66	66	67	67	68	68	184
	15-05	62	63	64	64	65	65	66	66	67	67	68	68	185
	15-06	62	62	63	63	64	64	65	66	66	67	67	68	186
	15-07	61	62	62	63	63	64	64	65	65	66	66	67	187
	15-08	61	62	62	63	63	64	64	65	65	66	66	67	188
	15-09	60	61	61	62	62	63	64	64	65	65	66	66	189
	15-10	60	60	61	61	62	62	63	63	64	64	65	66	190
	15-11	60	60	61	61	62	62	63	63	64	64	65	65	191
	TOTAL MONTHS	108	109	110	111	112	113	114	115	116	117	118	119	

MA 9-0 / CA 13-0

MENTAL AGE

YEARS MONTHS	9 0	9 1	9 2	9 3	9 4	9 5	9 6	9 7	9 8	9 9	9 10	9 11	
16–00 / 16–02	59	59	60	60	61	62	62	63	63	64	64	65	192 / 194
16–03 / 16–07	58	59	59	60	60	61	61	62	62	63	64	64	195 / 199
16–08 / 17–00	57	58	58	59	59	60	60	61	61	62	63	63	200 / 204
17–01 / 17–05	56	57	57	58	58	59	59	60	60	61	62	62	205 / 209
17–06 / 17–10	55	56	56	57	57	58	58	59	59	60	61	61	210 / 214
17–11 / 18–00	55	56	56	57	57	58	58	59	59	60	61	61	215 / 216
TOTAL MONTHS	108	109	110	111	112	113	114	115	116	117	118	119	

CHRONOLOGICAL AGE

MENTAL AGE

YEARS / MONTHS	10-0	10-1	10-2	10-3	10-4	10-5	10-6	10-7	10-8	10-9	10-10	10-11	TOTAL MONTHS
5–00													60
5–01													61
5–02													62
5–03													63
5–04													64
5–05													65
5–06													66
5–07													67
5–08													68
5–09													69
5–10													70
5–11													71
6–00													72
6–01													73
6–02	169	170											74
6–03	166	168	169	171									75
6–04	164	165	166	168	169								76
6–05	161	162	164	165	167	168	170						77
6–06	158	160	161	163	164	165	167	168	170				78
6–07	156	157	159	160	162	163	164	166	167	168	170		79
6–08	154	155	156	158	159	160	162	163	164	166	167	169	80
6–09	151	153	154	155	157	158	159	161	162	163	165	166	81
6–10	149	151	152	153	155	156	157	158	160	161	162	164	82
6–11	147	148	150	151	152	154	155	156	157	159	160	161	83
7–00	145	146	148	149	150	151	153	154	155	156	158	159	84
7–01	143	144	145	147	148	149	150	152	153	154	155	157	85
7–02	141	142	143	145	146	147	148	150	151	152	153	154	86
7–03	139	140	141	143	144	145	146	147	149	150	151	152	87
7–04	137	138	139	141	142	143	144	145	147	148	149	150	88
7–05	135	136	138	139	140	141	142	143	145	146	147	148	89
7–06	133	135	136	137	138	139	140	141	143	144	145	146	90
7–07	132	133	134	135	136	137	138	140	141	142	143	144	91
7–08	130	131	132	133	134	136	137	138	139	140	141	142	92
7–09	128	129	130	132	133	134	135	136	137	138	139	140	93
7–10	127	128	129	130	131	132	133	134	135	136	137	139	94
7–11	125	126	127	128	129	130	131	133	134	135	136	137	95
TOTAL MONTHS	120	121	122	123	124	125	126	127	128	129	130	131	

CHRONOLOGICAL AGE

MA 10–0 / CA 5–0

YEARS / MONTHS	10 0	10 1	10 2	10 3	10 4	10 5	10 6	10 7	10 8	10 9	10 10	10 11	TOTAL MONTHS
8–00	123	125	126	127	128	129	130	131	132	133	134	135	96
8–01	122	123	124	125	126	127	128	129	130	131	133	134	97
8–02	121	122	123	124	125	126	127	128	129	130	131	132	98
8–03	119	120	121	122	123	124	125	126	127	128	129	130	99
8–04	118	119	120	121	122	123	124	125	126	127	128	129	100
8–05	117	118	119	120	121	122	123	124	125	126	127	128	101
8–06	115	116	117	118	119	120	121	122	123	124	125	126	102
8–07	114	115	116	117	118	119	120	121	122	123	124	125	103
8–08	113	114	115	116	117	118	119	120	120	121	122	123	104
8–09	112	113	114	115	115	116	117	118	119	120	121	122	105
8–10	111	111	112	113	114	115	116	117	118	119	120	121	106
8–11	109	110	111	112	113	114	115	116	117	118	119	120	107
9–00	108	109	110	111	112	113	114	115	116	116	117	118	108
9–01	107	108	109	110	111	112	113	114	114	115	116	117	109
9–02	106	107	108	109	110	111	112	112	113	114	115	116	110
9–03	105	106	107	108	109	110	110	111	112	113	114	115	111
9–04	104	105	106	107	108	109	109	110	111	112	113	114	112
9–05	103	104	105	106	107	108	108	109	110	111	112	113	113
9–06	102	103	104	105	106	107	107	108	109	110	111	112	114
9–07	101	102	103	104	105	106	106	107	108	109	110	111	115
9–08	101	101	102	103	104	105	106	106	107	108	109	110	116
9–09	100	101	101	102	103	104	105	105	106	107	108	109	117
9–10	99	100	100	101	102	103	104	104	105	106	107	108	118
9–11	98	99	100	100	101	102	103	104	104	105	106	107	119
10–00	97	98	99	100	100	101	102	103	104	104	105	106	120
10–01	97	97	98	99	100	100	101	102	103	104	104	105	121
10–02	96	97	97	98	99	100	100	101	102	103	103	104	122
10–03	95	96	97	97	98	99	100	100	101	102	103	104	123
10–04	95	95	96	97	98	98	99	100	101	101	102	103	124
10–05	94	95	95	96	97	98	98	99	100	101	101	102	125
10–06	93	94	95	95	96	97	98	98	99	100	101	101	126
10–07	93	93	94	95	96	96	97	98	98	99	100	101	127
10–08	92	93	93	94	95	96	96	97	98	98	99	100	128
10–09	91	92	93	94	94	95	96	96	97	98	99	99	129
10–10	91	92	92	93	94	94	95	96	97	97	98	99	130
10–11	90	91	92	92	93	94	94	95	96	97	97	98	131
TOTAL MONTHS	120	121	122	123	124	125	126	127	128	129	130	131	

CHRONOLOGICAL AGE

MA 10–0 / CA 8–0

YEARS MONTHS	10 0	10 1	10 2	10 3	10 4	10 5	10 6	10 7	10 8	10 9	10 10	10 11	
11–00	90	91	91	92	93	93	94	95	95	96	97	97	132
11–01	89	90	91	91	92	93	93	94	95	95	96	97	133
11–02	89	89	90	91	91	92	93	93	94	95	95	96	134
11–03	88	89	90	90	91	92	92	93	94	94	95	96	135
11–04	88	88	89	90	90	91	92	92	93	94	94	95	136
11–05	87	88	88	89	90	90	91	92	92	93	94	94	137
11–06	87	87	88	89	89	90	91	91	92	93	93	94	138
11–07	86	87	88	88	89	89	90	91	91	92	93	93	139
11–08	86	86	87	88	88	89	90	90	91	91	92	93	140
11–09	85	86	86	87	88	88	89	90	90	91	92	92	141
11–10	85	85	86	87	87	88	89	89	90	90	91	92	142
11–11	84	85	86	86	87	87	88	89	89	90	91	91	143
12–00	84	85	85	86	86	87	88	88	89	89	90	91	144
12–01	83	84	85	85	86	86	87	88	88	89	89	90	145
12–02	83	84	84	85	85	86	87	87	88	88	89	90	146
12–03	83	83	84	84	85	86	86	87	87	88	89	89	147
12–04	82	83	83	84	84	85	86	86	87	87	88	89	148
12–05	82	82	83	83	84	85	85	86	86	87	88	88	149
12–06	81	82	82	83	84	84	85	85	86	86	87	88	150
12–07	81	81	82	83	83	84	84	85	85	86	87	87	151
12–08	80	81	81	82	83	83	84	84	85	86	86	87	152
12–09	80	80	81	82	82	83	83	84	84	85	86	86	153
12–10	79	80	81	81	82	82	83	84	84	85	85	86	154
12–11	79	80	80	81	81	82	83	83	84	84	85	85	155
13–00	79	79	80	80	81	82	82	83	83	84	84	85	156
13–01	78	79	79	80	80	81	82	82	83	83	84	84	157
13–02	78	79	79	80	80	81	82	82	83	83	84	84	158
13–03	78	78	79	79	80	80	81	82	82	83	83	84	159
13–04	77	78	78	79	79	80	81	81	82	82	83	83	160
13–05	77	78	78	79	79	80	81	81	82	82	83	83	161
13–06	77	77	78	78	79	79	80	81	81	82	82	83	162
13–07	76	77	77	78	78	79	79	80	81	81	82	82	163
13–08	76	77	77	78	78	79	79	80	81	81	82	82	164
13–09	76	76	77	77	78	78	79	80	80	81	81	82	165
13–10	75	76	76	77	77	78	79	79	80	80	81	81	166
13–11	75	76	76	77	77	78	78	79	80	80	81	81	167
TOTAL MONTHS	120	121	122	123	124	125	126	127	128	129	130	131	

CHRONOLOGICAL AGE

MA 10–0 / CA 11–0

YEARS MONTHS	10 0	10 1	10 2	10 3	10 4	10 5	10 6	10 7	10 8	10 9	10 10	10 11	TOTAL MONTHS
14–00	75	75	76	76	77	77	78	79	79	80	80	81	168
14–01	74	75	75	76	76	77	78	78	79	79	80	80	169
14–02	74	75	75	76	76	77	77	78	79	79	80	80	170
14–03	74	74	75	75	76	76	77	78	78	79	79	80	171
14–04	73	74	74	75	76	76	77	77	78	78	79	79	172
14–05	73	74	74	75	75	76	77	77	78	78	79	79	173
14–06	73	73	74	74	75	76	76	77	77	78	78	79	174
14–07	72	73	74	74	75	75	76	76	77	77	78	78	175
14–08	72	73	73	74	75	75	76	76	77	77	78	78	176
14–09	72	73	73	74	74	75	75	76	76	77	77	78	177
14–10	72	72	73	73	74	74	75	75	76	76	77	77	178
14–11	72	72	73	73	74	74	75	75	76	76	77	77	179
15–00	71	72	72	73	73	74	74	75	75	76	76	77	180
15–01	70	71	72	72	73	73	74	74	75	75	76	76	181
15–02	70	71	71	72	72	73	73	74	75	75	76	76	182
15–03	70	70	71	71	72	72	73	73	74	74	75	75	183
15–04	69	70	70	71	71	72	72	73	73	74	74	75	184
15–05	69	69	70	70	71	71	72	73	73	74	74	75	185
15–06	68	69	69	70	70	71	71	72	72	73	73	74	186
15–07	68	68	69	69	70	70	71	71	72	72	73	73	187
15–08	67	68	68	69	69	70	71	71	72	72	73	73	188
15–09	67	67	68	68	69	69	70	70	71	71	72	73	189
15–10	66	67	67	68	68	69	69	70	70	71	71	72	190
15–11	66	66	67	67	68	69	69	70	70	71	71	72	191
16–00 / 16–02	65	66	66	67	67	68	68	69	69	70	71	71	192 / 194
16–03 / 16–07	65	65	66	66	67	67	68	69	69	70	70	71	195 / 199
16–08 / 17–00	64	64	65	65	66	66	67	68	68	69	69	70	200 / 204
17–01 / 17–05	63	63	64	64	65	65	66	67	67	68	68	69	205 / 209
17–06 / 17–10	62	62	63	63	64	64	65	66	66	67	67	68	210 / 214
17–11 / 18–00	62	62	63	63	64	64	65	66	66	67	67	68	215 / 216
TOTAL MONTHS	120	121	122	123	124	125	126	127	128	129	130	131	

CHRONOLOGICAL AGE

YEARS MONTHS	11 0	11 1	11 2	11 3	11 4	11 5	11 6	11 7	11 8	11 9	11 10	11 11	
5–00													60
5–01													61
5–02													62
5–03													63
5–04													64
5–05													65
5–06													66
5–07													67
5–08													68
5–09													69
5–10													70
5–11													71
6–00													72
6–01													73
6–02													74
6–03													75
6–04													76
6–05													77
6–06													78
6–07													79
6–08	170												80
6–09	167	169	170										81
6–10	165	166	168	169	170								82
6–11	163	164	165	166	168	169	170						83
7–00	160	161	163	164	165	167	168	169	170				84
7–01	158	159	160	162	163	164	165	167	168	169	170		85
7–02	156	157	158	159	161	162	163	164	166	167	168	169	86
7–03	154	155	156	157	158	160	161	162	163	164	166	167	87
7–04	151	153	154	155	156	157	158	160	161	162	163	164	88
7–05	149	150	152	153	154	155	156	157	159	160	161	162	89
7–06	147	148	150	151	152	153	154	155	157	158	159	160	90
7–07	145	146	148	149	150	151	152	153	154	156	157	158	91
7–08	143	145	146	147	148	149	150	151	152	154	155	156	92
7–09	141	143	144	145	146	147	148	149	150	151	153	154	93
7–10	140	141	142	143	144	145	146	147	148	150	151	152	94
7–11	138	139	140	141	142	143	144	145	147	148	149	150	95
	132	133	134	135	136	137	138	139	140	141	142	143	TOTAL MONTHS

CHRONOLOGICAL AGE

MA 11–0 / CA 5–0

YEARS MONTHS	11 0	11 1	11 2	11 3	11 4	11 5	11 6	11 7	11 8	11 9	11 10	11 11	
8–00	136	137	138	139	140	141	143	144	145	146	147	148	96
8–01	135	136	137	138	139	140	141	142	143	144	145	146	97
8–02	133	134	135	136	137	138	139	140	141	142	143	144	98
8–03	131	132	133	135	136	137	138	139	140	141	142	143	99
8–04	130	131	132	133	134	135	136	137	138	139	140	141	100
8–05	129	130	131	132	132	133	134	135	136	137	138	139	101
8–06	127	128	129	130	131	132	133	134	135	136	137	138	102
8–07	126	127	128	129	130	131	132	133	133	134	135	136	103
8–08	124	125	126	127	128	129	130	131	132	133	134	135	104
8–09	123	124	125	126	127	128	129	130	131	132	132	133	105
8–10	122	123	124	125	125	126	127	128	129	130	131	132	106
8–11	120	121	122	123	124	125	126	127	128	129	130	131	107
9–00	119	120	121	122	123	124	125	126	126	127	128	129	108
9–01	118	119	120	121	122	123	123	124	125	126	127	128	109
9–02	117	118	119	119	120	121	122	123	124	125	126	127	110
9–03	116	117	117	118	119	120	121	122	123	124	124	125	111
9–04	115	116	116	117	118	119	120	121	122	122	123	124	112
9–05	114	114	115	116	117	118	119	120	120	121	122	123	113
9–06	113	113	114	115	116	117	118	118	119	120	121	122	114
9–07	111	112	113	114	115	116	116	117	118	119	120	121	115
9–08	110	111	112	113	114	115	115	116	117	118	119	120	116
9–09	110	110	111	112	113	114	114	115	116	117	118	118	117
9–10	108	109	110	111	112	113	113	114	115	116	117	117	118
9–11	108	108	109	110	111	112	112	113	114	115	116	116	119
10–00	107	107	108	109	110	111	111	112	113	114	115	115	120
10–01	106	107	107	108	109	110	111	111	112	113	114	114	121
10–02	105	106	107	107	108	109	110	110	111	112	113	113	122
10–03	104	105	106	107	107	108	109	110	110	111	112	113	123
10–04	104	104	105	106	107	107	108	109	110	110	111	112	124
10–05	103	103	104	105	106	106	107	108	109	109	110	111	125
10–06	102	103	104	104	105	106	106	107	108	109	109	110	126
10–07	101	102	103	104	104	105	106	106	107	108	109	109	127
10–08	101	101	102	103	103	104	105	106	106	107	108	109	128
10–09	100	101	101	102	103	104	104	105	106	106	107	108	129
10–10	99	100	101	101	102	103	104	104	105	106	106	107	130
10–11	99	99	100	101	101	102	103	104	104	105	106	106	131
	132	133	134	135	136	137	138	139	140	141	142	143	TOTAL MONTHS

CHRONOLOGICAL AGE

CHRONOLOGICAL AGE — YEARS MONTHS	11-0	11-1	11-2	11-3	11-4	11-5	11-6	11-7	11-8	11-9	11-10	11-11	TOTAL MONTHS
11–00	98	99	99	100	101	101	102	103	104	104	105	106	132
11–01	97	98	99	99	100	101	101	102	103	103	104	105	133
11–02	97	97	98	99	99	100	101	102	102	103	104	104	134
11–03	96	97	98	98	99	100	100	101	102	102	103	104	135
11–04	96	96	97	98	98	99	100	100	101	102	102	103	136
11–05	95	96	96	97	98	98	99	100	100	101	102	102	137
11–06	94	95	96	96	97	98	98	99	100	100	101	102	138
11–07	94	95	95	96	97	97	98	98	99	100	100	101	139
11–08	93	94	95	95	96	97	97	98	98	99	100	100	140
11–09	93	93	94	95	95	96	97	97	98	98	99	100	141
11–10	92	93	94	94	95	95	96	97	97	98	99	99	142
11–11	92	92	93	94	94	95	96	96	97	97	98	99	143
12–00	91	92	92	93	94	94	95	96	96	97	97	98	144
12–01	91	91	92	93	93	94	94	95	96	96	97	97	145
12–02	90	91	91	92	93	93	94	94	95	96	96	97	146
12–03	90	90	91	92	92	93	93	94	95	95	96	96	147
12–04	89	90	90	91	92	92	93	93	94	95	95	96	148
12–05	89	89	90	90	91	92	92	93	93	94	95	95	149
12–06	88	89	89	90	91	91	92	92	93	94	94	95	150
12–07	88	88	89	90	90	91	91	92	93	93	94	94	151
12–08	87	88	88	89	90	90	91	91	92	93	93	94	152
12–09	87	87	88	89	89	90	90	91	91	92	93	93	153
12–10	86	87	88	88	89	89	90	90	91	92	92	93	154
12–11	86	87	87	88	88	89	89	90	91	91	92	92	155
13–00	85	86	87	87	88	88	89	89	90	91	91	92	156
13–01	85	86	86	87	87	88	88	89	90	90	91	91	157
13–02	85	86	86	87	87	88	88	89	90	90	91	91	158
13–03	84	85	86	86	87	87	88	88	89	89	90	91	159
13–04	84	84	85	86	86	87	87	88	88	89	90	90	160
13–05	84	84	85	86	86	87	87	88	88	89	90	90	161
13–06	83	84	84	85	86	86	87	87	88	88	89	89	162
13–07	83	83	84	85	85	86	86	87	87	88	88	89	163
13–08	83	83	84	84	85	86	86	87	87	88	88	89	164
13–09	82	83	83	84	85	85	86	86	87	87	88	88	165
13–10	82	82	83	84	84	85	85	86	86	87	87	88	166
13–11	82	82	83	83	84	84	85	86	86	87	87	88	167
TOTAL MONTHS	132	133	134	135	136	137	138	139	140	141	142	143	

MA 11–0 / CA 11–0

YEARS	11	11	11	11	11	11	11	11	11	11	11	11	
MONTHS	0	1	2	3	4	5	6	7	8	9	10	11	
14–00	81	82	82	83	83	84	85	85	86	86	87	87	168
14–01	81	81	82	82	83	84	84	85	85	86	86	87	169
14–02	81	81	82	82	83	84	84	85	85	86	86	87	170
14–03	80	81	81	82	82	83	84	84	85	85	86	86	171
14–04	80	80	81	81	82	83	83	84	84	85	85	86	172
14–05	80	80	81	81	82	83	83	84	84	85	85	86	173
14–06	79	80	80	81	82	82	83	83	84	84	85	85	174
14–07	79	79	80	81	81	82	82	83	83	84	84	85	175
14–08	79	79	80	80	81	82	82	83	83	84	84	85	176
14–09	78	79	80	80	81	81	82	82	83	83	84	84	177
14–10	78	79	79	80	80	81	81	82	82	83	83	84	178
14–11	78	78	79	80	80	81	81	82	82	83	83	84	179
15–00	78	78	79	79	80	80	81	81	82	82	83	83	180
15–01	77	77	78	78	79	80	80	81	81	82	82	83	181
15–02	77	77	78	78	79	79	80	80	81	81	82	83	182
15–03	76	77	77	78	78	79	79	80	80	81	81	82	183
15–04	75	76	76	77	77	78	79	79	80	80	81	81	184
15–05	75	76	76	77	77	78	78	79	79	80	81	81	185
15–06	75	75	76	76	77	77	78	78	79	79	80	80	186
15–07	74	74	75	75	76	77	77	78	78	79	79	80	187
15–08	74	74	75	75	76	76	77	77	78	79	79	80	188
15–09	73	74	74	75	75	76	76	77	77	78	78	79	189
15–10	72	73	73	74	75	75	76	76	77	77	78	78	190
15–11	72	73	73	74	74	75	75	76	76	77	78	78	191
16–00 } 16–02 }	72	72	73	73	74	74	75	75	76	76	77	77	{ 192 { 194
16–03 } 16–07 }	71	72	72	73	73	74	74	75	75	76	76	77	{ 195 { 199
16–08 } 17–00 }	70	71	71	72	73	73	74	74	75	75	76	76	{ 200 { 204
17–01 } 17–05 }	69	70	70	71	72	72	73	73	74	74	75	75	{ 205 { 209
17–06 } 17–10 }	68	69	69	70	71	71	72	72	73	73	74	74	{ 210 { 214
17–11 } 18–00 }	68	69	69	70	71	71	72	72	73	73	74	74	{ 215 { 216
TOTAL MONTHS	132	133	134	135	136	137	138	139	140	141	142	143	

CHRONOLOGICAL AGE

CHRONOLOGICAL AGE YEARS / MONTHS	12 0	12 1	12 2	12 3	12 4	12 5	12 6	12 7	12 8	12 9	12 10	12 11	TOTAL MONTHS
7–00													84
7–01													85
7–02	170												86
7–03	168	169	170										87
7–04	166	167	168	169	170								88
7–05	163	165	166	167	168	169	170						89
7–06	161	162	163	165	166	167	168	169	170				90
7–07	159	160	161	162	164	165	166	167	168	169	170		91
7–08	157	158	159	160	161	163	164	165	166	167	168	169	92
7–09	155	156	157	158	159	160	161	163	164	165	166	167	93
7–10	153	154	155	156	157	158	159	160	162	163	164	165	94
7–11	151	152	153	154	155	156	157	158	159	161	162	163	95
8–00	149	150	151	152	153	154	155	156	157	158	160	161	96
8–01	147	148	149	150	151	152	153	155	156	157	158	159	97
8–02	145	146	147	149	150	151	152	153	154	155	156	157	98
8–03	144	145	146	147	148	149	150	151	152	153	154	155	99
8–04	142	143	144	145	146	147	148	149	150	151	152	153	100
8–05	140	141	142	143	144	145	146	147	148	149	150	151	101
8–06	139	140	141	142	143	144	145	146	147	148	149	150	102
8–07	137	138	139	140	141	142	143	144	145	146	147	148	103
8–08	136	137	138	139	140	141	142	142	143	144	145	146	104
8–09	134	135	136	137	138	139	140	141	142	143	144	145	105
8–10	133	134	135	136	137	138	138	139	140	141	142	143	106
8–11	132	132	133	134	135	136	137	138	139	140	141	142	107
9–00	130	131	132	133	134	135	136	136	137	138	139	140	108
9–01	129	130	131	132	132	133	134	135	136	137	138	139	109
9–02	127	128	129	130	131	132	133	134	135	135	136	137	110
9–03	126	127	128	129	130	131	132	132	133	134	135	136	111
9–04	125	126	127	128	129	129	130	131	132	133	134	135	112
9–05	124	125	126	126	127	128	129	130	131	132	132	133	113
9–06	123	124	124	125	126	127	128	129	129	130	131	132	114
9–07	121	122	123	124	125	126	126	127	128	129	130	131	115
9–08	120	121	122	123	124	124	125	126	127	128	129	129	116
9–09	119	120	121	122	123	123	124	125	126	127	127	128	117
9–10	118	119	120	121	121	122	123	124	125	125	126	127	118
9–11	117	118	119	120	120	121	122	123	123	124	125	126	119
TOTAL MONTHS	144	145	146	147	148	149	150	151	152	153	154	155	

171

MA 12–0 / CA 7–0

MENTAL AGE

YEARS MONTHS	12 0	12 1	12 2	12 3	12 4	12 5	12 6	12 7	12 8	12 9	12 10	12 11	
10–00	116	117	118	118	119	120	121	122	122	123	124	125	120
10–01	115	116	117	118	118	119	120	121	121	122	123	124	121
10–02	114	115	116	117	117	118	119	120	120	121	122	123	122
10–03	113	114	115	116	116	117	118	119	119	120	121	122	123
10–04	113	113	114	115	116	116	117	118	119	119	120	121	124
10–05	112	112	113	114	115	115	116	117	118	118	119	120	125
10–06	111	112	112	113	114	115	115	116	117	117	118	119	126
10–07	110	111	112	112	113	114	114	115	116	117	117	118	127
10–08	109	110	111	111	112	113	114	114	115	116	116	117	128
10–09	108	109	110	111	111	112	113	113	114	115	116	116	129
10–10	108	108	109	110	111	111	112	113	113	114	115	115	130
10–11	107	108	108	109	110	110	111	112	113	113	114	115	131
11–00	106	107	108	108	109	110	110	111	112	112	113	114	132
11–01	106	106	107	108	108	109	110	110	111	112	112	113	133
11–02	105	106	106	107	108	108	109	110	110	111	112	112	134
11–03	104	105	106	106	107	108	108	109	110	110	111	112	135
11–04	104	104	105	106	106	107	108	108	109	109	110	111	136
11–05	103	103	104	105	105	106	107	107	108	109	109	110	137
11–06	102	103	104	104	105	105	106	107	107	108	109	109	138
11–07	102	102	103	104	104	105	106	106	107	107	108	109	139
11–08	101	102	102	103	104	104	105	105	106	107	107	108	140
11–09	100	101	102	102	103	103	104	105	105	106	107	107	141
11–10	100	100	101	102	102	103	104	104	105	105	106	107	142
11–11	99	100	100	101	102	102	103	104	104	105	105	106	143
12–00	99	99	100	100	101	102	102	103	104	104	105	105	144
12–01	98	99	99	100	100	101	102	102	103	104	104	105	145
12–02	98	98	99	99	100	101	101	102	102	103	104	104	146
12–03	97	98	98	99	99	100	101	101	102	102	103	104	147
12–04	96	97	98	98	99	99	100	101	101	102	102	103	148
12–05	96	96	97	98	98	99	99	100	101	101	102	102	149
12–06	95	96	97	97	98	98	99	99	100	101	101	102	150
12–07	95	95	96	97	97	98	98	99	100	100	101	101	151
12–08	94	95	95	96	97	97	98	98	99	100	100	101	152
12–09	94	94	95	95	96	97	97	98	98	99	100	100	153
12–10	93	94	94	95	96	96	97	97	98	98	99	100	154
12–11	93	93	94	95	95	96	96	97	97	98	99	99	155
	144	145	146	147	148	149	150	151	152	153	154	155	TOTAL MONTHS

CHRONOLOGICAL AGE

MA 12–0 / CA 10–0

CHRONOLOGICAL AGE

YEARS MONTHS	12 0	12 1	12 2	12 3	12 4	12 5	12 6	12 7	12 8	12 9	12 10	12 11	
13–00	92	93	93	94	95	95	96	96	97	97	98	99	156
13–01	92	92	93	93	94	95	95	96	96	97	97	98	157
13–02	92	92	93	93	94	95	95	96	96	97	97	98	158
13–03	91	92	92	93	93	94	95	95	96	96	97	97	159
13–04	91	91	92	92	93	93	94	95	95	96	96	97	160
13–05	91	91	92	92	93	93	94	95	95	96	96	97	161
13–06	90	91	91	92	92	93	93	94	95	95	96	96	162
13–07	90	90	91	91	92	92	93	93	94	95	95	96	163
13–08	90	90	91	91	92	92	93	93	94	95	95	96	164
13–09	89	90	90	91	91	92	92	93	93	94	95	95	165
13–10	88	89	90	90	91	91	92	92	93	93	94	95	166
13–11	88	89	89	90	91	91	92	92	93	93	94	94	167
14–00	88	88	89	90	90	91	91	92	92	93	93	94	168
14–01	87	88	88	89	90	90	91	91	92	92	93	93	169
14–02	87	88	88	89	90	90	91	91	92	92	93	93	170
14–03	87	87	88	88	89	90	90	91	91	92	92	93	171
14–04	86	87	87	88	89	89	90	90	91	91	92	92	172
14–05	86	87	87	88	89	89	90	90	91	91	92	92	173
14–06	86	86	87	87	88	89	89	90	90	91	91	92	174
14–07	85	86	86	87	88	88	89	89	90	90	91	91	175
14–08	85	86	86	87	88	88	89	89	90	90	91	91	176
14–09	85	85	86	86	87	88	88	89	89	90	90	91	177
14–10	84	85	85	86	87	87	88	88	89	89	90	90	178
14–11	84	85	85	86	87	87	88	88	89	89	90	90	179
15–00	84	84	85	86	86	87	87	88	88	89	89	90	180
15–01	83	84	84	85	85	86	86	87	87	88	89	89	181
15–02	83	84	84	85	85	86	86	87	87	88	88	89	182
15–03	82	83	83	84	85	85	86	86	87	87	88	88	183
15–04	82	82	83	83	84	84	85	85	86	87	87	88	184
15–05	82	82	83	83	84	84	85	85	86	86	87	87	185
15–06	81	81	82	83	83	84	84	85	85	86	86	87	186
15–07	80	81	81	82	82	83	83	84	84	85	86	86	187
15–08	80	81	81	82	82	83	83	84	84	85	85	86	188
15–09	79	80	80	81	82	82	83	83	84	84	85	85	189
15–10	79	79	80	80	81	81	82	82	83	83	84	85	190
15–11	79	79	80	80	81	81	82	82	83	83	84	84	191
	144	145	146	147	148	149	150	151	152	153	154	155	TOTAL MONTHS

MA 12–0 / CA 13–0

YEARS MONTHS	12 0	12 1	12 2	12 3	12 4	12 5	12 6	12 7	12 8	12 9	12 10	12 11	
16–00 ⎰ 16–02 ⎱	78	78	79	79	80	81	81	82	82	83	83	84	⎰ 192 ⎱ 194
16–03 ⎰ 16–07 ⎱	77	78	78	79	79	80	80	81	81	82	83	83	⎰ 195 ⎱ 199
16–08 ⎰ 17–00 ⎱	77	78	78	79	79	80	80	81	81	82	83	83	⎰ 200 ⎱ 204
17–01 ⎰ 17–05 ⎱	76	77	77	78	78	79	79	80	80	81	82	82	⎰ 205 ⎱ 209
17–06 ⎰ 17–10 ⎱	75	76	76	77	77	78	78	79	79	80	81	81	⎰ 210 ⎱ 214
17–11 ⎰ 18–00 ⎱	75	76	76	77	77	78	78	79	79	80	81	81	⎰ 215 ⎱ 216
	144	145	146	147	148	149	150	151	152	153	154	155	TOTAL MONTHS

CHRONOLOGICAL AGE

MENTAL AGE

YEARS MONTHS	13 0	13 1	13 2	13 3	13 4	13 5	13 6	13 7	13 8	13 9	13 10	13 11	
7–00													84
7–01													85
7–02													86
7–03													87
7–04													88
7–05													89
7–06													90
7–07													91
7–08	170												92
7–09	168	169	170										93
7–10	166	167	168	169	170								94
7–11	164	165	166	167	168	169	170						95
8–00	162	163	164	165	166	167	168	169	170				96
8–01	160	161	162	163	164	165	166	167	168	169	170		97
8–02	158	159	160	161	162	163	164	165	166	167	168	169	98
8–03	156	157	158	159	160	161	162	163	164	165	166	167	99
8–04	154	155	156	157	158	159	160	161	162	163	164	165	100
8–05	152	153	154	155	156	157	158	159	160	161	162	163	101
8–06	151	152	153	154	155	156	157	158	159	160	160	161	102
8–07	149	150	151	152	153	154	155	156	157	158	159	160	103
8–08	147	148	149	150	151	152	153	154	155	156	157	158	104
8–09	146	147	148	149	149	150	151	152	153	154	155	156	105
8–10	144	145	146	147	148	149	150	151	152	152	153	154	106
8–11	143	144	144	145	146	147	148	149	150	151	152	153	107
9–00	141	142	143	144	145	146	146	147	148	149	150	151	108
9–01	140	141	141	142	143	144	145	146	147	148	149	149	109
9–02	138	139	140	141	142	143	143	144	145	146	147	148	110
9–03	137	138	139	139	140	141	142	143	144	145	146	146	111
9–04	135	136	137	138	139	140	141	141	142	143	144	145	112
9–05	134	135	136	137	138	138	139	140	141	142	143	144	113
9–06	133	134	135	135	136	137	138	139	140	140	141	142	114
9–07	131	132	133	134	135	136	136	137	138	139	140	141	115
9–08	130	131	132	133	134	134	135	136	137	138	139	139	116
9–09	129	130	131	132	132	133	134	135	136	136	137	138	117
9–10	128	129	129	130	131	132	133	133	134	135	136	137	118
9–11	127	127	128	129	130	131	131	132	133	134	135	135	119
	156	157	158	159	160	161	162	163	164	165	166	167	TOTAL MONTHS

CHRONOLOGICAL AGE

175

MA 13–0 / CA 7–0

YEARS MONTHS	13 0	13 1	13 2	13 3	13 4	13 5	13 6	13 7	13 8	13 9	13 10	13 11	
10–00	126	126	127	128	129	129	130	131	132	133	133	134	120
10–01	125	125	126	127	128	128	129	130	131	132	132	133	121
10–02	123	124	125	126	127	127	128	129	130	130	131	132	122
10–03	123	123	124	125	126	126	127	128	129	129	130	131	123
10–04	122	122	123	124	125	125	126	127	128	128	129	130	124
10–05	121	121	122	123	124	124	125	126	127	127	128	129	125
10–06	120	120	121	122	123	123	124	125	126	126	127	128	126
10–07	119	120	120	121	122	122	123	124	125	125	126	127	127
10–08	118	119	119	120	121	121	122	123	124	124	125	126	128
10–09	117	118	118	119	120	121	121	122	123	123	124	125	129
10–10	116	117	118	118	119	120	120	121	122	123	123	124	130
10–11	115	116	117	117	118	119	119	120	121	122	122	123	131
11–00	115	115	116	117	117	118	119	119	120	121	121	122	132
11–01	114	114	115	116	116	117	118	118	119	120	120	121	133
11–02	113	114	114	115	116	116	117	118	118	119	120	120	134
11–03	112	113	114	114	115	116	116	117	118	118	119	120	135
11–04	111	112	113	113	114	115	115	116	117	117	118	119	136
11–05	111	111	112	113	113	114	115	115	116	117	117	118	137
11–06	110	111	111	112	113	113	114	115	115	116	117	117	138
11–07	109	110	111	111	112	113	113	114	114	115	116	116	139
11–08	109	109	110	111	111	112	112	113	114	114	115	116	140
11–09	108	109	109	110	110	111	112	112	113	114	114	115	141
11–10	107	108	109	109	110	110	111	112	112	113	114	114	142
11–11	107	107	108	109	109	110	110	111	112	112	113	113	143
12–00	106	107	107	108	108	109	110	110	111	112	112	113	144
12–01	105	106	107	107	108	108	109	110	110	111	111	112	145
12–02	105	105	106	107	107	108	108	109	110	110	111	111	146
12–03	104	105	105	106	107	107	108	108	109	110	110	111	147
12–04	104	104	105	105	106	107	107	108	108	109	110	110	148
12–05	103	104	104	105	105	106	107	107	108	108	109	110	149
12–06	102	103	104	104	105	105	106	107	107	108	108	109	150
12–07	102	103	103	104	104	105	105	106	107	107	108	108	151
12–08	101	102	102	103	104	104	105	105	106	107	107	108	152
12–09	101	101	102	102	103	104	104	105	105	106	107	107	153
12–10	100	101	101	102	103	103	104	104	105	105	106	107	154
12–11	100	100	101	101	102	103	103	104	104	105	105	106	155
	156	157	158	159	160	161	162	163	164	165	166	167	TOTAL MONTHS

CHRONOLOGICAL AGE

MENTAL AGE

CHRONOLOGICAL AGE

YEARS / MONTHS	13 0	13 1	13 2	13 3	13 4	13 5	13 6	13 7	13 8	13 9	13 10	13 11	
13-00	99	100	100	101	101	102	103	103	104	104	105	105	156
13-01	99	99	100	100	101	101	102	103	103	104	104	105	157
13-02	99	99	100	100	101	101	102	103	103	104	104	105	158
13-03	98	98	99	100	100	101	101	102	102	103	104	104	159
13-04	97	98	99	99	100	100	101	101	102	102	103	104	160
13-05	97	98	99	99	100	100	101	101	102	102	103	104	161
13-06	97	97	98	98	99	100	100	101	101	102	102	103	162
13-07	96	97	97	98	98	99	100	100	101	101	102	102	163
13-08	96	97	97	98	98	99	100	100	101	101	102	102	164
13-09	96	96	97	97	98	98	99	100	100	101	101	102	165
13-10	95	96	96	97	97	98	98	99	100	100	101	101	166
13-11	95	96	96	97	97	98	98	99	99	100	101	101	167
14-00	94	95	96	96	97	97	98	98	99	99	100	101	168
14-01	94	94	95	96	96	97	97	98	98	99	99	100	169
14-02	94	94	95	96	96	97	97	98	98	99	99	100	170
14-03	93	94	95	95	96	96	97	97	98	98	99	99	171
14-04	93	93	94	95	95	96	96	97	97	98	98	99	172
14-05	93	93	94	95	95	96	96	97	97	98	98	99	173
14-06	92	93	93	94	95	95	96	96	97	97	98	98	174
14-07	92	92	93	93	94	95	95	96	96	97	97	98	175
14-08	92	92	93	93	94	95	95	96	96	97	97	98	176
14-09	91	92	92	93	93	94	95	95	96	96	97	97	177
14-10	91	91	92	92	93	94	94	95	95	96	96	97	178
14-11	91	91	92	92	93	93	94	95	95	96	96	97	179
15-00	90	91	91	92	92	93	94	94	95	95	96	96	180
15-01	90	90	91	91	92	92	93	93	94	94	95	95	181
15-02	90	90	91	91	92	92	93	93	94	94	95	95	182
15-03	89	89	90	90	91	91	92	93	93	94	94	95	183
15-04	88	89	89	90	90	91	91	92	92	93	93	94	184
15-05	88	89	89	90	90	91	91	92	92	93	93	94	185
15-06	87	88	88	89	89	90	90	91	92	92	93	93	186
15-07	87	87	88	88	89	89	90	90	91	91	92	92	187
15-08	86	87	88	88	89	89	90	90	91	91	92	92	188
15-09	86	86	87	87	88	88	89	89	90	91	91	92	189
15-10	85	86	86	87	87	88	88	89	89	90	90	91	190
15-11	85	85	86	87	87	88	88	89	89	90	90	91	191
TOTAL MONTHS	156	157	158	159	160	161	162	163	164	165	166	167	

MA 13-0 / CA 13-0

YEARS MONTHS	13 0	13 1	13 2	13 3	13 4	13 5	13 6	13 7	13 8	13 9	13 10	13 11	
16–00 〉 16–02 〈	84	85	85	86	86	87	87	88	88	89	90	90	〈 192 〉 194
16–03 〉 16–07 〈	84	84	85	85	86	86	87	88	88	89	89	90	〈 195 〉 199
16–08 〉 17–00 〈	84	84	85	85	86	86	87	88	88	89	89	90	〈 200 〉 204
17–01 〉 17–05 〈	83	83	84	84	85	85	86	87	87	88	88	89	〈 205 〉 209
17–06 〉 17–10 〈	82	82	83	83	84	84	85	86	86	87	87	88	〈 210 〉 214
17–11 〉 18–00 〈	82	82	83	83	84	84	85	86	86	87	87	88	〈 215 〉 216
	156	157	158	159	160	161	162	163	164	165	166	167	TOTAL MONTHS

CHRONOLOGICAL AGE

YEARS / MONTHS	14 0	14 1	14 2	14 3	14 4	14 5	14 6	14 7	14 8	14 9	14 10	14 11	TOTAL MONTHS
8–00													96
8–01													97
8–02	170												98
8–03	168	169	170										99
8–04	166	167	168	169	170								100
8–05	164	165	166	167	168	169	170						101
8–06	162	163	164	165	166	167	168	169	170				102
8–07	161	162	163	163	164	165	166	167	168	169	170		103
8–08	159	160	161	162	163	164	164	165	166	167	168	169	104
8–09	157	158	159	160	161	162	163	164	165	166	166	167	105
8–10	155	156	157	158	159	160	161	162	163	164	165	166	106
8–11	154	155	155	156	157	158	159	160	161	162	163	164	107
9–00	152	153	154	155	156	156	157	158	159	160	161	162	108
9–01	150	151	152	153	154	155	156	157	158	158	159	160	109
9–02	149	150	151	151	152	153	154	155	156	157	158	159	110
9–03	147	148	149	150	151	152	153	153	154	155	156	157	111
9–04	146	147	148	148	149	150	151	152	153	154	154	155	112
9–05	144	145	146	147	148	149	149	150	151	152	153	154	113
9–06	143	144	145	146	146	147	148	149	150	151	151	152	114
9–07	142	142	143	144	145	146	147	147	148	149	150	151	115
9–08	140	141	142	143	143	144	145	146	147	148	148	149	116
9–09	139	140	140	141	142	143	144	145	145	146	147	148	117
9–10	137	138	139	140	141	142	142	143	144	145	146	146	118
9–11	136	137	138	139	139	140	141	142	143	143	144	145	119
10–00	135	136	137	137	138	139	140	141	141	142	143	144	120
10–01	134	135	135	136	137	138	139	139	140	141	142	142	121
10–02	133	133	134	135	136	137	137	138	139	140	140	141	122
10–03	132	132	133	134	135	135	136	137	138	138	139	140	123
10–04	131	131	132	133	134	134	135	136	137	137	138	139	124
10–05	129	130	131	132	132	133	134	135	135	136	137	138	125
10–06	129	129	130	131	131	132	133	134	134	135	136	137	126
10–07	128	128	129	130	130	131	132	133	133	134	135	135	127
10–08	126	127	128	129	129	130	131	131	132	133	134	134	128
10–09	126	126	127	128	128	129	130	131	131	132	133	133	129
10–10	125	125	126	127	127	128	129	130	130	131	132	132	130
10–11	124	124	125	126	126	127	128	128	129	130	131	131	131
TOTAL MONTHS	168	169	170	171	172	173	174	175	176	177	178	179	

CHRONOLOGICAL AGE

179

MA 14–0 / CA 8–0

YEARS MONTHS	14 0	14 1	14 2	14 3	14 4	14 5	14 6	14 7	14 8	14 9	14 10	14 11	
11–00	123	123	124	125	126	126	127	128	128	129	130	130	132
11–01	122	123	123	124	125	125	126	127	127	128	129	129	133
11–02	121	122	122	123	124	124	125	126	126	127	128	128	134
11–03	120	121	122	122	123	124	124	125	126	126	127	128	135
11–04	119	120	121	121	122	123	123	124	125	125	126	127	136
11–05	119	119	120	121	121	122	122	123	124	124	125	126	137
11–06	118	118	119	120	120	121	122	122	123	124	124	125	138
11–07	117	118	118	119	120	120	121	122	122	123	123	124	139
11–08	116	117	118	118	119	119	120	121	121	122	123	123	140
11–09	115	116	117	117	118	119	119	120	121	121	122	122	141
11–10	115	115	116	117	117	118	119	119	120	120	121	122	142
11–11	114	115	115	116	117	117	118	118	119	120	120	121	143
12–00	113	114	115	115	116	116	117	118	118	119	120	120	144
12–01	113	113	114	114	115	116	116	117	118	118	119	119	145
12–02	112	113	113	114	114	115	116	116	117	118	118	119	146
12–03	111	112	113	113	114	114	115	116	116	117	117	118	147
12–04	111	111	112	113	113	114	114	115	116	116	117	117	148
12–05	110	111	111	112	112	113	114	114	115	115	116	117	149
12–06	110	110	111	111	112	112	113	114	114	115	115	116	150
12–07	109	110	110	111	111	112	112	113	114	114	115	115	151
12–08	108	109	109	110	111	111	112	112	113	114	114	115	152
12–09	108	108	109	109	110	111	111	112	112	113	113	114	153
12–10	107	108	108	109	109	110	111	111	112	112	113	113	154
12–11	107	107	108	108	109	109	110	111	111	112	112	113	155
13–00	106	107	107	108	108	109	109	110	111	111	112	112	156
13–01	105	106	107	107	108	108	109	109	110	110	111	112	157
13–02	105	106	107	107	108	108	109	109	110	110	111	112	158
13–03	105	105	106	106	107	108	108	109	109	110	110	111	159
13–04	104	105	105	106	106	107	107	108	109	109	110	110	160
13–05	104	105	105	106	106	107	107	108	109	109	110	110	161
13–06	103	104	105	105	106	106	107	107	108	108	109	110	162
13–07	103	103	104	105	105	106	106	107	107	108	108	109	163
13–08	103	103	104	105	105	106	106	107	107	108	108	109	164
13–09	102	103	103	104	105	105	106	106	107	107	108	108	165
13–10	102	102	103	103	104	104	105	106	106	107	107	108	166
13–11	102	102	103	103	104	104	105	106	106	107	107	108	167
TOTAL MONTHS	168	169	170	171	172	173	174	175	176	177	178	179	

CHRONOLOGICAL AGE

CHRONOLOGICAL AGE

YEARS / MONTHS	14 0	14 1	14 2	14 3	14 4	14 5	14 6	14 7	14 8	14 9	14 10	14 11	
14–00	101	102	102	103	103	104	104	105	105	106	107	107	168
14–01	101	101	102	102	103	103	104	104	105	105	106	107	169
14–02	101	101	102	102	103	103	104	104	105	105	106	107	170
14–03	100	101	101	102	102	103	103	104	104	105	105	106	171
14–04	99	100	100	101	102	102	103	103	104	104	105	105	172
14–05	99	100	100	101	102	102	103	103	104	104	105	105	173
14–06	99	99	100	100	101	102	102	103	103	104	104	105	174
14–07	98	99	99	100	100	101	102	102	103	103	104	104	175
14–08	98	99	99	100	100	101	102	102	103	103	104	104	176
14–09	98	98	99	99	100	100	101	102	102	103	103	104	177
14–10	97	98	98	99	99	100	100	101	102	102	103	103	178
14–11	97	98	98	99	99	100	100	101	102	102	103	103	179
15–00	97	97	98	98	99	99	100	100	101	102	102	103	180
15–01	96	97	97	98	98	99	99	100	100	101	101	102	181
15–02	96	96	97	98	98	99	99	100	100	101	101	102	182
15–03	95	96	96	97	97	98	98	99	99	100	101	101	183
15–04	94	95	96	96	97	97	98	98	99	99	100	100	184
15–05	94	95	95	96	96	97	98	98	99	99	100	100	185
15–06	94	94	95	95	96	96	97	97	98	98	99	99	186
15–07	93	93	94	95	95	96	96	97	97	98	98	99	187
15–08	93	93	94	94	95	95	96	97	97	98	98	99	188
15–09	92	93	93	94	94	95	95	96	96	97	97	98	189
15–10	91	92	92	93	94	94	95	95	96	96	97	97	190
15–11	91	92	92	93	93	94	94	95	96	96	97	97	191
16–00 / 16–02	91	91	92	92	93	93	94	94	95	95	96	96	192 / 194
16–03 / 16–07	90	91	91	92	93	93	94	94	95	95	96	96	195 / 199
16–08 / 17–00	90	91	91	92	92	93	93	94	94	95	95	96	200 / 204
17–01 / 17–05	89	90	90	91	92	92	93	93	94	94	95	95	205 / 209
17–06 / 17–10	88	89	89	90	91	91	92	92	93	93	94	94	210 / 214
17–11 / 18–00	88	89	89	90	91	91	92	92	93	93	94	94	215 / 216
	168	169	170	171	172	173	174	175	176	177	178	179	TOTAL MONTHS

MA 14–0 / CA 14–0

MENTAL AGE

YEARS MONTHS	15 0	15 1	15 2	15 3	15 4	15 5	15 6	15 7	15 8	15 9	15 10	15 11	TOTAL MONTHS
8–00													96
8–01													97
8–02													98
8–03													99
8–04													100
8–05													101
8–06													102
8–07													103
8–08	170												104
8–09	168	169	170										105
8–10	166	167	168	169	170								106
8–11	165	166	167	167	168	169	170						107
9–00	163	164	165	166	167	167	168	169	170				108
9–01	161	162	163	164	165	166	167	167	168	169	170		109
9–02	159	160	161	162	163	164	165	166	167	167	168	169	110
9–03	158	159	160	160	161	162	163	164	165	166	167	167	111
9–04	156	157	158	159	160	161	161	162	163	164	165	166	112
9–05	155	155	156	157	158	159	160	161	161	162	163	164	113
9–06	153	154	155	156	156	157	158	159	160	161	162	162	114
9–07	152	152	153	154	155	156	157	157	158	159	160	161	115
9–08	150	151	152	153	153	154	155	156	157	157	158	159	116
9–09	149	149	150	151	152	153	154	154	155	156	157	158	117
9–10	147	148	149	150	150	151	152	153	154	154	155	156	118
9–11	146	147	147	148	149	150	151	151	152	153	154	155	119
10–00	144	145	146	147	148	148	149	150	151	152	152	153	120
10–01	143	144	145	146	146	147	148	149	149	150	151	152	121
10–02	142	143	143	144	145	146	147	147	148	149	150	150	122
10–03	141	142	142	143	144	145	145	146	147	148	148	149	123
10–04	140	140	141	142	143	143	144	145	146	146	147	148	124
10–05	138	139	140	141	141	142	143	144	144	145	146	147	125
10–06	137	138	139	140	140	141	142	142	143	144	145	145	126
10–07	136	137	138	138	139	140	141	141	142	143	143	144	127
10–08	135	136	137	137	138	139	139	140	141	142	142	143	128
10–09	134	135	135	136	137	138	138	139	140	140	141	142	129
10–10	133	134	134	135	136	137	137	138	139	139	140	141	130
10–11	132	133	133	134	135	135	136	137	138	138	139	140	131
TOTAL MONTHS	180	181	182	183	184	185	186	187	188	189	190	191	

CHRONOLOGICAL AGE

YEARS MONTHS	15 0	15 1	15 2	15 3	15 4	15 5	15 6	15 7	15 8	15 9	15 10	15 11	
11–00	131	132	132	133	134	134	135	136	136	137	138	139	132
11–01	130	131	131	132	133	133	134	135	135	136	137	137	133
11–02	129	130	130	131	132	132	133	134	134	135	136	137	134
11–03	128	129	130	130	131	132	132	133	134	134	135	136	135
11–04	127	128	129	129	130	131	131	132	133	133	134	135	136
11–05	126	127	128	128	129	130	130	131	132	132	133	134	137
11–06	126	126	127	128	128	129	129	130	131	131	132	133	138
11–07	125	125	126	127	127	128	129	129	130	131	131	132	139
11–08	124	125	125	126	126	127	128	128	129	130	130	131	140
11–09	123	124	124	125	126	126	127	127	128	129	129	130	141
11–10	122	123	124	124	125	125	126	127	127	128	129	129	142
11–11	122	122	123	123	124	125	125	126	127	127	128	128	143
12–00	121	121	122	123	123	124	124	125	126	126	127	127	144
12–01	120	121	121	122	122	123	124	124	125	125	126	127	145
12–02	119	120	121	121	122	122	123	124	124	125	125	126	146
12–03	119	119	120	120	121	122	122	123	123	124	125	125	147
12–04	118	119	119	120	120	121	122	122	123	123	124	125	148
12–05	117	118	118	119	120	120	121	121	122	123	123	124	149
12–06	117	117	118	118	119	120	120	121	121	122	123	123	150
12–07	116	117	117	118	118	119	120	120	121	121	122	122	151
12–08	115	116	116	117	118	118	119	119	120	121	121	122	152
12–09	115	115	116	116	117	118	118	119	119	120	120	121	153
12–10	114	115	115	116	116	117	117	118	119	119	120	120	154
12–11	113	114	115	115	116	116	117	117	118	119	119	120	155
13–00	113	113	114	115	115	116	116	117	117	118	119	119	156
13–01	112	113	113	114	114	115	116	116	117	117	118	118	157
13–02	112	113	113	114	114	115	116	116	117	117	118	118	158
13–03	111	112	113	113	114	114	115	115	116	117	117	118	159
13–04	111	111	112	113	113	114	114	115	115	116	116	117	160
13–05	111	111	112	113	113	114	114	115	115	116	116	117	161
13–06	110	111	111	112	112	113	114	114	115	115	116	116	162
13–07	110	110	111	111	112	112	113	113	114	115	115	116	163
13–08	110	110	111	111	112	112	113	113	114	115	115	116	164
13–09	109	109	110	111	111	112	112	113	113	114	114	115	165
13–10	108	109	109	110	111	111	112	112	113	113	114	114	166
13–11	108	109	109	110	110	111	112	112	113	113	114	114	167
	180	181	182	183	184	185	186	187	188	189	190	191	TOTAL MONTHS

CHRONOLOGICAL AGE

MA 15–0 / CA 11–0

CHRONOLOGICAL AGE

YEARS MONTHS	15 0	15 1	15 2	15 3	15 4	15 5	15 6	15 7	15 8	15 9	15 10	15 11	
14–00	108	108	109	109	110	110	111	112	112	113	113	114	168
14–01	107	108	108	109	109	110	110	111	111	112	113	113	169
14–02	107	108	108	109	109	110	110	111	111	112	113	113	170
14–03	107	107	108	108	109	109	110	110	111	111	112	113	171
14–04	106	106	107	108	108	109	109	110	110	111	111	112	172
14–05	106	106	107	108	108	109	109	110	110	111	111	112	173
14–06	105	106	106	107	108	108	109	109	110	110	111	111	174
14–07	105	105	106	106	107	107	108	109	109	110	110	111	175
14–08	105	105	106	106	107	108	108	109	109	110	110	111	176
14–09	104	105	105	106	106	107	107	108	109	109	110	110	177
14–10	104	104	105	105	106	106	107	107	108	108	109	110	178
14–11	104	104	105	105	106	106	107	107	108	109	109	110	179
15–00	103	104	104	105	105	106	106	107	107	108	108	109	180
15–01	102	103	103	104	105	105	106	106	107	107	108	108	181
15–02	102	103	103	104	104	105	106	106	107	107	108	108	182
15–03	102	102	103	103	104	104	105	105	106	106	107	107	183
15–04	101	101	102	102	103	103	104	105	105	106	106	107	184
15–05	101	101	102	102	103	103	104	104	105	106	106	107	185
15–06	100	101	101	102	102	103	103	104	104	105	105	106	186
15–07	99	100	100	101	101	102	102	103	104	104	105	105	187
15–08	99	100	100	101	101	102	102	103	103	104	105	105	188
15–09	98	99	100	100	101	101	102	102	103	103	104	104	189
15–10	98	98	99	99	100	100	101	101	102	102	103	104	190
15–11	98	98	99	99	100	100	101	101	102	102	103	103	191
16–00 } 16–02 {	97	97	98	98	99	100	100	101	101	102	102	103	{ 192 } 194
16–03 } 16–07 {	97	97	98	98	99	99	100	100	101	101	102	102	{ 195 } 199
16–08 } 17–00 {	96	97	97	98	98	99	99	100	100	101	102	102	{ 200 } 204
17–01 } 17–05 {	96	97	97	98	98	99	99	100	100	101	102	102	{ 205 } 209
17–06 } 17–10 {	95	96	96	97	97	98	98	99	99	100	101	101	{ 210 } 214
17–11 } 18–00 {	95	96	96	97	97	98	98	99	99	100	101	101	{ 215 } 216
	180	181	182	183	184	185	186	187	188	189	190	191	TOTAL MONTHS

YEARS MONTHS	16 0	16 1	16 2	16 3	16 4	16 5	16 6	16 7	16 8	16 9	16 10	16 11	TOTAL MONTHS
8-00													96
8-01													97
8-02													98
8-03													99
8-04													100
8-05													101
8-06													102
8-07													103
8-08													104
8-09													105
8-10													106
8-11													107
9-00													108
9-01													109
9-02	170												110
9-03	168	169	170										111
9-04	167	167	168	169	170								112
9-05	165	166	167	167	168	169	170						113
9-06	163	164	165	166	167	167	168	169	170				114
9-07	162	162	163	164	165	166	167	167	168	169	170		115
9-08	160	161	162	162	163	164	165	166	167	167	168	169	116
9-09	158	159	160	161	162	163	163	164	165	166	167	167	117
9-10	157	158	158	159	160	161	162	162	163	164	165	166	118
9-11	155	156	157	158	159	159	160	161	162	163	163	164	119
10-00	154	155	155	156	157	158	159	159	160	161	162	163	120
10-01	153	153	154	155	156	156	157	158	159	160	160	161	121
10-02	151	152	153	153	154	155	156	157	157	158	159	160	122
10-03	150	151	151	152	153	154	154	155	156	157	157	158	123
10-04	149	149	150	151	152	152	153	154	155	155	156	157	124
10-05	147	148	149	150	150	151	152	153	153	154	155	156	125
10-06	146	147	148	148	149	150	151	151	152	153	153	154	126
10-07	145	146	146	147	148	149	149	150	151	151	152	153	127
10-08	144	144	145	146	147	147	148	149	149	150	151	152	128
10-09	143	143	144	145	145	146	147	148	148	149	150	150	129
10-10	141	142	143	144	144	145	146	146	147	148	148	149	130
10-11	140	141	142	142	143	144	144	145	146	147	147	148	131
TOTAL MONTHS	192	193	194	195	196	197	198	199	200	201	202	203	

CHRONOLOGICAL AGE

MA 16–0 / CA 8–0

YEARS / MONTHS	16 0	16 1	16 2	16 3	16 4	16 5	16 6	16 7	16 8	16 9	16 10	16 11	
11–00	139	140	141	141	142	143	143	144	145	145	146	147	132
11–01	138	139	140	140	141	142	142	143	144	144	145	146	133
11–02	137	138	139	139	140	141	141	142	143	143	144	145	134
11–03	136	137	138	138	139	140	140	141	142	142	143	144	135
11–04	135	136	137	137	138	139	139	140	141	141	142	143	136
11–05	134	135	136	136	137	138	138	139	140	140	141	141	137
11–06	133	134	135	135	136	137	137	138	139	139	140	141	138
11–07	132	133	134	134	135	136	136	137	138	138	139	140	139
11–08	132	132	133	133	134	135	135	136	137	137	138	139	140
11–09	131	131	132	132	133	134	134	135	136	136	137	138	141
11–10	130	130	131	132	132	133	134	134	135	135	136	137	142
11–11	129	130	130	131	131	132	133	133	134	135	135	136	143
12–00	128	129	129	130	131	131	132	132	133	134	134	135	144
12–01	127	128	129	129	130	130	131	132	132	133	133	134	145
12–02	127	127	128	128	129	130	130	131	131	132	133	133	146
12–03	126	127	127	128	128	129	130	130	131	131	132	133	147
12–04	125	126	126	127	128	128	129	129	130	131	131	132	148
12–05	124	125	126	126	127	127	128	129	129	130	130	131	149
12–06	124	124	125	125	126	127	127	128	128	129	130	130	150
12–07	123	124	124	125	125	126	127	127	128	128	129	129	151
12–08	122	123	123	124	125	125	126	126	127	128	128	129	152
12–09	122	122	123	123	124	124	125	126	126	127	127	128	153
12–10	121	122	122	123	123	124	124	125	126	126	127	127	154
12–11	120	121	122	122	123	123	124	124	125	126	126	127	155
13–00	120	120	121	121	122	122	123	124	124	125	125	126	156
13–01	119	120	120	121	121	122	122	123	124	124	125	125	157
13–02	119	120	120	121	121	122	122	123	124	124	125	125	158
13–03	118	119	119	120	121	121	122	122	123	123	124	124	159
13–04	118	118	119	119	120	120	121	122	122	123	123	124	160
13–05	118	118	119	119	120	120	121	122	122	123	123	124	161
13–06	117	117	118	119	119	120	120	121	121	122	122	123	162
13–07	116	117	117	118	118	119	120	120	121	121	122	122	163
13–08	116	117	117	118	118	119	120	120	121	121	122	122	164
13–09	116	116	117	117	118	118	119	119	120	121	121	122	165
13–10	115	116	116	117	117	118	118	119	119	120	120	121	166
13–11	115	115	116	117	117	118	118	119	119	120	120	121	167
	192	193	194	195	196	197	198	199	200	201	202	203	TOTAL MONTHS

CHRONOLOGICAL AGE

MA 16–0 / CA 11–0

YEARS MONTHS (CHRONOLOGICAL AGE)	16 0	16 1	16 2	16 3	16 4	16 5	16 6	16 7	16 8	16 9	16 10	16 11	
14–00	114	115	115	116	116	117	118	118	119	119	120	120	168
14–01	114	114	115	115	116	116	117	118	118	119	119	120	169
14–02	114	114	115	115	116	116	117	118	118	119	119	120	170
14–03	113	114	114	115	115	116	116	117	117	118	119	119	171
14–04	112	113	114	114	115	115	116	116	117	117	118	118	172
14–05	112	113	114	114	115	115	116	116	117	117	118	118	173
14–06	112	112	113	113	114	115	115	116	116	117	117	118	174
14–07	111	112	112	113	113	114	115	115	116	116	117	117	175
14–08	111	112	112	113	113	114	115	115	116	116	117	117	176
14–09	111	111	112	112	113	113	114	114	115	116	116	117	177
14–10	110	111	111	112	112	113	113	114	114	115	115	116	178
14–11	110	111	111	112	112	113	113	114	114	115	115	116	179
15–00	110	110	111	111	112	112	113	113	114	114	115	115	180
15–01	109	109	110	110	111	111	112	113	113	114	114	115	181
15–02	109	109	110	110	111	111	112	112	113	114	114	115	182
15–03	108	108	109	110	110	111	111	112	112	113	113	114	183
15–04	107	108	108	109	109	110	110	111	111	112	113	113	184
15–05	107	108	108	109	109	110	110	111	111	112	112	113	185
15–06	106	107	107	108	109	109	110	110	111	111	112	112	186
15–07	106	106	107	107	108	108	109	109	110	110	111	111	187
15–08	106	106	107	107	108	108	109	109	110	110	111	111	188
15–09	105	105	106	106	107	107	108	109	109	110	110	111	189
15–10	104	105	105	106	106	107	107	108	108	109	109	110	190
15–11	104	105	105	106	106	107	107	108	108	109	109	110	191
16–00 } 16–02 }	103	104	104	105	105	106	106	107	107	108	109	109	{ 192 194
16–03 } 16–07 }	103	103	104	104	105	105	106	107	107	108	108	109	{ 195 199
16–08 } 17–00 }	103	103	104	104	105	105	106	107	107	108	108	109	{ 200 204
17–01 } 17–05 }	103	103	104	104	105	105	106	107	107	108	108	109	{ 205 209
17–06 } 17–10 }	102	102	103	103	104	104	105	106	106	107	107	108	{ 210 214
17–11 } 18–00 }	102	102	103	103	104	104	105	106	106	107	107	108	{ 215 216
	192	193	194	195	196	197	198	199	200	201	202	203	TOTAL MONTHS

MA 16–0 / CA 14–0

YEARS MONTHS	17-0	17-1	17-2	17-3	17-4	17-5	17-6	17-7	17-8	17-9	17-10	17-11	TOTAL MONTHS
8-00													96
8-01													97
8-02													98
8-03													99
8-04													100
8-05													101
8-06													102
8-07													103
8-08													104
8-09													105
8-10													106
8-11													107
9-00													108
9-01													109
9-02													110
9-03													111
9-04													112
9-05													113
9-06													114
9-07													115
9-08	170												116
9-09	168	169	170										117
9-10	167	167	168	169	170								118
9-11	165	166	167	167	168	169	170						119
10-00	163	164	165	166	167	167	168	169	170				120
10-01	162	163	163	164	165	166	167	167	168	169	170		121
10-02	160	161	162	163	163	164	165	166	167	167	168	169	122
10-03	159	160	161	161	162	163	164	164	165	166	167	167	123
10-04	158	158	159	160	161	161	162	163	164	164	165	166	124
10-05	156	157	158	158	159	160	161	161	162	163	164	164	125
10-06	155	156	156	157	158	159	159	160	161	162	162	163	126
10-07	154	154	155	156	157	157	158	159	159	160	161	162	127
10-08	152	153	154	154	155	156	157	157	158	159	159	160	128
10-09	151	152	153	153	154	155	155	156	157	157	158	159	129
10-10	150	151	151	152	153	153	154	155	155	156	157	158	130
10-11	149	149	150	151	151	152	153	153	154	155	156	156	131
TOTAL MONTHS	204	205	206	207	208	209	210	211	212	213	214	215	

CHRONOLOGICAL AGE

MA 17-0 / CA 8-0

MENTAL AGE

YEARS → MONTHS	17 0	17 1	17 2	17 3	17 4	17 5	17 6	17 7	17 8	17 9	17 10	17 11	
11–00	147	148	149	150	150	151	152	152	153	154	154	155	132
11–01	146	147	148	148	149	150	150	151	152	152	153	154	133
11–02	145	146	147	147	148	149	149	150	151	151	152	153	134
11–03	144	145	146	146	147	148	148	149	150	150	151	152	135
11–04	143	144	145	145	146	147	147	148	148	149	150	150	136
11–05	142	143	143	144	145	145	146	147	147	148	149	149	137
11–06	141	142	142	143	144	144	145	146	146	147	148	148	138
11–07	140	141	141	142	143	143	144	145	145	146	147	147	139
11–08	139	140	140	141	142	142	143	144	144	145	146	146	140
11–09	138	139	139	140	141	141	142	143	143	144	144	145	141
11–10	137	138	139	139	140	140	141	142	142	143	144	144	142
11–11	136	137	138	138	139	140	140	141	141	142	143	143	143
12–00	135	136	137	137	138	139	139	140	140	141	142	142	144
12–01	135	135	136	136	137	138	138	139	139	140	141	141	145
12–02	134	134	135	136	136	137	138	138	139	139	140	141	146
12–03	133	134	134	135	136	136	137	137	138	139	139	140	147
12–04	132	133	133	134	135	135	136	136	137	138	138	139	148
12–05	132	132	133	133	134	134	135	136	136	137	137	138	149
12–06	131	131	132	133	133	134	134	135	136	136	137	137	150
12–07	130	131	131	132	132	133	134	134	135	135	136	137	151
12–08	129	130	130	131	132	132	133	133	134	135	135	136	152
12–09	129	129	130	130	131	131	132	133	133	134	134	135	153
12–10	128	128	129	130	130	131	131	132	132	133	134	134	154
12–11	127	128	128	129	130	130	131	131	132	132	133	134	155
13–00	126	127	128	128	129	129	130	130	131	132	132	133	156
13–01	126	126	127	127	128	129	129	130	130	131	131	132	157
13–02	126	126	127	127	128	129	129	130	130	131	131	132	158
13–03	125	126	126	127	127	128	128	129	130	130	131	131	159
13–04	124	125	125	126	127	127	128	128	129	129	130	131	160
13–05	124	125	125	126	127	127	128	128	129	129	130	131	161
13–06	124	124	125	125	126	126	127	127	128	129	129	130	162
13–07	123	123	124	125	125	126	126	127	127	128	128	129	163
13–08	123	123	124	125	125	126	126	127	127	128	128	129	164
13–09	122	123	123	124	124	125	126	126	127	127	128	128	165
13–10	122	122	123	123	124	124	125	125	126	127	127	128	166
13–11	122	122	123	123	124	124	125	125	126	127	127	128	167
	204	205	206	207	208	209	210	211	212	213	214	215	TOTAL MONTHS

CHRONOLOGICAL AGE

189

MA 17–0 / CA 11–0

YEARS ↱ MONTHS ↱	17 0	17 1	17 2	17 3	17 4	17 5	17 6	17 7	17 8	17 9	17 10	17 11	
14–00	121	121	122	123	123	124	124	125	125	126	126	127	168
14–01	120	121	121	122	122	123	124	124	125	125	126	126	169
14–02	120	121	121	122	122	123	124	124	125	125	126	126	170
14–03	120	120	121	121	122	122	123	123	124	125	125	126	171
14–04	119	120	120	121	121	122	122	123	123	124	124	125	172
14–05	119	120	120	121	121	122	122	123	123	124	124	125	173
14–06	118	119	119	120	121	121	122	122	123	123	124	124	174
14–07	118	118	119	119	120	120	121	122	122	123	123	124	175
14–08	118	118	119	119	120	120	121	122	122	123	123	124	176
14–09	117	118	118	119	119	120	120	121	121	122	123	123	177
14–10	117	117	118	118	119	119	120	120	121	121	122	122	178
14–11	117	117	118	118	119	119	120	120	121	121	122	122	179
15–00	116	116	117	118	118	119	119	120	120	121	121	122	180
15–01	115	116	116	117	117	118	118	119	119	120	120	121	181
15–02	115	116	116	117	117	118	118	119	119	120	120	121	182
15–03	114	115	115	116	116	117	118	118	119	119	120	120	183
15–04	114	114	115	115	116	116	117	117	118	118	119	119	184
15–05	114	114	115	115	116	116	117	117	118	118	119	119	185
15–06	113	113	114	114	115	115	116	116	117	118	118	119	186
15–07	112	113	113	114	114	115	115	116	116	117	117	118	187
15–08	112	112	113	114	114	115	115	116	116	117	117	118	188
15–09	111	112	112	113	113	114	114	115	115	116	116	117	189
15–10	110	111	111	112	113	113	114	114	115	115	116	116	190
15–11	110	111	111	112	112	113	114	114	115	115	116	116	191
16–00 } 16–02 }	110	110	111	111	112	112	113	113	114	114	115	115	{ 192 { 194
16–03 } 16–07 }	109	110	110	111	112	112	113	113	114	114	115	115	{ 195 { 199
16–08 } 17–00 }	109	110	110	111	112	112	113	113	114	114	115	115	{ 200 { 204
17–01 } 17–05 }	109	110	110	111	112	112	113	113	114	114	115	115	{ 205 { 209
17–06 } 17–10 }	108	109	109	110	111	111	112	112	113	113	114	114	{ 210 { 214
17–11 } 18–00 }	108	109	109	110	111	111	112	112	113	113	114	114	{ 215 { 216
	204	205	206	207	208	209	210	211	212	213	214	215	↱ TOTAL MONTHS

CHRONOLOGICAL AGE

MA 17–0 / CA 14–0

YEARS / MONTHS	18 0	18 1	18 2	18 3	18 4	18 5	18 6	18 7	18 8	18 9	18 10	18 11	
10-00													120
10-01													121
10-02	170												122
10-03	168	169	170										123
10-04	167	167	168	169	170								124
10-05	165	166	167	167	168	169	170						125
10-06	164	165	165	166	167	167	168	169	170				126
10-07	162	163	164	165	165	166	167	167	168	169	170		127
10-08	161	162	162	163	164	165	165	166	167	167	168	169	128
10-09	160	160	161	162	162	163	164	165	165	166	167	167	129
10-10	158	159	160	160	161	162	162	163	164	165	165	166	130
10-11	157	158	158	159	160	160	161	162	162	163	164	165	131
11-00	156	156	157	158	158	159	160	161	161	162	163	163	132
11-01	154	155	156	157	157	158	159	159	160	161	161	162	133
11-02	153	154	155	155	156	157	157	158	159	159	160	161	134
11-03	152	153	154	154	155	156	156	157	158	158	159	160	135
11-04	151	152	152	153	154	154	155	156	156	157	158	158	136
11-05	150	151	151	152	153	153	154	155	155	156	157	157	137
11-06	149	150	150	151	152	152	153	153	154	155	155	156	138
11-07	148	149	149	150	150	151	152	152	153	154	154	155	139
11-08	147	147	148	149	149	150	151	151	152	153	153	154	140
11-09	146	146	147	148	148	149	150	150	151	151	152	153	141
11-10	145	145	146	147	147	148	149	149	150	150	151	152	142
11-11	144	144	145	146	146	147	148	148	149	149	150	151	143
12-00	143	143	144	145	145	146	147	147	148	148	149	150	144
12-01	142	143	143	144	144	145	146	146	147	147	148	149	145
12-02	141	142	142	143	144	144	145	145	146	147	147	148	146
12-03	140	141	142	142	143	143	144	145	145	146	146	147	147
12-04	139	140	141	141	142	142	143	144	144	145	145	146	148
12-05	139	139	140	140	141	142	142	143	143	144	145	145	149
12-06	138	138	139	140	140	141	141	142	143	143	144	144	150
12-07	137	138	138	139	139	140	141	141	142	142	143	144	151
12-08	136	137	137	138	139	139	140	140	141	142	142	143	152
12-09	136	136	137	137	138	138	139	140	140	141	141	142	153
12-10	135	135	136	137	137	138	138	139	139	140	141	141	154
12-11	134	135	135	136	136	137	138	138	139	139	140	140	155
	216	217	218	219	220	221	222	223	224	225	226	227	TOTAL MONTHS

CHRONOLOGICAL AGE

MA 18-0 / CA 10-0

YEARS / MONTHS	18 0	18 1	18 2	18 3	18 4	18 5	18 6	18 7	18 8	18 9	18 10	18 11	
13–00	133	134	134	135	136	136	137	137	138	138	139	140	156
13–01	133	133	134	134	135	135	136	137	137	138	138	139	157
13–02	133	133	134	134	135	135	136	137	137	138	138	139	158
13–03	132	132	133	134	134	135	135	136	136	137	137	138	159
13–04	131	132	132	133	133	134	134	135	136	136	137	137	160
13–05	131	132	132	133	133	134	134	135	136	136	137	137	161
13–06	130	131	131	132	133	133	134	134	135	135	136	136	162
13–07	130	130	131	131	132	132	133	134	134	135	135	136	163
13–08	130	130	131	131	132	132	133	134	134	135	135	136	164
13–09	129	129	130	131	131	132	132	133	133	134	134	135	165
13–10	128	129	129	130	130	131	132	132	133	133	134	134	166
13–11	128	129	129	130	130	131	131	132	133	133	134	134	167
14–00	127	128	129	129	130	130	131	131	132	132	133	134	168
14–01	127	127	128	128	129	130	130	131	131	132	132	133	169
14–02	127	127	128	128	129	130	130	131	131	132	132	133	170
14–03	126	127	127	128	128	129	129	130	131	131	132	132	171
14–04	125	126	127	127	128	128	129	129	130	130	131	132	172
14–05	125	126	127	127	128	128	129	129	130	130	131	132	173
14–06	125	125	126	126	127	128	128	129	129	130	130	131	174
14–07	124	125	125	126	126	127	127	128	129	129	130	130	175
14–08	124	125	125	126	126	127	127	128	129	129	130	130	176
14–09	124	124	125	125	126	126	127	127	128	128	129	129	177
14–10	123	124	124	125	125	126	126	127	127	128	128	129	178
14–11	123	124	124	125	125	126	126	127	127	128	128	129	179
15–00	122	123	123	124	124	125	126	126	127	127	128	128	180
15–01	122	122	123	123	124	124	125	125	126	126	127	127	181
15–02	122	122	123	123	124	124	125	125	126	126	127	127	182
15–03	121	121	122	122	123	123	124	124	125	126	126	127	183
15–04	120	120	121	122	122	123	123	124	124	125	125	126	184
15–05	120	120	121	122	122	123	123	124	124	125	125	126	185
15–06	119	120	120	121	121	122	122	123	123	124	124	125	186
15–07	118	119	119	120	120	121	122	122	123	123	124	124	187
15–08	118	119	119	120	120	121	121	122	123	123	124	124	188
15–09	118	118	119	119	120	120	121	121	122	122	123	123	189
15–10	117	117	118	118	119	119	120	120	121	121	122	123	190
15–11	117	117	118	118	119	119	120	120	121	121	122	123	191
	216	217	218	219	220	221	222	223	224	225	226	227	TOTAL MONTHS

CHRONOLOGICAL AGE

MA 18–0 / CA 13–0

MENTAL AGE

YEARS MONTHS	18 0	18 1	18 2	18 3	18 4	18 5	18 6	18 7	18 8	18 9	18 10	18 11	
16–00 16–02	116	116	117	117	118	119	119	120	120	121	121	122	{192 {194
16–03 16–07	116	116	117	117	118	119	119	120	120	121	121	122	{195 {199
16–08 17–00	116	116	117	117	118	119	119	120	120	121	121	121	{200 {204
17–01 17–05	116	116	117	117	118	119	119	120	120	120	121	121	{205 {209
17–06 17–10	115	116	116	117	117	118	118	119	119	120	121	121	{210 {214
17–11 18–00	115	116	116	117	117	118	118	119	119	120	121	121	{215 {216
	216	217	218	219	220	221	222	223	224	225	226	227	TOTAL MONTHS

CHRONOLOGICAL AGE

MA 18–0 / CA 16–0

YEARS ⎨ MONTHS	19 0	19 1	19 2	19 3	19 4	19 5	19 6	19 7	19 8	19 9	19 10	19 11	
10–00													120
10–01													121
10–02													122
10–03													123
10–04													124
10–05													125
10–06													126
10–07													127
10–08	170	170											128
10–09	168	169	170	170									129
10–10	167	167	168	169	170	170							130
10–11	165	166	167	167	168	169	169	170					131
11–00	164	165	165	166	167	167	168	169	169	170			132
11–01	163	163	164	165	165	166	167	167	168	169	169	170	133
11–02	161	162	163	163	164	165	165	166	167	167	168	169	134
11–03	160	161	162	162	163	164	164	165	166	166	167	168	135
11–04	159	160	160	161	162	162	163	164	164	165	166	166	136
11–05	158	158	159	160	160	161	162	162	163	164	164	165	137
11–06	157	157	158	159	159	160	161	161	162	163	163	164	138
11–07	156	156	157	158	158	159	159	160	161	161	162	163	139
11–08	154	155	156	156	157	158	158	159	160	160	161	161	140
11–09	153	154	155	155	156	156	157	158	158	159	160	160	141
11–10	152	153	154	154	155	155	156	157	157	158	159	159	142
11–11	151	152	153	153	154	154	155	156	156	157	157	158	143
12–00	150	151	151	152	153	153	154	154	155	156	156	157	144
12–01	149	150	150	151	152	152	153	153	154	155	155	156	145
12–02	148	149	150	150	151	151	152	153	153	154	154	155	146
12–03	148	148	149	149	150	151	151	152	152	153	154	154	147
12–04	147	147	148	148	149	150	150	151	151	152	153	153	148
12–05	146	146	147	148	148	149	149	150	151	151	152	152	149
12–06	145	146	146	147	147	148	149	149	150	150	151	151	150
12–07	144	145	145	146	147	147	148	148	149	149	150	151	151
12–08	143	144	144	145	146	146	147	147	148	149	149	150	152
12–09	142	143	144	144	145	145	146	147	147	148	148	149	153
12–10	142	142	143	143	144	145	145	146	146	147	147	148	154
12–11	141	142	142	143	143	144	144	145	146	146	147	147	155
	228	229	230	231	232	233	234	235	236	237	238	239	TOTAL MONTHS

Left margin: CHRONOLOGICAL AGE

YEARS MONTHS	19 0	19 1	19 2	19 3	19 4	19 5	19 6	19 7	19 8	19 9	19 10	19 11	
13–00	140	141	141	142	142	143	144	144	145	145	146	146	156
13–01	139	140	140	141	142	142	143	143	144	145	145	146	157
13–02	139	140	140	141	142	142	143	143	144	145	145	146	158
13–03	139	139	140	140	141	141	142	143	143	144	144	145	159
13–04	138	138	139	140	140	141	141	142	142	143	143	144	160
13–05	138	138	139	140	140	141	141	142	142	143	143	144	161
13–06	137	138	138	139	139	140	140	141	141	142	143	143	162
13–07	136	137	137	138	139	139	140	140	141	141	142	142	163
13–08	136	137	137	138	139	139	140	140	141	141	142	142	164
13–09	136	136	137	137	138	138	139	139	140	141	141	142	165
13–10	135	135	136	137	137	138	138	139	139	140	140	141	166
13–11	135	135	136	136	137	138	138	139	139	140	140	141	167
14–00	134	135	135	136	136	137	137	138	138	139	140	140	168
14–01	133	134	134	135	136	136	137	137	138	138	139	139	169
14–02	133	134	134	135	136	136	137	137	138	138	139	139	170
14–03	133	133	134	134	135	135	136	137	137	138	138	139	171
14–04	132	133	133	134	134	135	135	136	136	137	138	138	172
14–05	132	133	133	134	134	135	135	136	136	137	138	138	173
14–06	131	132	132	133	134	134	135	135	136	136	137	137	174
14–07	131	131	132	132	133	133	134	135	135	136	136	137	175
14–08	131	131	132	132	133	133	134	135	135	136	136	137	176
14–09	130	131	131	132	132	133	133	134	134	135	135	136	177
14–10	129	130	130	131	132	132	133	133	134	134	135	135	178
14–11	129	130	130	131	132	132	133	133	134	134	135	135	179
15–00	129	129	130	130	131	131	132	132	133	134	134	135	180
15–01	128	128	129	130	130	131	131	132	132	133	133	134	181
15–02	128	128	129	130	130	131	131	132	132	133	133	134	182
15–03	127	128	128	129	129	130	130	131	131	132	132	133	183
15–04	126	127	127	128	128	129	130	130	131	131	132	132	184
15–05	126	127	127	128	128	129	129	130	131	131	132	132	185
15–06	125	126	127	127	128	128	129	129	130	130	131	131	186
15–07	125	125	126	126	127	127	128	128	129	129	130	131	187
15–08	125	125	126	126	127	127	128	128	129	129	130	130	188
15–09	124	124	125	125	126	127	127	128	128	129	129	130	189
15–10	123	124	124	125	125	126	126	127	127	128	128	129	190
15–11	123	124	124	125	125	126	126	127	127	128	128	129	191
TOTAL MONTHS	228	229	230	231	232	233	234	235	236	237	238	239	

CHRONOLOGICAL AGE

195

MA 19–0 / CA 13–0

YEARS MONTHS	19 0	19 1	19 2	19 3	19 4	19 5	19 6	19 7	19 8	19 9	19 10	19 11	TOTAL MONTHS
16–00 } 16–02 }	122	123	123	124	124	125	125	126	126	127	128	128	{ 192 { 194
16–03 } 16–07 }	122	123	123	124	124	125	125	126	126	127	128	128	{ 195 { 199
16–08 } 17–00 }	122	122	123	123	124	124	125	126	126	127	127	128	{ 200 { 204
17–01 } 17–05 }	122	122	123	123	124	124	125	126	126	127	127	128	{ 205 { 209
17–06 } 17–10 }	122	122	123	123	124	124	125	126	126	127	127	128	{ 210 { 214
17–11 } 18–00 }	122	122	123	123	124	124	125	126	126	127	127	128	{ 215 { 216
	228	229	230	231	232	233	234	235	236	237	238	239	TOTAL MONTHS

CHRONOLOGICAL AGE

YEARS MONTHS	20 0	20 1	20 2	20 3	20 4	20 5	20 6	20 7	20 8	20 9	20 10	20 11	
11–00													132
11–01													133
11–02	170												134
11–03	168	169	170										135
11–04	167	168	168	169	170	170							136
11–05	166	166	167	168	168	169	170	170					137
11–06	164	165	166	166	167	168	168	169	170				138
11–07	163	164	165	165	166	167	167	168	168	169	170		139
11–08	162	163	163	164	165	165	166	167	167	168	168	169	140
11–09	161	161	162	163	163	164	165	165	166	167	167	168	141
11–10	160	160	161	162	162	163	164	164	165	165	166	167	142
11–11	159	159	160	161	161	162	162	163	164	164	165	166	143
12–00	158	158	159	159	160	161	161	162	162	163	164	164	144
12–01	157	157	158	158	159	160	160	161	161	162	163	163	145
12–02	156	156	157	158	158	159	159	160	161	161	162	162	146
12–03	155	155	156	157	157	158	158	159	160	160	161	161	147
12–04	154	154	155	156	156	157	157	158	159	159	160	160	148
12–05	153	154	154	155	155	156	156	157	158	158	159	159	149
12–06	152	153	153	154	154	155	156	156	157	157	158	159	150
12–07	151	152	152	153	154	154	155	155	156	156	157	158	151
12–08	150	151	152	152	153	153	154	154	155	156	156	157	152
12–09	149	150	151	151	152	152	153	153	154	155	155	156	153
12–10	149	149	150	150	151	151	152	153	153	154	154	155	154
12–11	148	148	149	150	150	151	151	152	152	153	154	154	155
13–00	147	148	148	149	149	150	150	151	152	152	153	153	156
13–01	146	147	147	148	148	149	150	150	151	151	152	152	157
13–02	146	147	147	148	148	149	150	150	151	151	152	152	158
13–03	145	146	146	147	148	148	149	149	150	150	151	152	159
13–04	145	145	146	146	147	147	148	148	149	150	150	151	160
13–05	145	145	146	146	147	147	148	148	149	150	150	151	161
13–06	144	145	145	145	146	147	147	148	148	149	149	150	162
13–07	143	144	144	145	145	146	146	147	147	148	149	149	163
13–08	143	144	144	145	145	146	146	147	147	148	149	149	164
13–09	142	143	143	144	144	145	146	146	147	147	148	148	165
13–10	141	142	143	143	144	144	145	145	146	146	147	148	166
13–11	141	142	143	143	144	144	145	145	146	146	147	148	167
	240	241	242	243	244	245	246	247	248	249	250	251	TOTAL MONTHS

CHRONOLOGICAL AGE

MA 20–0 / CA 11–0

CHRONOLOGICAL AGE

YEARS MONTHS	20 0	20 1	20 2	20 3	20 4	20 5	20 6	20 7	20 8	20 9	20 10	20 11	
14–00	141	141	142	142	143	143	144	145	145	146	146	147	168
14–01	140	140	141	142	142	143	143	144	144	145	145	146	169
14–02	140	140	141	142	142	143	143	144	144	145	145	146	170
14–03	139	140	140	141	141	142	143	143	144	144	145	145	171
14–04	139	139	140	140	141	141	142	142	143	144	144	144	172
14–05	139	139	140	140	141	141	142	142	143	144	144	144	173
14–06	138	138	139	139	140	141	141	142	142	143	143	144	174
14–07	137	138	138	139	139	140	140	141	142	142	143	143	175
14–08	137	138	138	139	139	140	140	141	142	142	143	143	176
14–09	136	137	138	138	139	139	140	140	141	141	142	142	177
14–10	136	136	137	137	138	139	139	140	140	141	141	142	178
14–11	136	136	137	137	138	139	139	140	140	141	141	142	179
15–00	135	136	136	137	137	138	138	139	139	140	140	141	180
15–01	134	135	135	136	136	137	138	138	139	139	140	140	181
15–02	134	135	135	136	136	137	138	138	139	139	140	140	182
15–03	134	134	135	135	136	136	137	137	138	138	139	139	183
15–04	133	133	134	134	135	135	136	136	137	137	138	139	184
15–05	133	133	134	134	135	135	136	136	137	137	138	139	185
15–06	132	132	133	133	134	135	135	136	136	137	137	138	186
15–07	131	132	132	133	133	134	134	135	135	136	136	137	187
15–08	131	132	132	133	133	134	134	135	135	136	136	137	188
15–09	130	131	131	132	132	133	133	134	134	135	136	136	189
15–10	129	130	130	131	132	132	133	133	134	134	135	135	190
15–11	129	130	130	131	131	132	133	133	134	134	135	135	191
16–00 / 16–02	129	129	130	130	131	131	132	132	133	133	134	134	192 / 194
16–03 / 16–07	129	129	130	130	131	131	132	132	133	133	134	134	195 / 199
16–08 / 17–00	128	129	129	130	131	131	132	132	133	133	134	134	200 / 204
17–01 / 17–05	128	129	129	130	131	131	132	132	133	133	134	134	205 / 209
17–06 / 17–10	128	129	129	130	131	131	132	132	133	133	134	134	210 / 214
17–11 / 18–00	128	129	129	130	131	131	132	132	133	133	134	134	215 / 216
TOTAL MONTHS	240	241	242	243	244	245	246	247	248	249	250	251	

MA 20–0 / CA 14–0

YEARS MONTHS	21 0	21 1	21 2	21 3	20 4	21 5	21 6	21 7	21 8	21 9	21 10	21 11	
11–00													132
11–01													133
11–02													134
11–03													135
11–04													136
11–05													137
11–06													138
11–07													139
11–08	170												140
11–09	168	169	170										141
11–10	167	168	169	169	170								142
11–11	166	167	167	168	169	169	170						143
12–00	165	166	166	167	167	168	169	169	170				144
12–01	164	164	165	166	166	167	168	168	169	169	170		145
12–02	163	164	164	165	165	166	167	167	168	168	169	170	146
12–03	162	163	163	164	164	165	166	166	167	167	168	169	147
12–04	161	162	162	163	163	164	165	165	166	166	167	168	148
12–05	160	161	161	162	162	163	164	164	165	165	166	167	149
12–06	159	160	160	161	162	162	163	163	164	164	165	166	150
12–07	158	159	159	160	161	161	162	162	163	164	164	165	151
12–08	157	158	159	159	160	160	161	161	162	163	163	164	152
12–09	156	157	158	158	159	159	160	160	161	162	162	163	153
12–10	156	156	157	157	158	158	159	160	160	161	161	162	154
12–11	155	155	156	156	157	158	158	159	159	160	160	161	155
13–00	154	154	155	156	156	157	157	158	158	159	159	160	156
13–01	153	154	154	155	155	156	156	157	158	158	159	159	157
13–02	153	154	154	155	155	156	156	157	158	158	159	159	158
13–03	152	153	153	154	154	155	156	156	157	157	158	158	159
13–04	151	152	152	153	154	154	155	155	156	156	157	157	160
13–05	151	152	152	153	154	154	155	155	156	156	157	157	161
13–06	150	151	152	152	153	153	154	154	155	155	156	157	162
13–07	150	150	151	151	152	152	153	154	154	155	155	156	163
13–08	150	150	151	151	152	152	153	154	154	155	155	156	164
13–09	149	149	150	151	151	152	152	153	153	154	154	155	165
13–10	148	149	149	150	150	151	151	152	153	153	154	154	166
13–11	148	149	149	150	150	151	151	152	152	153	154	154	167
	252	253	254	255	256	257	258	259	260	261	262	263	TOTAL MONTHS

CHRONOLOGICAL AGE

MA 21–0 / CA 11–0

YEARS MONTHS	21-0	21-1	21-2	21-3	21-4	21-5	21-6	21-7	21-8	21-9	21-10	21-11	
14–00	148	148	148	149	149	150	151	151	152	152	153	153	168
14–01	147	147	148	148	149	149	150	150	151	151	152	153	169
14–02	147	147	148	148	149	149	150	150	151	151	152	153	170
14–03	146	146	147	147	148	149	149	150	150	151	151	152	171
14–04	145	146	146	147	147	148	148	149	149	150	150	151	172
14–05	145	146	146	147	147	148	148	149	149	150	150	151	173
14–06	144	145	145	146	147	147	148	148	149	149	150	150	174
14–07	144	144	145	145	146	146	147	147	148	148	149	150	175
14–08	144	144	145	145	146	146	147	147	148	148	149	150	176
14–09	143	143	144	145	145	146	146	147	147	148	148	149	177
14–10	142	143	143	144	144	145	146	146	147	147	148	148	178
14–11	142	143	143	144	144	145	146	146	147	147	148	148	179
15–00	142	142	143	143	144	144	145	145	146	146	147	147	180
15–01	141	141	142	142	143	143	144	144	145	146	146	147	181
15–02	141	141	142	142	143	143	144	144	145	146	146	147	182
15–03	140	140	141	141	142	143	143	144	144	145	145	146	183
15–04	139	140	140	141	141	142	142	143	143	144	144	145	184
15–05	139	140	140	141	141	142	142	143	143	144	144	145	185
15–06	138	139	139	140	140	141	141	142	142	143	144	144	186
15–07	137	138	138	139	140	140	141	141	142	142	143	143	187
15–08	137	138	138	139	140	140	141	141	142	142	143	143	188
15–09	137	137	138	138	139	139	140	140	141	141	142	142	189
15–10	136	136	137	137	138	138	139	139	140	141	141	142	190
15–11	136	136	137	137	138	138	139	139	140	140	141	142	191
16–00 } 16–02	135	135	136	136	137	138	138	139	139	140	140	141	{ 192 194
16–03 } 16–07	135	135	136	136	137	138	138	139	139	140	140	141	{ 195 199
16–08 } 17–00	135	135	136	136	137	138	138	139	139	140	140	141	{ 200 204
17–01 } 17–05	135	135	136	136	137	138	138	139	139	140	140	141	{ 205 209
17–06 } 17–10	135	135	136	136	137	138	138	139	139	140	140	141	{ 210 214
17–11 } 18–00	135	135	136	136	137	138	138	139	139	140	140	141	{ 215 216
	252	253	254	255	256	257	258	259	260	261	262	263	TOTAL MONTHS

CHRONOLOGICAL AGE

CHRONOLOGICAL AGE YEARS MONTHS	22 0	22 1	22 2	22 3	22 4	22 5	22 6	22 7	22 8	22 9	22 10	22 11	
11–00													132
11–01													133
11–02													134
11–03													135
11–04													136
11–05													137
11–06													138
11–07													139
11–08													140
11–09													141
11–10													142
11–11													143
12–00													144
12–01													145
12–02	170												146
12–03	169	170											147
12–04	168	169	169	170									148
12–05	167	168	168	169	170	170							149
12–06	166	167	167	168	169	169	170						150
12–07	165	166	166	167	168	168	169	169	170				151
12–08	164	165	166	166	167	167	168	168	169	170	170		152
12–09	163	164	164	165	166	166	167	167	168	169	169		153
12–10	162	163	164	164	165	165	166	166	167	168	168		154
12–11	162	162	163	163	164	164	165	166	166	167	167		155
13–00	161	161	162	162	163	163	164	165	165	166	166		156
13–01	160	160	161	161	162	163	163	164	164	165	165		157
13–02	160	160	161	161	162	163	163	164	164	165	165		158
13–03	159	159	160	161	161	162	162	163	163	164	165		159
13–04	158	159	159	160	160	161	161	162	163	163	164		160
13–05	158	159	159	160	160	161	161	162	163	163	164		161
13–06	157	158	158	159	159	160	161	161	162	162	163		162
13–07	156	157	157	158	159	159	160	160	161	161	162		163
13–08	156	157	157	158	159	159	160	160	161	161	162		164
13–09	156	156	157	157	158	158	159	159	160	160	161		165
13–10	155	155	156	156	157	157	158	159	159	160	160		166
13–11	155	155	156	156	157	157	158	159	159	160	160		167
TOTAL MONTHS	264	265	266	267	268	269	270	271	272	273	274		

MA 22–0 / CA 11–0

YEARS MONTHS	22 0	22 1	22 2	22 3	22 4	22 5	22 6	22 7	22 8	22 9	22 10	22 11	TOTAL MONTHS
14–00	154	154	155	156	156	157	157	158	158	159	159		168
14–01	153	154	154	155	155	156	156	157	158	158	159		169
14–02	153	154	154	155	155	156	156	157	158	158	159		170
14–03	152	153	153	154	155	155	156	156	157	157	158		171
14–04	152	152	153	153	154	154	155	155	156	156	157		172
14–05	152	152	153	153	154	154	155	155	156	156	157		173
14–06	151	151	152	152	153	154	154	155	155	156	156		174
14–07	150	151	151	152	152	153	153	154	155	155	155		175
14–08	150	151	151	152	152	153	153	154	155	155	155		176
14–09	149	150	150	151	152	152	153	153	154	155	155		177
14–10	149	149	150	150	151	151	152	152	153	154	154		178
14–11	149	149	150	150	151	151	152	152	153	154	154		179
15–00	148	148	149	150	150	151	151	152	152	153	153		180
15–01	147	148	148	149	149	150	150	151	151	152	152		181
15–02	147	148	148	149	149	150	150	151	151	152	152		182
15–03	146	147	147	148	148	149	149	150	151	151	152		183
15–04	145	146	147	147	148	148	149	149	150	150	151		184
15–05	145	146	147	147	148	148	149	149	150	150	151		185
15–06	145	145	146	146	147	147	148	148	149	149	150		186
15–07	144	144	145	145	146	146	147	147	148	149	149		187
15–08	144	144	145	145	146	146	147	147	148	149	149		188
15–09	143	143	144	145	145	146	146	147	147	148	148		189
15–10	142	143	143	144	144	145	145	146	146	147	147		190
15–11	142	143	143	144	144	145	145	146	146	147	147		191
16–00 } 16–02	141	142	142	143	143	144	144	145	145	146	147		{ 192 194
16–03 } 16–07	141	142	142	143	143	144	144	145	145	146	147		{ 195 199
16–08 } 17–00	141	142	142	143	143	144	144	145	145	146	147		{ 200 204
17–01 } 17–05	141	142	142	143	143	144	144	145	145	146	147		{ 205 209
17–06 } 17–10	141	142	142	143	143	144	144	145	145	146	147		{ 210 214
17–11 } 18–00	141	142	142	143	143	144	144	145	145	146	147		{ 215 216
	264	265	266	267	268	269	270	271	272	273	274		TOTAL MONTHS

CHRONOLOGICAL AGE

MA 22–0 / CA 14–0

202

APPENDIX C

Constants for Converting Stanford-Binet Conventional IQs into Stanford-Binet Deviation IQs[14]

In instances in which a conventional IQ score has been obtained on a Stanford-Binet scale it may be more convenient to transform it directly into a deviation IQ than to derive the mental age score and enter Appendix B. The following tables of constants are provided for this purpose, and so that DIQs can be computed for the extreme cases for which values are not available from the deviation IQ tables. [At some ages *corrected* constants must be used for DIQs below 50, as is indicated in the tables (cf., p. 52). The corrected constants are presented in Appendix D.]

To apply these tables in the transformation of a conventional to a deviation IQ:

(1) subtract the mean for the subject's chronological age group from the conventional IQ,

(2) multiply the remainder by the accompanying K, and

(3) add 100;

$$DIQ = [(\text{conventional IQ} - \text{mean}) \times K] + 100, \text{ where K is } \frac{16}{SD}.$$

To obtain conventional IQs after age 13 corrected CA divisors must be used in the traditional $\frac{MA}{CA}$ formula. To facilitate computation, these divisors appear in the tables for the ages at which they are required.

In some instances a DIQ obtained with these tables will differ by one IQ point from the value read from Appendix B. Such differences are a result of automatic rounding of numbers during machine processing of data.

[14] This table, which was developed by the writer in establishing the deviation IQ tables for the Stanford-Binet scales, appears in the manual for the third revision of the scales as its Appendix A (55, pp. 339–341). IQ lower limits and corrected CA divisors have been added to extend its usefulness.

APPENDIX C

Constants for Converting Conventional IQs into Deviation IQs

Lowest conventional IQ to which a constant can be applied follows K, under
IQ Lower Limit; for lower values refer to Appendix D

CA	Mean	K	IQ Lower Limit	Corrected CA Divisor (months)	CA	Mean	K	IQ Lower Limit	Corrected CA Divisor (months)
2–00	102	.99	—	—	6–00	100	1.11	—	—
2–01	102	.97	—	—	6–01	100	1.11	—	—
2–02	103	.95	—	—	6–02	100	1.11	—	—
2–03	103	.93	—	—	6–03	100	1.10	—	—
2–04	103	.91	—	—	6–04	100	1.10	—	—
2–05	103	.89	—	—	6–05	100	1.10	—	—
2–06	103	.87	—	—	6–06	100	1.09	—	—
2–07	103	.87	—	—	6–07	100	1.09	—	—
2–08	104	.87	—	—	6–08	100	1.08	—	—
2–09	104	.87	—	—	6–09	100	1.08	—	—
2–10	104	.88	—	—	6–10	101	1.08	—	—
2–11	104	.88	—	—	6–11	101	1.07	—	—
3–00	104	.88	—	—	7–00	101	1.07	—	—
3–01	104	.89	—	—	7–01	101	1.06	—	—
3–02	104	.89	—	—	7–02	101	1.06	—	—
3–03	103	.90	—	—	7–03	101	1.06	—	—
3–04	103	.91	—	—	7–04	101	1.05	27	—
3–05	102	.92	—	—	7–05	101	1.05	27	—
3–06	102	.92	—	—	7–06	101	1.04	27	—
3–07	102	.93	—	—	7–07	102	1.04	32	—
3–08	102	.94	—	—	7–08	102	1.04	32	—
3–09	102	.95	—	—	7–09	102	1.03	32	—
3–10	102	.96	—	—	7–10	102	1.03	32	—
3–11	102	.97	—	—	7–11	102	1.02	32	—
4–00	102	.98	—	—	8–00	102	1.02	32	—
4–01	102	.99	—	—	8–01	102	1.02	29	—
4–02	101	1.00	—	—	8–02	102	1.01	29	—
4–03	101	1.01	—	—	8–03	102	1.01	29	—
4–04	101	1.02	—	—	8–04	102	1.01	29	—
4–05	101	1.03	—	—	8–05	102	1.00	29	—
4–06	101	1.04	—	—	8–06	102	1.00	29	—
4–07	101	1.04	—	—	8–07	102	.99	29	—
4–08	101	1.05	—	—	8–08	102	.99	29	—
4–09	101	1.06	—	—	8–09	102	.99	29	—
4–10	100	1.07	—	—	8–10	103	.99	29	—
4–11	100	1.08	—	—	8–11	103	.98	29	—
5–00	100	1.09	—	—	9–00	103	.98	29	—
5–01	100	1.09	—	—	9–01	103	.98	29	—
5–02	100	1.10	—	—	9–02	103	.98	29	—
5–03	100	1.11	—	—	9–03	103	.97	29	—
5–04	100	1.11	—	—	9–04	103	.97	29	—
5–05	100	1.12	—	—	9–05	103	.97	29	—
5–06	100	1.12	—	—	9–06	103	.96	20	—
5–07	100	1.12	—	—	9–07	103	.96	20	—
5–08	100	1.12	—	—	9–08	103	.96	20	—
5–09	100	1.12	—	—	9–09	103	.95	20	—
5–10	100	1.12	—	—	9–10	103	.95	20	—
5–11	100	1.12	—	—	9–11	103	.95	20	—

Constants for Converting Conventional IQs into Deviation IQs

Lowest conventional IQ to which a constant can be applied follows K, under
IQ Lower Limit, for lower values refer to Appendix D

CA	Mean	K	IQ Lower Limit	Corrected CA Divisor (months)	CA	Mean	K	IQ Lower Limit	Corrected CA Divisor (months)
10–00	103	.94	20	—	14–00	101	.90	—	164
10–01	103	.94	20	—	14–01	101	.90	—	165
10–02	103	.94	20	—	14–02	101	.90	—	165
10–03	103	.94	20	—	14–03	101	.91	—	166
10–04	103	.93	25	—	14–04	101	.91	—	167
10–05	103	.93	25	—	14–05	101	.91	—	167
10–06	103	.93	25	—	14–06	101	.91	—	168
10–07	102	.92	25	—	14–07	101	.91	—	169
10–08	102	.92	25	—	14–08	101	.91	—	169
10–09	102	.92	25	—	14–09	101	.91	—	170
10–10	102	.91	29	—	14–10	101	.92	—	171
10–11	102	.91	29	—	14–11	101	.92	—	171
11–00	102	.91	30	—	15–00	102	.92	—	172
11–01	102	.90	28	—	15–01	102	.92	—	173
11–02	102	.90	28	—	15–02	102	.92	—	173
11–03	102	.90	28	—	15–03	102	.93	—	174
11–04	102	.90	27	—	15–04	102	.93	—	175
11–05	102	.90	27	—	15–05	102	.93	—	175
11–06	102	.90	27	—	15–06	102	.93	—	176
11–07	102	.89	27	—	15–07	102	.94	—	177
11–08	102	.89	27	—	15–08	103	.94	—	177
11–09	102	.89	27	—	15–09	103	.94	—	178
11–10	102	.89	27	—	15–10	103	.94	—	179
11–11	102	.89	27	—	15–11	103	.95	—	179
12–00	102	.88	27	—	16–00	103	.95		
12–01	102	.88	27	—	16–01	103	.95	—	180
12–02	102	.88	27	—	16–02	103	.95		
12–03	101	.88	27	—	16–03	104	.96		
12–04	101	.88	27	—	16–04	104	.96		
12–05	101	.89	25	—	16–05	104	.96	—	180
12–06	101	.89	25	—	16–06	104	.96		
12–07	101	.89	25	—	16–07	104	.96		
12–08	101	.89	25	—	16–08	104	.98		
12–09	101	.89	25	—	16–09	104	.98		
12–10	101	.89	25	—	16–10	104	.98	—	180
12–11	101	.89	25	—	16–11	104	.98		
13–00	101	.89	25	156	17–00	104	.98		
13–01	101	.89	25	157	17–01	104	.98		
13–02	101	.89	25	157	17–02	104	.98		
13–03	101	.89	25	158	17–03	104	.98	—	180
13–04	101	.89	25	159	17–04	104	.98		
13–05	101	.89	25	159	17–05	104	.98		
13–06	101	.90	20	160	17–06	105	1.00		
13–07	101	.90	20	161	17–07	105	1.00		
13–08	101	.90	20	161	17–08	105	1.00		
13–09	101	.90	20	162	17–09	105	1.00	—	180
13–10	101	.90	20	163	17–10	105	1.00		
13–11	101	.90	20	163	17–11	105	1.00		
					18–00	105	1.00		

APPENDIX D

Constants for Converting Stanford-Binet Conventional IQs
Between −4 and −5 Standard Deviations into
Stanford-Binet Deviation IQs

The age differences in the constants which are used to transform conventional into deviation IQs (cf., Appendix C) reflect age differences in variability of the intelligence quotient. These age differences in variability appear to be due chiefly to the varying concentration of average-difficulty items along the mental age scale. By minus four standard deviations these differing constants are being applied to scores obtained on the same area of the mental age scale and not to different areas varying in the concentration of average-difficulty items. Therefore, it is necessary to modify the constants at certain ages for conventional IQs below −4 SDs. The corrected constants, together with the IQs to which they apply, are in the following table. The constants at adjacent years are also included in order to facilitate the interpolation of constants for fractions of a year.

206

APPENDIX D

Constants for Converting Conventional IQs between
—4 and —5 SDs into Deviation IQs

		CHRONOLOGICAL AGE (in Years)							
		7	8	9	10	11	12	13	14
INTELLIGENCE QUOTIENT	20	—	—	—	.94	.93	.91	.91	.90
	21	—	—	.97	.94	.93	.91	.90	.90
	22	—	—	.97	.94	.93	.91	.90	.90
	23	—	1.01	.97	.94	.93	.91	.90	.90
	24	—	1.01	.97	.94	.93	.91	.90	.90
	25	1.07	1.01	.97	.94	.93	.90	.89	—
	26	1.07	1.01	.97	.94	.92	.90	.89	—
	27	1.07	1.01	.97	.94	.92	.89	.89	—
	28	1.07	1.01	.97	.94	.92	.88	—	—
	29	1.07	1.01	.97	.94	.92	.88	—	—
	30	1.07	1.01	.98	.94	.91	—	—	—
	31	1.07	1.01	.98	.94	.91	—	—	—
	32	1.07	1.02	.98	.94	.91	—	—	—

Change in Conventional and Deviation IQs for Different Age Intervals Subsequent to Tests at Nineteen Different Ages: Berkeley Growth Study Sample

In this section the amount of change between tests for subjects tested at frequent intervals from infancy through adolescence is tabulated. The amount of change from the age specified in a table's heading to each of the ages indicated in its left-hand margin appears in the body of that table.

The IQ changes in part A of the tables *should not* be used in practical situations because these values confound actual changes in relative position with scoring inadequacies inherent in the conventional IQ concept. Before using the values in part B of the tables to qualify the performance of individual subjects, the reader should be thoroughly familiar with the material in Chapters 9, 10, and 11, especially that on pages 82–83 and 93–95.

APPENDIX E.1

Change in IQs of Individuals Tested at 1 Month and at Subsequent Ages:
BGS Sample

Years and Months	A. Conventional IQ Score Changes						N	B. Deviation IQ Score Changes					
	Median	Quartiles I	Quartiles III	Range	Mean	S.D.		Median	Quartiles I	Quartiles III	Range	Mean	S.D.
0–3	12	7	20	2–40	13.9	9.0	52	9	3	18	1–30	11.5	9.0
0–6	10	6	24	0–49	15.9	13.0	48	14	4	21	1–45	14.8	11.8
0–9	10	5	22	0–49	14.2	11.5	47	13	6	23	0–47	15.2	10.6
1–0	12	5	20	1–53	15.2	12.5	45	16	9	21	0–54	16.1	11.2
1–6	11	6	25	0–55	15.8	13.8	45						
2–0	14	5	26	3–58	18.0	15.2	41	15	6	25	0–75	18.2	15.7
2–6	17	7	28	0–71	21.2	16.6	41	13	7	23	1–50	15.7	11.7
3–0	24	8	34	0–64	23.2	17.7	40	15	7	22	0–73	16.6	13.0
4–0	20	9	28	1–63	21.4	16.1	37	17	7	28	0–81	18.9	15.7
5–0	15	8	23	0–57	18.9	16.4	39	12	7	24	1–77	17.8	15.7
6–0	26	12	39	2–70	28.0	19.0	40	14	7	31	0–90	21.8	20.3
7–0	26	13	42	4–74	30.1	19.1	39	18	10	33	1–89	22.5	17.3
8–0	29	20	42	2–83	32.3	20.4	39	14	8	31	1–67	21.0	16.8
9–0	33	19	48	1–80	34.7	22.5	37	19	8	32	0–71	21.9	16.2
10–0	34	20	48	2–109	37.8	25.6	40	17	10	31	0–73	22.9	20.3
11–0	35	21	48	1–93	36.9	22.3	37	17	8	30	0–60	19.8	15.7
12–0	30	14	50	1–87	33.3	23.6	35	15	6	26	1–60	18.4	15.5
14–0	32	20	43	1–83	33.7	21.1	33	12	7	28	0–55	17.6	14.6
17–0	33	20	47	5–71	34.0	18.6	34	19	9	27	0–76	21.4	16.3

APPENDIX E.2

Change in IQs of Individuals Tested at 3 Months and at Subsequent Ages: BGS Sample

Years and Months	A Conventional IQ Score Changes							B Deviation IQ Score Changes					
	Median	Quartiles I	Quartiles III	Range	Mean	S.D.	N	Median	Quartiles I	Quartiles III	Range	Mean	S.D.
0–6	11	5	19	1–38	12.7	9.1	57	12	8	21	0–45	14.6	10.2
0–9	9	4	16	1–34	10.7	8.8	56	14	7	22	0–56	15.5	11.7
1–0	8	4	18	0–39	11.3	9.6	53	12	6	25	1–50	17.0	13.5
1–6	9	4	22	0–54	13.8	12.9	51						
2–0	19	11	28	0–66	21.8	16.2	48	15	9	36	2–64	21.6	17.4
2–6	18	15	31	0–75	23.1	18.1	47	13	6	26	0–67	17.9	15.4
3–0	28	13	40	3–71	27.7	17.1	48	15	9	23	0–47	17.6	12.2
4–0	18	13	31	0–61	22.4	13.9	45	16	6	29	1–62	19.8	15.5
5–0	18	8	31	1–63	19.8	14.6	47	16	6	26	0–66	19.0	16.0
6–0	29	20	40	0–82	30.2	17.5	48	15	9	32	0–87	22.4	19.0
7–0	29	18	41	2–72	31.4	17.0	46	18	8	28	0–74	22.4	18.6
8–0	35	16	47	0–74	33.8	18.9	47	19	8	33	0–65	21.7	16.9
9–0	39	20	55	2–82	37.3	21.7	45	20	8	34	0–69	22.9	17.2
10–0	38	21	55	1–101	39.9	22.6	47	19	8	34	0–74	22.8	18.8
11–0	41	23	54	0–90	39.8	22.5	45	18	6	35	0–72	21.6	17.5
12–0	39	20	53	5–89	37.5	20.5	43	17	5	31	1–74	20.6	16.8
14–0	35	23	50	1–82	36.0	20.6	37	12	7	30	0–51	18.3	15.0
17–0	40	24	51	2–71	37.4	19.2	40	17	7	34	0–76	20.3	16.5

APPENDIX E.3

Change in IQs of Individuals Tested at 6 Months and at Subsequent Ages: BGS Sample

Years and Months	A Conventional IQ Score Changes						N	B Deviation IQ Score Changes					
	Median	Quartiles I	Quartiles III	Range	Mean	S.D.		Median	Quartiles I	Quartiles III	Range	Mean	S.D.
0–9	7	2	12	0–24	7.8	6.3	52	10	4	13	0–43	10.2	8.4
1–0	7	4	12	0–28	8.5	6.1	49	8	4	15	0–34	10.4	8.7
1–6	9	4	17	0–31	11.2	8.4	47						
2–0	11	3	25	1–58	15.8	15.4	45	16	10	28	0–54	19.7	13.4
2–6	16	6	29	1–61	18.2	14.3	44	15	8	23	1–37	15.4	9.8
3–0	18	10	36	0–56	21.6	15.8	44	15	9	21	1–38	16.0	10.2
4–0	14	9	28	0–59	18.3	13.0	41	12	4	27	0–55	16.6	13.9
5–0	16	5	26	0–50	16.6	13.7	43	17	12	26	1–44	19.0	11.0
6–0	24	10	40	1–77	26.1	18.2	44	21	13	33	1–68	23.7	15.2
7–0	24	10	42	1–72	26.8	17.5	42	23	9	31	0–62	21.9	15.4
8–0	24	14	41	1–83	29.0	19.4	43	18	9	31	0–71	21.4	15.7
9–0	30	17	46	4–79	33.4	21.1	42	17	10	31	0–67	22.2	15.7
10–0	38	19	52	0–116	36.7	24.7	43	21	12	32	0–86	25.1	19.0
11–0	40	21	51	0–83	36.8	22.0	42	18	10	32	0–48	20.8	13.1
12–0	33	18	49	5–77	34.4	20.6	40	20	9	27	0–62	20.2	14.2
14–0	36	20	44	1–73	33.0	19.3	34	16	7	30	0–72	20.3	16.5
17–0	34	22	48	2–78	33.8	18.9	36	19	5	31	2–60	21.6	15.7

APPENDIX E.4

Change in IQs of Individuals Tested at 9 Months and at Subsequent Ages: BGS Sample

Years and Months	A Conventional IQ Score Changes							B Deviation IQ Score Changes					
	Median	Quartiles I	Quartiles III	Range	Mean	S.D.	N	Median	Quartiles I	Quartiles III	Range	Mean	S.D.
1-0	4	2	6	0-15	4.8	3.7	52	8	4	14	0-28	9.7	7.1
1-6	6	2	13	0-37	8.4	7.6	49						
2-0	12	7	22	1-51	15.4	11.6	46	15	6	27	1-59	17.3	13.0
2-6	17	8	23	0-45	16.9	12.1	45	12	3	23	0-36	13.0	10.9
3-0	22	8	31	0-45	20.3	12.4	46	11	8	20	0-33	13.9	7.7
4-0	15	10	21	3-43	16.0	8.7	44	12	6	19	1-46	15.0	11.7
5-0	9	5	20	1-40	13.3	10.8	45	11	6	24	1-44	15.2	11.4
6-0	22	13	32	2-61	23.9	14.3	46	15	7	24	0-63	18.7	15.4
7-0	25	14	32	1-55	24.1	13.3	44	15	4	25	0-50	17.0	13.6
8-0	24	16	37	1-67	26.4	16.3	45	15	5	28	0-52	16.6	13.1
9-0	30	14	47	0-65	31.0	17.8	43	15	6	25	1-48	17.6	13.4
10-0	28	18	47	3-100	34.2	21.0	45	17	9	28	2-77	21.3	16.5
11-0	35	22	46	0-83	34.3	18.3	43	13	7	24	1-59	16.6	13.3
12-0	32	21	43	1-74	31.9	16.4	42	12	6	22	0-51	15.2	12.3
14-0	34	13	43	1-73	30.7	16.4	35	10	5	23	0-56	14.7	12.8
17-0	34	23	40	5-59	31.6	13.6	38	12	6	23	0-59	16.6	13.9

APPENDIX E.5

Change in IQs of Individuals Tested at 1 Year and at Subsequent Ages: BGS Sample

Years and Months	A Conventional IQ Score Changes						N	B Deviation IQ Score Changes					
	Median	Quartiles I	Quartiles III	Range	Mean	S.D.		Median	Quartiles I	Quartiles III	Range	Mean	S.D.
1-6	5	2	12	0-32	7.4	6.8	49	11	4	21	0-48	14.1	11.8
2-0	12	7	19	0-48	14.6	10.8	46	11	4	19	0-30	12.3	8.3
2-6	16	5	24	0-44	15.7	11.6	45	11	6	16	2-36	12.3	8.5
3-0	20	10	30	0-45	20.0	11.5	46	9	4	22	0-50	13.1	11.5
4-0	14	10	20	0-42	15.0	8.3	44	14	7	22	0-53	15.5	11.5
5-0	9	4	20	0-39	12.3	10.7	45	16	10	28	1-66	20.5	14.6
6-0	21	13	34	1-60	23.8	13.7	46	15	10	26	2-56	18.6	13.3
7-0	23	12	33	0-55	23.8	13.3	44	13	7	24	1-71	18.2	15.1
8-0	24	15	36	1-66	26.5	15.6	45	17	9	26	1-67	19.6	14.2
9-0	31	15	44	0-62	30.3	17.9	43	14	7	30	0-80	19.6	18.1
10-0	30	20	44	1-99	34.0	20.3	45	12	6	24	1-68	17.6	15.4
11-0	33	20	46	0-76	34.4	17.4	43	16	5	25	0-62	17.3	14.2
12-0	30	18	44	2-67	31.4	17.2	42	11	6	28	1-68	16.5	15.4
14-0	31	19	44	1-66	30.9	16.1	35	14	5	26	1-75	16.6	14.9
17-0	34	24	41	2-52	31.6	13.5	38						

APPENDIX E.6

Change in IQs of Individuals Tested at 1 Year–6 Months and at Subsequent Ages: BGS Sample

| Years and Months | A Conventional IQ Score Changes | | | | | | | B Deviation IQ Score Changes | | | | | |
	Median	Quartiles I	Quartiles III	Range	Mean	S.D.	N	Median	Quartiles I	Quartiles III	Range	Mean	S.D.
2-0	11	6	15	0–52	13.4	10.8	45	10	5	18	0–59	13.2	11.2
2-6	14	10	19	0–46	15.6	9.6	46	8	4	19	0–47	11.6	10.7
3-0	18	11	27	4–41	19.3	10.6	45	9	6	18	0–49	12.2	10.0
4-0	11	7	18	0–41	13.6	9.5	43	10	4	19	2–41	13.5	11.0
5-0	9	6	14	0–51	11.4	10.5	45	10	5	18	0–51	13.3	12.0
6-0	19	12	34	0–58	23.0	15.0	45	18	9	27	0–52	20.1	14.1
7-0	21	9	36	0–55	22.5	14.0	43	15	5	29	0–51	17.7	14.2
8-0	24	17	36	0–74	26.8	16.3	44	13	6	22	2–60	17.9	15.9
9-0	23	17	45	0–74	28.8	19.6	42	17	8	27	1–53	20.0	15.0
10-0	26	14	46	8–90	33.4	21.4	44	20	5	30	1–65	20.4	17.0
11-0	28	19	45	3–88	33.2	19.1	42	17	6	29	1–60	19.0	15.9
12-0	26	17	40	0–79	30.8	18.9	41	12	7	24	1–56	17.3	15.4
14-0	31	21	40	1–78	31.2	17.2	37	11	6	22	0–54	17.0	15.6
17-0	30	19	39	3–64	29.7	15.0	38	12	5	26	0–52	17.2	14.4

Change in IQs of Individuals Tested at 2 Years and at Subsequent Ages: BGS Sample

Years and Months	A Conventional IQ Score Changes							N	B Deviation IQ Score Changes					
	Median	Quartiles		Range	Mean	S.D.			Median	Quartiles		Range	Mean	S.D.
		I	III							I	III			
2–6	6	2	11	0–19	7.1	5.7		42	8	2	17	1–34	9.8	8.3
3–0	8	2	12	0–31	8.5	7.2		44	7	5	17	0–39	10.6	9.1
4–0	8	4	12	0–27	8.8	6.1		41	11	6	22	0–34	13.5	9.0
5–0	10	5	15	1–36	11.0	7.4		43	14	7	24	1–49	15.9	11.5
6–0	10	3	18	0–38	12.2	10.2		43	11	6	27	0–45	16.6	12.4
7–0	14	6	17	0–33	13.3	8.8		41	13	9	19	0–41	16.3	10.3
8–0	14	8	26	0–48	16.8	12.7		42	16	6	24	1–51	16.5	12.6
9–0	16	8	30	1–49	19.7	14.1		40	14	6	28	1–44	17.1	12.6
10–0	20	9	31	1–77	21.8	16.2		42	14	9	21	0–61	17.7	13.4
11–0	22	11	30	0–55	22.7	14.1		40	12	6	22	1–48	15.2	12.3
12–0	17	8	29	1–57	20.2	14.0		39	13	7	22	1–50	15.5	10.9
14–0	23	11	27	1–41	20.4	12.2		33	13	7	18	0–34	14.2	9.4
17–0	20	11	26	1–43	18.9	11.0		36	14	8	18	0–40	14.5	9.5

APPENDIX E.8

Change in IQs of Individuals Tested at 2 Years–6 Months and at Subsequent Ages: BGS Sample

Years and Months	A Conventional IQ Score Changes							B Deviation IQ Score Changes					
	Median	Quartiles I	Quartiles III	Range	Mean	S.D.	N	Median	Quartiles I	Quartiles III	Range	Mean	S.D.
3-0	6	3	11	0–29	7.5	6.4	45	6	4	11	0–24	7.6	5.8
4-0	8	3	14	1–24	8.8	6.6	42	9	5	12	1–28	10.3	7.0
5-0	9	4	14	1–33	10.3	7.4	43	8	5	16	0–32	11.2	8.7
6-0	10	4	19	0–36	11.9	9.2	43	14	8	28	0–47	16.8	12.2
7-0	10	7	16	1–33	12.3	8.5	42	15	8	23	2–40	16.1	10.3
8-0	14	7	26	0–42	16.6	11.6	42	12	4	24	0–38	14.3	11.9
9-0	18	7	28	0–42	18.3	13.0	41	14	9	25	1–39	16.2	10.7
10-0	20	7	31	1–75	22.0	16.9	42	16	7	23	1–61	17.6	14.1
11-0	22	13	29	0–52	22.0	13.0	42	16	8	25	3–40	17.6	10.1
12-0	20	6	29	0–50	19.5	12.9	40	16	6	22	1–39	14.8	10.0
14-0	20	11	27	3–42	19.5	10.9	37	15	9	20	1–34	15.4	9.3
17-0	17	10	24	3–37	18.3	10.4	37	11	6	18	1–40	14.0	10.2

APPENDIX E.9

Change in IQs of Individuals Tested at 3 Years and at Subsequent Ages:
BGS Sample

Years and Months	A Conventional IQ Score Changes						N	B Deviation IQ Score Changes					
	Median	Quartiles I	III	Range	Mean	S.D.		Median	Quartiles I	III	Range	Mean	S.D.
4-0	9	4	13	0–27	9.4	6.5	45	8	4	11	0–31	9.0	7.3
5-0	12	6	18	0–32	12.9	8.2	46	10	5	17	0–31	11.4	8.3
6-0	10	4	15	1–30	10.5	7.2	46	11	6	23	0–39	14.8	11.2
7-0	10	4	17	0–34	11.0	7.9	45	13	6	24	0–41	14.9	10.8
8-0	11	3	24	1–37	13.7	11.8	45	10	3	24	0–37	14.0	11.9
9-0	14	4	24	1–48	15.8	12.8	44	12	5	24	0–44	15.0	11.8
10-0	15	5	23	0–61	18.3	15.7	45	12	6	25	0–54	16.2	14.0
11-0	20	10	26	0–55	19.8	13.3	44	16	8	22	0–48	16.8	11.5
12-0	16	7	25	0–58	17.6	12.5	42	13	7	22	0–50	14.8	10.5
14-0	16	11	25	1–41	17.8	10.5	37	13	8	24	1–35	15.3	9.4
17-0	16	9	22	1–44	16.3	9.8	40	13	8	18	0–39	14.1	9.4

217

APPENDIX E.10

Change in IQs of Individuals Tested at 4 Years and at Subsequent Ages: BGS Sample

| Years and Months | A Conventional IQ Score Changes | | | | | | | B Deviation IQ Score Changes | | | | | |
	Median	Quartiles I	Quartiles III	Range	Mean	S.D.	N	Median	Quartiles I	Quartiles III	Range	Mean	S.D.
5-0	6	2	11	0-19	7.2	5.2	44	8	3	16	0-27	9.6	7.4
6-0	12	3	18	0-24	11.2	7.6	44	15	8	20	0-30	14.0	8.6
7-0	10	5	15	0-29	10.9	7.5	43	11	6	16	0-34	12.5	8.5
8-0	13	6	24	1-38	15.4	10.5	43	12	5	19	1-32	12.3	9.0
9-0	18	7	30	1-39	18.7	12.1	42	14	6	19	1-32	13.7	8.7
10-0	19	10	31	0-57	21.3	14.1	43	12	5	23	1-37	14.0	11.8
11-0	24	10	31	2-50	23.0	12.6	42	16	8	22	1-32	14.9	9.1
12-0	20	8	31	2-41	20.2	12.6	41	15	4	19	0-30	13.3	8.7
14-0	20	11	30	1-39	19.8	11.4	35	13	8	21	2-32	14.2	7.7
17-0	20	13	27	0-34	19.3	8.9	38	12	6	18	2-34	12.6	8.0

APPENDIX E.11

Change in IQs of Individuals Tested at 5 Years and at Subsequent Ages:

BGS Sample

Years and Months	A Conventional IQ Score Changes						N	B Deviation IQ Score Changes					
	Median	Quartiles I	Quartiles III	Range	Mean	S.D.		Median	Quartiles I	Quartiles III	Range	Mean	S.D.
6-0	12	8	18	2–32	13.8	7.3	46	6	4	13	0–27	9.3	7.2
7-0	12	8	18	0–32	13.6	8.5	44	8	3	15	0–26	9.1	6.7
8-0	15	10	23	0–43	16.9	10.2	45	9	4	16	0–34	10.1	7.6
9-0	20	9	29	0–47	20.0	12.6	43	10	5	16	1–37	10.4	7.4
10-0	20	14	32	0–66	23.9	14.0	45	8	5	14	1–40	11.0	8.8
11-0	24	12	37	3–53	24.3	12.9	43	12	4	16	1–33	11.2	7.4
12-0	22	12	33	1–56	21.9	12.0	42	8	4	13	1–37	9.7	7.8
14-0	18	10	32	1–45	20.8	12.2	36	9	6	16	1–25	10.6	7.3
17-0	19	10	31	0–42	20.1	12.2	39	9	6	17	1–27	10.8	7.0

APPENDIX E.12

Change in IQs of Individuals Tested at 6 Years and at Subsequent Ages: BGS Sample

Years and Months	A Conventional IQ Score Changes							N	B Deviation IQ Score Changes					
	Median	Quartiles		Range	Mean	S.D.			Median	Quartiles		Range	Mean	S.D.
		I	III							I	III			
7–0	5	2	9	0–14	5.8	4.2		45	8	3	13	0–20	7.9	5.9
8–0	8	3	12	0–32	8.9	6.5		46	8	3	14	0–29	9.4	7.7
9–0	11	5	16	0–37	11.6	7.7		44	7	2	16	0–29	9.2	7.9
10–0	13	4	20	0–39	12.4	9.8		46	8	4	13	0–22	8.5	5.9
11–0	14	6	22	0–49	14.8	10.4		44	9	4	16	0–36	10.7	8.6
12–0	10	5	18	1–33	12.9	9.2		42	8	3	13	0–42	9.8	8.5
14–0	12	4	18	0–38	12.4	9.0		36	6	3	16	0–36	9.9	9.6
17–0	8	5	18	0–32	11.4	8.6		39	10	5	14	0–34	11.1	7.8

APPENDIX E.13

Change in IQs of Individuals Tested at 7 Years and at Subsequent Ages: BGS Sample

Years and Months	A Conventional IQ Score Changes						N	B Deviation IQ Score Changes					
	Median	Quartiles I	Quartiles III	Range	Mean	S.D.		Median	Quartiles I	Quartiles III	Range	Mean	S.D.
8-0	6	2	12	0–30	7.7	6.9	45	8	5	13	1–30	9.3	6.1
9-0	10	6	16	0–30	11.8	7.6	44	9	4	14	0–28	9.9	6.9
10-0	10	6	19	0–44	13.1	10.0	45	7	4	14	0–24	9.2	7.1
11-0	12	4	21	0–35	13.6	10.4	44	9	5	14	1–28	10.4	6.5
12-0	11	5	19	1–32	12.8	8.8	41	8	5	12	1–30	9.8	6.9
14-0	8	5	14	1–34	10.9	8.0	37	8	3	13	1–32	9.6	7.5
17-0	9	4	14	0–31	10.0	7.4	40	8	2	14	1–27	9.2	7.4

APPENDIX E.14

Change in IQs of Individuals Tested at 8 Years and at Subsequent Ages: BGS Sample

Years and Months	A Conventional IQ Score Changes							B Deviation IQ Score Changes					
	Median	Quartiles I	Quartiles III	Range	Mean	S.D.	N	Median	Quartiles I	Quartiles III	Range	Mean	S.D.
9–0	6	3	10	0–21	7.3	6.2	45	7	3	10	0–19	7.1	5.5
10–0	6	5	13	0–36	9.6	8.6	46	5	2	11	0–32	7.6	7.5
11–0	9	5	17	1–25	10.8	7.4	44	8	4	14	0–21	8.6	6.0
12–0	6	3	15	0–24	9.1	7.1	42	6	4	12	0–22	8.0	5.5
14–0	6	3	12	0–22	7.5	6.0	36	6	3	10	0–20	7.1	5.4
17–0	8	3	12	0–23	9.0	6.6	39	9	4	11	0–25	8.7	6.3

APPENDIX E.15

Change in IQs of Individuals Tested at 9 Years and at Subsequent Ages:
BGS Sample

Years and Months	A Conventional IQ Score Changes						N	B Deviation IQ Score Changes					
	Median	Quartiles I	III	Range	Mean	S.D.		Median	Quartiles I	III	Range	Mean	S.D.
10–0	5	2	11	0–37	7.9	8.0	44	5	2	10	0–33	7.2	7.4
11–0	5	2	10	0–29	6.8	6.3	43	4	2	10	0–27	6.1	5.6
12–0	6	2	10	0–31	7.0	6.2	40	6	4	8	0–29	7.0	5.6
14–0	9	4	13	0–23	9.1	6.2	35	9	4	14	1–22	9.3	5.8
17–0	10	6	14	1–23	9.6	5.5	38	10	5	14	0–22	9.6	5.7

Change in IQs of Individuals Tested at 10 Years and at Subsequent Ages: BGS Sample

Years and Months	A Conventional IQ Score Changes						N	B Deviation IQ Score Changes					
	Median	Quartiles I	III	Range	Mean	S.D.		Median	Quartiles I	III	Range	Mean	S.D.
11–0	6	2	10	0–18	6.5	4.9	44	5	3	10	0–18	6.2	4.4
12–0	5	2	10	0–27	6.9	6.3	42	5	2	9	0–26	6.7	6.0
14–0	7	3	13	0–21	8.2	5.7	36	8	3	12	0–20	7.7	5.6
17–0	8	5	15	1–28	10.1	6.8	39	7	5	14	1–26	9.5	6.4

Change in IQs of Individuals Tested at 11 Years and at Subsequent Ages: BGS Sample

Years and Months	A Conventional IQ Score Changes						N	B Deviation IQ Score Changes					
	Median	Quartiles I	III	Range	Mean	S.D.		Median	Quartiles I	III	Range	Mean	S.D.
12–0	5	3	10	0–18	6.3	4.7	42	4	3	9	0–16	5.8	4.2
14–0	6	4	11	1–16	7.5	4.1	37	6	4	9	0–14	6.4	3.7
17–0	7	5	12	0–24	8.6	6.1	39	7	4	10	1–21	7.8	5.4

APPENDIX E.18

Change in IQs of Individuals Tested at 12 Years and at Subsequent Ages: BGS Sample

Years and Months	A Conventional IQ Score Changes						N	B Deviation IQ Score Changes					
	Median	Quartiles I	III	Range	Mean	S.D.		Median	Quartiles I	III	Range	Mean	S.D.
14-0	6	3	8	0–19	6.5	4.2	35	6	3	7	0–16	5.6	3.6
17-0	7	3	14	0–21	7.9	5.7	37	6	3	11	0–18	7.1	4.9

APPENDIX E.19

Change in IQs of Individuals Tested at 14 Years and at Subsequent Ages: BGS Sample

Years and Months	A Conventional IQ Score Changes						N	B Deviation IQ Score Changes					
	Median	Quartiles I	III	Range	Mean	S.D.		Median	Quartiles I	III	Range	Mean	S.D.
17-0	5	2	8	0–18	6.1	5.0	36	5	2	8	0–18	5.8	4.7

Index

of Stanford-Binet, 25–29; conventional IQ means and SDs with age, 19–21; correlations between age levels, 10; correlations between IQs, tabular presentation, 12–13; description of sample, 7–9, 112; DIQ means and SDs, 20–21; effect of use of different tests, 28–29; graphic comparison of change in conventional and deviation IQ, 36; intercorrelations among age level test scores, 12–13; Institute of Human Development (Institute of Child Welfare), 2, 112; Lability scores for individual subjects, 42–45, definition, 14; McNemar's corrections applied to IQs, 32; mean change in IQ score, cause of, 16–18; means — scores corrected by McNemar's technique, 32; mental age gains, related to ability, 55, comparison for groups of same age, 55–56, standard score value, 57, 60, table of comparison, 57–63; mental tests administered, 9; practice effects, 22; principal investigator (Dr. Nancy Bayley), 7; research and testing program, 7–8; stability of DIQ, 22–24; variability change with age, 8, 16–19; variability corrections of IQs at all ages, 33–35

Bishton, R. (10), 115; Effects of home environment on achievement, 74

Bradway, Katherine P. (11, 12), 115, 116; Follow-up on 1937 standardization samples of Stanford-Binet, 10; Age change in conventional IQ, 14, 25–29

Brown, F. (13), 116; Variability explanations, 31

Butler, A. J. (48), 117; WISC on below average groups, 107

California First Year Mental Scale, 9, 14, 18, 20; standardization sample, 20

California Guidance Study, 10, 55

California Pre-School Scale, 9, 14, 18, 20, 21, 22, 25; standardization sample, 21

Cartee, J. (58), 118; Comparison of WISC with the Stanford-Binet, 107

Change in conventional IQ, 2; as a measure of change in relative position, 18–19; effect of biases on change estimation, 105; effect of heterogeneity in

age, 14; factors related to, 79–80; related to percentile change, 18. *See also* Conventional IQ, change

Change in conventional and deviation IQ, 22; graphic comparison, 23; tables of change, 209–225. *See also* Stability of intelligence; Conventional IQ; *and* Deviation IQ

Change in deviation IQ, corrected, 24; effect of biases on change estimation, 105; factors related to, 79–80; tables of change, 25–29, 209–225, uncorrected, 25–29. *See also* Deviation IQ, change

Chronological age divisors for the Stanford-Binet scales, 89, 203–205

Clark, S. (37), 117; Differential performance on items, 77

Clarke, A. D. B. (14), 116; Age changes in conventional IQ, 14

Clarke, A. M. (14), 116; Age changes in conventional IQ, 14

Classification on basis of IQ and DIQ, 72, 98–100; graphic presentation, 70

Cohen, B. D. (15), 116; WISC compared with other tests, 107

Collier, Mary J. (15), 116; WISC compared with other tests, 107

Common elements; *see* Overlap hypothesis

Composition of intelligence, 1, 80

Conrad, H. S. (16, 34, 35), 116, 117; Composition of intelligence, 1; Duration of mental growth, 52

Consistency of ability with age; *see* Stability of intelligence; Conventional IQ; *and* Deviation IQ

Conventional IQ, age change in meaning, 6, 18; age changes in variability, 16, 30–31, graphic illustration, 31; causes of change in means with age, 16–18, 48–49; changes related to level and test construction, 18–19, effect of DIQ transformation, 22, effect of variability correction, 34–36, meaning of, 29, 1937 standardization samples of Stanford-Binet, 25–29, *see also* Stability of intelligence; compared with DIQ, 6, 70–72, for individual subjects, 42–45; computation, 15; correlation between means and SDs, 41; distribution with

age — error of measurement, 37, related to ability, 38; Reliability of conventional IQ, average difference and ability levels, 38–39, different ability levels, 35–36, effect of age increase in MA distribution, 39–40, effect of method of computing, 35–36, 39–40; Spread of performance, 38; Variability of conventional IQ, explanation, 31–32

Means and SDs of conventional IQs, correlation between, 41

Measures of mental test performance, 69

Mental age scores, 3, 48–49, 75–77, 92; age distribution, increase with age, 39, graphic illustration, 53; change as related to IQ change, 75, illustrative examples, 63, 75; conventional vs. corrected, 3, 48–49, 114; corrected mental age scores, 48, 49, 75–76, 122–123, extensions to higher levels, 49, 76–77, illustration of use, 92, interpretation, 75–76, 122, meaning, 49, practical value, 77–78, procedure for determining corrected scores, 92–93, restrictions on use, 75–76, table of, Appendix A, 122–123; corrections required, 48–50; DIQ, comparison in interpreting scores, 77, case study example, 78; differences between ability groups, 3, 55–57; errors of measurement, 39–40, increase with age, 37–38; equivalence of mental age units, 57–63; extension to higher age levels, 3, 92, 122; gains related to ability, graphic illustration, 55–56, standard score value of gains, 57, 60, table of comparison, 58–59; practical uses, 77–78; related to reading ability, 75–76; reliability, 37–38; retention in Stanford-Binet scales, 76; school grouping on basis of, 77; uncorrected, overestimate at age levels, 76, 85–86, 113; *Wechsler Intelligence Scale for Children*, 107–111, computational illustration, 110

Mental development, growth and maturing; *see* Mental age scores; *and* Rate of mental maturing

Mental tests, functions of, 63, 80; interpretation for parents, 78; predictive value of, 10, 80–82. *See also* Stability of intelligence

Merrill, Maud A. (54, 55), 118; Array distributions of test-retest scores, 15; Conventional IQ, assumption of constant SD, 30; Mental age scores, 92, overcorrection, 76; Pinneau Revised IQ Tables — manual for 1960 revision of Stanford-Binet scale, 52; Reliability of IQ at different ability levels, 35, effect of age increase in MA distribution, 39–40, effect of method of computing, 35–36; Variability changes in conventional IQ, 18, 30

Morphett, M. V. (40), 117; MA related to reading readiness, 75–76

Nelson, Virginia L. (50), 117; Fels Study — test-retest relationships, 10; IQ variability changes related to developmental processes, 29

Neurological defects and predictive value of IQ, 80, 96–97

Noller, P. A. (61), 118; Comparison of WISC with the Stanford-Binet, 107

Oakland Growth Study, *see* Adolescent Growth Study

O'Connor, J. P. (27), 116; Overlap hypothesis, 63

Overlap hypothesis, 2, 54–55, 61, 63

Parental expectations, 72–74

Parents, providing tests results to, 78

Percentile change in relation to change in conventional IQ, 18

Percentile equivalents for DIQs, 72–73

Pinneau, S. R. (41, 42, 43, 44, 45, 46), 117; Deviation IQ percentile chart, 73; Deviation IQ tables (Pinneau Revised IQ Tables), 52–53, 114, 124–202; Errors of measurement of MA, 37, 46; Lability scores, conventional and deviation IQ, 42, ff.; Mental age scores, corrected values for Stanford-Binet scales, 122–123, extension of concept, 76–77; Mental growth, related to ability level, 62–63; Reliability, and MA distribution, 37, 46, effect of item weighting, 37, 46, of IQ at different levels, 36–37; Stability of IQ, 1, 40–41; Variability related to mental growth, 31, corrections at all ages, 33–34, graphic illustration of effects, 35

Pintner, R. (47), 117; Percentile chart and supplementary guide for 1937 revision of the Stanford-Binet scale, 72

Practice effects of BGS sample, 22

Predicting later scores, reservations regarding, 81; required information, 81; standard error of estimate, 82

Predictive value of IQ, 79–80; preschool tests, predicting mature ability, 80, 97–98

Progressive Education, 98–102

Rate of mental maturing, related to ability level, 63–64. *See also* Mental age scores, gains

Reading and ability, 75–76, 99

Regression equation, 81

Relative standing; *see* Deviation IQ

Reliability of IQ, ability level related to, 40–41; average difference and variance method, 38–39, effect of combining age samples, 39; effect of item weighting, 36–37; explanation of age changes, 39; MAs — effect on of item weighting, 37, function of the IQ technique, 39–40

Revised IQ tables, *see* Deviation IQ tables

Russell, D. H. (21), 116; Reading readiness, 77

Sandercock, Marian G. (48), 117; WISC and Stanford-Binet on below average groups, 107

School, frustration in relation to curriculum, 74–75. *See also* Educational applications

Schramm, T. A. (61), 118; Comparison of WISC with the Stanford-Binet, 107

Simmons, Katherine (17), 116; Brush Foundation, 10

Skipping, 100–102

Sloan, W. (49), 117; Age change in IQ, 14

Sontag, L. W. (50), 117; Fels Study — test-retest relationships, 10; IQ variability changes related to developmental processes, 29

Spaulding, Patricia J. (51), 117

Stability of intelligence, 1–2; ability level differences, 40–41; changes in conventional IQ, 10, 14–15, 208–225; change in DIQ, 22–29, 208–225; comparison of conventional and deviation IQ, 22–23; comparison of ability groups, 35–37; comparison of conventional and deviation IQ for individual subjects, 41–45; construction of scale, 45–47; correlation between means and SDs, 41; correlation studies, 10; effect of, of item weighting, 35–38, of method of deriving IQ, 39; factors relating to, age of testing, 1, 11, age change in means, 16, change in test, 28–29, test interval, 11; graphic comparison of change in conventional and deviation IQ, 23; implications of tables of IQ change, 93–95; measures of, correlation and IQ change, 2, 10; standard score measures of intelligence, 19–20; variability changes, 31–35. *See also* Deviation IQ

Stanford-Binet scales, age changes in variability, 18; explanations for variability changes, 18; 1916 revision, 14, 33; 1937 revision, 2, 3, 6, ff, 9, ff, 19, 37, 112, ff; 1960 revision, 2, 3, 49, 55, 114. *See also* Terman *and* Merrill

Subjects of samples, Berkeley Growth Study, 7–9; 1937 standardization of Stanford-Binet, 6–7

Terman, L. M. (52, 53, 54, 55), 118; Age changes in variability, 30; Array of distributions of test-retest scores, 15; Conventional IQ, assumption of constant SD, 30; IQ classification method, 72; Mental age scores, 92; Reliability of conventional IQ, effect of IQ technique, 35–36, effect on increase in MA distribution with age, 39–40; Stanford-Binet, 1916 scale, 14, 1937 scale, 6; Use of Pinneau Revised IQ Tables, 52

Testing of pre-adoptive children, 96–98

Thompson, C. G. (57), 118; Reading readiness, 76

Thompson, Clare W. (12, 56), 116, 118; Differential performance of ability groups on same items, 77; Follow-up on 1937 standardization samples of Stanford-Binet, 10

Triggs, Frances O. (58), 118; Comparison of WISC with the Stanford-Binet, 107

Variability change in IQ, relation to age, 30–31; corrections, McNemar, 32–33, at all ages, 33–35, effect on extreme scores, 52, smoothed and unsmoothed SDs for the Stanford-Binet, 19, 31; effect of difficulty of items, 32

Washburne, C. (40), 117; MA related to reading readiness, 75–76

Wechsler, D. (59, 60), 118; *Wechsler Intelligence Scale for Children*, 106, ff

Wechsler Intelligence Scale for Children, 106, ff; comparability of WISC and the Stanford-Binet, 107; mental age scores 107–110, computational illustration 110, 122; stability of WISC scores, 107

Weider, A. (61), 118; Comparison of WISC with the Stanford-Binet, 107

Wrightstone, J. W. (36), 117; Comparison of WISC with the Stanford-Binet, 107

Young, Florence M. (2), 115; Change in IQ score with age, 14

NOTES

NOTES